When Rebels Become Stakeholders

When Rebels Become Stakeholders

Democracy, Agency and Social Change in India

SUBRATA K. MITRA
V. B. SINGH

●SAGE www.sagepublications.com
Los Angeles ● London ● New Delhi ● Singapore ● Washington DC

Copyright © Subrata K. Mitra and V. B. Singh, 2009

All rights reserved. No part of this book may be reproduced or utilized in any form or by any means, electronic or mechanical, including photocopying, recording or by any information storage or retrieval system, without permission in writing from the publisher.

First published in 2009 by

SAGE Publications India Pvt Ltd
B1/I-1 Mohan Cooperative Industrial Area
Mathura Road, New Delhi 110 044, India
www.sagepub.in

SAGE Publications Inc
2455 Teller Road
Thousand Oaks, California 91320, USA

SAGE Publications Ltd
1 Oliver's Yard, 55 City Road
London EC1Y 1SP, United Kingdom

SAGE Publications Asia-Pacific Pte Ltd
33 Pekin Street
#02-01 Far East Square
Singapore 048763

Published by Vivek Mehra for SAGE Publications India Pvt Ltd, photo typeset in 11/13pt Berkeley by Star Compugraphics Private Limited, Delhi and printed at Chaman Enterprises, New Delhi.

Library of Congress Cataloging-in-Publication Data Available

ISBN: 978-81-7829-945-7 (HB)

The SAGE Team: Elina Majumdar, Sushmita Banerjee, Anju Saxena and Trinankur Banerjee

*Dedicated to the memory of
Tejeshwar Singh*

Contents

List of Tables ix
List of Figures xiv
Preface xv

1 Introduction: Democracy and the Puzzle of *Orderly* Social Change 1

2 The Context of Social Change: Interfacing Society and State in India 23

3 Continuity and Change in Indian Politics: An Inter-generational Analysis 41

4 The Elements of Political Agency and the Limits of Consensus 63

5 Political Competition, Social Cleavages and Institutionalisation of the Party System 87

6 Re-inventing the Nation: The Dialectics of Nation and Region in India 123

7 Poverty, Welfare and Social Opportunity in India 147

8 Building Social Capital from Above and Below: Locality, Region and Trust in India 176

9 India at Sixty: Social Change and the Resilience of Democracy 201

10 Beyond India: Democracy and Social Change in Comparative Perspective 228

Appendix 1:	*Note on Methodology*	246
Appendix 2:	*2.1 Survey Instrument, 1996*	260
	2.2 Survey Instrument, 2004	277
	2.3 Accommodation	294
Appendix 3:	*Tables*	296

Bibliography	301
Index	315
About the Authors	320

List of Tables

1.1	Efficacy of Vote (in per cent)	14
1.2	Legitimacy of the Institutional Arrangement (in per cent)	14
1.3	Subjects into Citizens (in per cent)	15
1.4	Social Base of Citizenship: Time Series, Cross-section Profile	16
2.1	Trust in Institutions 1996	37
2.2	Normative Evaluation of Democracy 2004	38
2.3	Kashmir: Challenge to India's Statehood	38
3.1	Level of Education by Generation (in per cent) 2004	50
3.2	Effect of Vote by Generation (in per cent) 2004	50
3.3	Parties' Attention to People by Generation (in per cent) 1996	51
3.4	Importance of Election by Generation (in per cent) 1996	51
3.5	Trust in Institutions by Generations (in per cent) 1996	52
3.6	Attitudes Towards Ayodhya Incident by Generation (in per cent) 1996	53
3.7	Policy Towards Pakistan by Generation (in per cent) 1996	54
3.8	Resolution of Kashmir Issue by Generation (in per cent) 2004	55
3.9	No Need of Atomic Bomb by Generation (in per cent) 2004	55
3.10	Separate Civil Code by Generation (in per cent) 1996	56
3.11	Reservation for Women by Generation (in per cent) 2004	56
3.12	Needs of Muslims Neglected by Generation (in per cent) 2004	57

3.13	Economic Satisfaction by Generation (in per cent) 2004	58
3.14	Privatisation by Generation (in per cent) 2004	58
3.15	No Free Trade to Foreign Companies by Generation (in per cent) 2004	59
3.16	Limited Ownership by Generation (in per cent) 2004	59
3.17	Government Better Without Parties by Generation (in per cent) 2004	60
3.18	Party Support by Generation (in per cent) 2004	60
4.1	Timing of Voting Preference (in per cent)	65
4.2	Timing of Voting Decision by Sub-categories: Comparing 1996 and 2004	67
4.3	Interest in Election Campaign (in per cent)	69
4.4	Attendance of Election Meetings during Campaign (in per cent)	70
4.5	Campaign Exposure (in per cent)	71
4.6	Visits by Candidate, Party Worker and Canvasser (in per cent)	73
4.7	Guided in Voting Decision (in per cent)	75
4.8	Index of Political Information (in per cent) 1996	77
4.8a	Index of Political Information Per Social Group (in per cent) 1996	78
4.9	Financial Satisfaction during the Last Few Years (in per cent)	79
4.10	Present Financial Situation (in per cent)	80
4.11	Future Financial Situation (in per cent)	81
4.12	Financial Satisfaction (in per cent)	83
5.1	Social Bases of Political Parties (1996–2004) (in per cent)	97
5.2	Efficacy of Vote (in per cent)	103
5.2a	Efficacy of Vote by Party	105
5.3	Usefulness of Political Parties (in per cent)	106
5.4	Legitimacy (in per cent)	107
5.4a	Legitimacy by Party	109
5.5	Partisan Response to the Demolition of Babri Mosque (in per cent) 1996	111

5.6	Partisan Opinion on Resolution of Kashmir Problem (in per cent)	113
5.7	India should Develop Friendly Relations with Pakistan (in per cent)	115
5.8	Need for Separate Civil Code for Every Community by Party Support (in per cent)	117
5.9	Issue Positions: Rebels, Stakeholders and Others	118
5.10	Party Support: Rebels, Stakeholders and Others	119
6.1	Concern about Central and State Government (in per cent)	128
6.2	Loyalty to Region First and then to India (in per cent)	129
6.3	Regional Parties Provide Better Government (in per cent)	130
6.4	Loyal to Region by 'Regional Parties Provide Better Government' (in per cent)	130
6.5	Trust in Local/State/Central Government (in per cent) 1996	131
6.6	Loyalty to Region by Trust in Different Levels of Governments (in per cent) 1996	131
6.7	Regionalists by Caste (in per cent)	133
6.8	Regionalists by Religion (in per cent)	134
6.9	Regionalists by Level of Education (in per cent)	135
6.10	Sense of Political Efficacy of Regionalists (in per cent)	136
6.11	Sense of Financial Satisfaction of Regionalists (in per cent)	137
6.12	Regionalists and their Attitudes Towards Communal Accommodation (in per cent)	138
6.13	Regionalists' Attitudes Towards Kashmir Issue (in per cent)	139
6.14	Regionalists and Partisan Preference (in per cent)	140
6.15	Self-rule and Shared-rule: Regionalists Cross-tabulated by Stakeholders (1996 and 2004)	143
7.1	Cross-tabulation of Class with Caste (in per cent)	152
7.2	Cross-tabulation of Class with Education (in per cent)	153

7.3	Perception of Financial Satisfaction by Socio-demographic Groups (in per cent)	155
7.4	Social Profiles of the Most and Least Deprived (in per cent)	158
7.5	'Ownership should be Limited' by Social Background (in per cent)	163
7.6	No Free Trade for Foreign Companies by Social Background (in per cent)	167
7.7	Privatise Government Companies by Social Background (in per cent)	169
7.8	Deprivation and Attitudes Towards Social Policy (in per cent) 1996	171
8.1	Regional Variation in Trust in Central, State and Local Government (1996)	186
8.2	Trust in Local Government across Regions and Socio-economic Strata	193
9.1	Evaluation of Different Institutions and Actors	208
9.2	Caste and Political Competition	216
9.3	The Politics of Community Formation	217
9.4	Mean and Standard Deviation on the Accommodation Scale 1996	221
10.1	Preference for Democracy as Compared to Authoritarianism	230
10.2	Competing Paradigms of State–Society Interaction: A Classificatory Scheme	234

Tables in the Appendix

A1.1	State-wise Distribution of Sampled Units and Respondents	248
A1.2	Comparable Figures for the Sample and the Universe	250
A1.3	List of Sampled Constituencies Lok Sabha and Vidhan Sabha	251

A2.3.1	Questions for Accomodation Scale	294
A3.1	Election Data, Indian Parliamentary Elections, 1952–2004	296
A3.2	Participation Trends in Major Assembly Elections, 1952–2006	296
A3.3	Percentage Turnout in Assembly Elections, 1984–2006	297
A3.4	Summary of Lok Sabha Elections, 1952–1971 (Seats and per cent of Vote)	298
A3.5	Summary of Lok Sabha Elections, 1977–2004 (Seats and per cent of Vote)	299
A3.6	Multiple Correlation of the Components of Democracy and Social Change (1996)	300

List of Figures

1.1	A Dynamic Neo-institutional Model of Democracy and Orderly Social Change	11
2.1	The *Jajmani* System	31
2.2	The Breakdown of the Pyramid of Social Dominance	32
2.3	Local Elites and the Regional Policy Environment	34
4.1	Timing of Voting Preference	66
4.2	Interest in Election Campaign	68
5.1	Per cent of Votes of the Congress, Relative to the Largest Non-Congress Party or Coalition	94
6.1	Votes and Seats Share of National Parties in Lok Sabha (1952–2004)	127

Preface

When Rebels Become Stakeholders explores the agency of ordinary men and women in the making of democratic social change in India. The study is specific to India, but the issues we examine here are of general interest. In contrast to the majority of post-colonial states, India has achieved both democracy *and* social change. We focus on the political skills of India's voters and their leaders instead of the *essence* of Indian culture to explain this remarkable phenomenon. The book draws on public opinion derived from three national surveys of the Indian electorate, held in 1971, 1996 and 2004 to explain this complex theme.

Books, like people, have complex genealogies. Many of the ideas and events we analyse here represent our collaboration over the past three decades. The book draws on our individual and joint research, but most particularly on *Democracy and Social Change in India: A Cross-section Analysis of the Indian Electorate* (Sage, 1999). A fortuitous conversation with Mr Tejeshwar Singh in 2005 in the crammed and convivial set up of his office at SAGE, the seat of independent Indian publishing for an entire generation, led us to rethink our initial design. The book that resulted has been enriched through the addition of new survey data from 2004, made available by Lokniti, Delhi. We take this opportunity to thank its directors, Peter de Souza and Yogendra Yadav and National Co-ordinator Sanjay Kumar for their generous help. Conversations with Dhirubhai Sheth—over the past many years since the inception of this project—have helped sharpen our arguments. Himanshu Bhattacharya has helped us from the outset with statistical analysis. Our two organisations, the South Asia Institute of the University of Heidelberg and the Centre for the Study of Developing Societies, Delhi, have been most helpful with institutional support.

Mike Enskat, Anja Kluge, Malte Pehl and Clemens Spiess have rendered valuable help with previous drafts of this text. Despite the heavy demand on his time, Ashok R. Chandran, our first editor at SAGE, has set the pace, and made the text accessible through his gentle, imaginative, effective and unobtrusive editing. Dr Sugata Ghosh, our commissioning editor at SAGE has seen the manuscript into publication during the final stages of the book with exemplary speed and attention to details. We would like to express our gratitude to all these friends.

Opinions, attitudes and values of ordinary people form the basis of this book. Our access to the voter would not have been possible, had it not been for the efforts of the investigators of Lokniti. We owe them a special vote of thanks. In transforming the fruits of their diligent labour into a form that makes it accessible to the elector and the scholar, we hope, we will strengthen the vital chain that connects information and the elector, and makes democracy work.

The book has been written with students of Indian democracy, and of comparative politics, in view. We hope that the book will provide the students of Indian society and politics with analytical tools that would make it possible for them to look beyond the uniqueness of India and instead think of this country as a unique set of common attributes, rather like any large, complex society ensconced in an ancient, continuous civilisation. Thanks to the popularity of public opinion polls which have become part of India's electoral landscape, the role of individual attitudes, expectations, values and distribution of opinion in the making of major political decisions is seen today as part and parcel of the democratic process. Still, for many specialists the individual often disappears and reappears as part of collective categories, ethnic groups or even becomes indistinguishable, lost in the *janta*—a collective of an undifferentiated, essentialised, static mass. In presenting survey data on individual attitudes, opinions and preferences into tabular form, arranged in terms of problems, concepts and socio-demographic categories, and bringing the individual back in again, the volume attempts to resist this tendency.

We dedicate this study to the memory of Mr Tejeshwar Singh, in homage to his contribution to Indian social science publication. The high standard of engagement, honesty and professionalism that he has set will continue to be a source of inspiration to others.

Subrata K. Mitra
V.B. Singh

1

Introduction: Democracy and the Puzzle of *Orderly* Social Change

The Puzzle

India has achieved a social revolution within the span of the six decades following Independence. During this relatively short time, the country has witnessed tumultuous changes in social hierarchy, literacy, relation of gender and power, urbanisation and most importantly, in political participation of marginal social groups. The Indian story, affecting one-fifth of mankind, is a major contribution to the history of democracy and social change of the twentieth century. It is an important political phenomenon in its own right. But it deserves serious scholarly attention for a second reason as well. In contrast to the liberal democratic states of Europe where social change had preceded democratisation, India has experienced democracy and social change concurrently. This simultaneous rather than sequential occurrence of social and democratic change makes the Indian case particularly interesting for the comparative politics of democracy and social change.

We explore the agency of ordinary men and women in the making of democratic and orderly social change in India. While agency, reflecting the democratic spirit of our times, is a much-discussed theme in contemporary social sciences, connecting the rationality of ordinary men and women to the explaining of the electoral participation and rapid structural change in the life of a country of continental proportions is specific to this study. The book analyses this intricate theme on the basis of attitudinal data, derived from three national surveys of the Indian electorate, held in 1971, 1996 and 2004.

The Context: Twentieth Century India and Eighteenth Century Europe

In historical perspective, democracy and social change have been unhappy bedfellows most of the time. The eighteenth century Europe, caught in the throes of industrialisation, rapid and forced migration, cities beset with squalor, food riots and machine breaking, witnessed violent skirmishes between working men and women, on the one hand—asserting their rights—and on the other, the owners of land and capital, who frequently, with the help of the machinery of the state, tried to fend them off, often with the accompaniment of the brutal use of force. The fortunate few who survived these battles eventually went on to become stakeholders in society, equipped with the right to vote, property, representation and eventually, a share in political power (Gilmour 1992, Hobsbawm and Rudé 1968, Moore 1966, Tilly 1975). A similar process is in course in contemporary post-colonial, post-communist and post-occupation societies as well but with a difference. Modern forms of communication and warfare have endowed the skirmishes with an unprecedented intensity, international networks and often, with the form of ethnic conflicts. The contemporary changing societies, like their European counterparts of the eighteenth century, are faced with the need to undergo massive changes in the structure of the economy, social relations and hierarchy of power. But democracy's mixed message puts them in a double bind. While their efforts to promote *entitlement* accelerate expectations and *enfranchisement* adds political muscle to popular demands, *empowerment*, the third element of the democratic triad helps mobilise opposition to policies that hurt entrenched interests. In the democratic caravan, the slowest runners—veto players in their own right—set the pace. As a result, attempts at change of any serious consequence get stymied. Worse, the rational expectation of resistance becomes an argument to abort proposals of structural change at an embryonic stage.

One does not need to go far to seek supportive evidence. Thanks to the meticulous documentation of the disorder that has accompanied structural change, historical and cross-national comparisons reveal a systematic pattern of riots, risings and revolution coinciding with attempts to transform ownership, social status, mores, custom, convention, tradition or social hierarchy.[1] Of course, attempts at change do not always fail. Mechanisms of conflict-resolution swing into action to absorb the shock. But, even in Western post-industrial societies with long established traditions of collective bargaining, democratic ardour dampens the enthusiasm for change. In the less developed world, where institutions are relatively new and fragile, where 'weak states' are locked into battle against 'strong societies,' both the resistance to change and the reaction to the resistance to change, can be even more drastic (Migdal 1988). 'Democracy', as Field Marshall Ayub Khan of Pakistan had warned when he dismissed the elected government 'does not work in a hot climate'.[2]

Scholarly pessimism about the chances of a smooth transition to democracy dominates analytic narratives of politics in transitional societies.[3] In contrast, the persistence of democratic institutions and significant social changes in India comes across as puzzling. In the dismal world of democratic social change, India remains the odd one out. During the 60 years since Independence, democratic institutions and practices have occasionally wilted but not withered away under the pressure of structural change. During this period, judging by the indicators such as urbanisation, industrialisation, literacy, women's empowerment and economic growth, social change in India has registered important gains. Far from remaining merely passive and a decorative backdrop to India's massive General Elections, former untouchables, backward classes, women, religious and ethnic minorities and people from peripheral geographic regions have moved into the mainstream of Indian politics as wielders of power. Democratic institutions such as elections, parties, legislatures, the judiciary and the politically accountable but professionally recruited bureaucracy have acted as active agents of change. However, barring the 19-month interlude of the Internal Emergency, 1975–77, India's democratic political system has not only survived; it has, in fact, managed to deepen and broaden its reach, adding a third, crucial level to the federal system that has seen the number of elected representatives of the people wielding real power go up from about 5000 to over 3 million during the past 15 years.[4] A whole range of other institutional innovations and constitutional changes have inducted the lower classes, rural leaders, women, former untouchables and backward classes into public sector employment, educational establishments and positions of power in the political system. The number of federal units has grown in a manner that empowers distinct cultural identities. The forces of law and order—the 'men on horseback' who have traditionally led the assault on democratic institutions in post-colonial societies—have been confined to the barracks most of the time.[5] The formal measures have been effectively complemented by the informal practice that has set the trend for the most comprehensive penetration of the Indian society by the winds of change, whose pace has been remarkably accelerated over the past decade through liberalisation of the economy and globalisation of Indian society and the market.

Why has India succeeded where others have failed? We argue in this book that the cohabitation of democracy and social change in India is not merely incidental or coincidental. Rather, the two are institutionally linked in a manner that is fundamentally causal, so much so that the weakening of the one renders the other ineffective. A number of fortuitous factors—among them, the early introduction of 'participation' under colonial rule, Partition of British India in a manner that reduced incoherence by removing the main challenger to the hegemony of the Indian National Congress while cementing its bonds with the national electorate, and the enduring ethos of consensus and accommodation, extended the requisite room to manoeuvre the creative forces of politics and institutional innovation to operate at their most effective during the formative years of the Republic. The book explores these larger themes by drawing on survey data that explore the causal connection between democracy and social transformation.

The main objective of this book is to join the debate on democracy and development[6] on the basis of a case study of the opinions and attitudes of the Indian voter. We argue that mass perception of institutions, policies and processes—so often dismissed as mere false consciousness or as the conditioned reflex of a gullible public, manipulated by the rhetoric of populist politicians—is our only window to the inner dynamics of democracy and social change. In this vein, we conceptualise perception as the key to the inner world of the actor. Popular perception as the key empirical evidence to test conjectures about the relationship of social power and political change has not received the scholarly attention that it deserves. Social attitudes—embodying a vast data base of political information, choices, opinions, attitudes, values with regard to social power, trust, status, aspirations and anxieties—play a critical role in our neo-institutional model of democracy and social change. This heuristic research design, discussed later in the chapter, seeks to interpret India's innovative political process in terms of India's new social elites—the 'stakeholders'—people who combine a sense of their own efficacy with a sense of legitimacy of the system—who play a crucial role in making orderly and democratic social change both possible and necessary. Indian *netas*—far more numerous in India than their equivalents in other contemporary changing societies—have learnt to combine governance with welfare and identity. Strategically placed at the crucial nodes of the system—in the localities, regions and at the national level—they and those competing to join them constitute India's political community, where a political culture of consensus, collaboration and competition has generated a sense of purpose and momentum, leading to orderly and democratic social change.

Drawing on the rich empirical base of the national surveys of the Indian electorate in 1971, 1996 and 2004, the book provides the 'missing links' in terms of the casual link that transforms rebels into stakeholders, which is the essence of the larger story of democratic social change in India.

A Case of Indian 'Exceptionalism'? Structural Change, Political Choice and the Rational Actor

India, for reasons explained in the preceding paragraph, has remained an anomaly in the field of the sociology of development, and for that reason, a focus of scholarly enquiry. More often than not, scholarly scepticism has been laced with a touch of pessimism. The Swedish economist Gunnar Myrdal (1968) thought it unlikely that the 'soft state' would be able to deliver hard, policy decisions with regard to change. The younger V. S. Naipaul, India's very own India-baiter during the troubled 1960s, had chimed in with dark forebodings (1964). Scepticism among early observers and foreign journalists (Harrison 1960) was the rule rather than the exception. This chorus of mostly negative views on the relationship of democracy and social change had found a law-like formulation by the Harvard political scientist Samuel P. Huntington (1968: 55) who foresaw a high probability of political collapse on the part of changing societies taking the democratic path.

The pessimistic prognosis emerging from comparative politics and developmental sociology was buttressed by the lessons of economic history. One of the most important voices was that of the Harvard economic historian Barrington Moore, whose influence continues to reverberate among the post-war generation of students of this field. In his magisterial summing up of three principal routes to social change, namely, the liberal, the communist and the fascist, Moore concluded that the poorest have always had to pay the price of social change. The victims of change, as we learn from the eighteenth century accounts of food riots and 'machine breaking' in Europe, have not, as one can expect from rational men and women, necessarily offered themselves up as willing cannon fodder to galloping industrialisation. The history of social change has thus been the history of social strife. Writing in the 1960s, Moore could only visualise misery, local strife and its containment by a powerful state and overall paralysis (1966, 1967).

In Pursuit of Lakshmi (1987) by Lloyd Rudolph and Susanne Rudolph added a new element to the debate on democracy and development by introducing the multiple roles of the state as a third player, transforming the dyadic conflict of classes, castes, regions, generations and identities into a triad of forces which makes coalition-building and compromise possible. In pre-industrial Europe as in post-Independence India, peasants, workers, forest dwellers and other victims of developmental projects (as in the

Sardar Sarovar project on the Narmada river in Gujarat, in western India, or the peasants' struggles of Andhra Pradesh, Bihar or West Bengal) have always known where their interests lie. Given a choice—and choice is what democracy is essentially about—they have voted in opposition to change. In this context, according to the Rudolphs, the intermediary role of the state in producing a political environment for orderly, democratic change has been essential. A fortuitous legacy of British rule, the state in India, 'avatars of Vishnu' in the delectable phrase of the Rudolph and Rudolph (1987: 401–402), has been a manifold presence—supporting the interests of peasants, owners, reformers, entrepreneurs, bureaucrats all at the same time—as and when the need for this has arisen. The high politics of the state has promoted change while maintaining continuity.

The mould was set by its colonial predecessor but the contents were added by the logic of popular rule. The vessel was there, into which the elites, whose ranks were continuously enriched through regular, fair, open and binding General Elections, poured new ideas and aspirations. The state in India had already acquired a distinct form by the time the power was transferred to the democratically elected Congress party. Reflecting the complex social base of the Indian National Congress, practically synonymous with the government in the 1950s, the state became a god of manifold attributes. From time to time, the process of dynamic change and social equilibrium appeared on the brink as the vessel threatened to overflow or to burst. But constitutional amendments, institutional innovation and the firm, disciplining hands of a state, parts of which enjoyed high political trust, maintained a dynamic equilibrium.

Post-Independence India thus began its political career with its own concept of social change—liberal in essence but radical in tone—as the moral basis of governance. Though Independence quickened the pace of state-driven, democratic social change; by itself, it was not so much an innovation as an appropriation of the political practice of the antecedent regime. At the outset, India, a society based on the hierarchy of caste status, assigned to the individual at birth, was juxtaposed with a legal and institutional structure whose mainstays were individual rights and their enforcement in a court of law. Reflecting its commitment to being a free society, the state opened up the competition to all ideological hues. Reacting to these stimuli, voices of the Left, Right and Centre surfaced regularly, and endowed India's political space with their richness and interaction in complex coalitions.[7]

The state in India, both in its political rhetoric and the policies that it followed gave full legitimacy to the agenda of social change, which corresponded to what Wilbert Moore has defined as the modernist programme, namely, '...the significant alteration of social structures (that is, of patterns of social action and interaction), including consequences and manifestations of such structures embodied in norms (rules of conduct), values, and cultural practices and symbols' (Moore 1960). As one could see from legislation, administrative directives and patterns of allocation, the desired transformation consisted in some directly observable phenomena such as social status, roles, norms, patterns of interaction, as well as non-tangibles such as dignity and empowerment. These normative aspects of social change came across as competing programmes in the foundational decade that followed Independence, voiced by different social groups, guided by their different interests and their perception of the social opportunity structure. Thanks to Nehru's uplifting rhetoric and the delicate balance of crass materialism and noble idealism, the Indian voter knew that the essence of politics consisted in both the distribution of resources and the redefinition of values. The spectrum of political parties, ranging from the revolutionary Left to the various shades of cultural and economic Right, provided articulate agency to the spread of opinion in the country. Between the ideological extremes were various shades of social democrats and centrists, dominated by the Indian National Congress, all competing for votes in the first General Election.

The question that arises here is why this potent mixture of pent-up demands from the lower social orders and their sudden empowerment through universal adult franchise kept the political pot simmering but did not let it boil over. Sharp differences were articulated, but mostly in terms of the orderly discourse of politics, neatly ranged within the paradigm of modernisation rather than the violent clashes that account for the majority of post-colonial democracies that fell by the wayside. The complex picture, presented by Rajni Kothari (1970) and W.H. Morris-Jones (1987) in their conceptualisation of the 'Congress System', got further complicated in the 1960s as the backward castes left the Congress in massive numbers for various regional and peasant parties, but after a break, during which governmental instability and a brief spell of authoritarian rule held the possibility of the breakdown of the Indian 'model' of democratic social change, the parties regrouped in terms of broadly-based coalitions—competing for the vote, but beholden to the same set of basic rules of the game—and brought India back into the mould of democracy and change.

In contemporary India, the debate on the modernisation paradigm has moved beyond the narrowly political. It now affects the broader issues of identity and the high politics of the state. The relatively new interest in indigenous values, identity and culture closely parallels developments in the world at large where the appeal of ethnicity and religion has overtaken the post-war emphases on economic development and class conflict as the dominant modes of political perception. This uncertainty about the terms of discourse is the predominant theme of Indian politics today as compared to the relatively consensual basis of Indian politics of the first decades following the end of British colonial rule. Still, the mould is set, the institutional arrangement of the state, its inner architecture of parties, interest groups and party-cleavage linkages have held. Quite remarkably for a developing country, the main policies of the state such as liberalisation of the economy, a cautious engagement with Pakistan in bilateral negotiations, cautious opening up of India's economy to international competition and nuclearisation have remained stable even as specific governments and coalitions come and go. In the following section, we discuss a formal model that underpins this process.

A Neo-institutional Model of Democratic Social Change

In Western Europe, full and free participation became a reality only after the structural changes in the economy and institutional arrangement were completed, and thus, were available only to the lucky survivors of the brutality of social transformation. In India, the introduction of mass democracy, rather than following structural change, preceded it. When Nehru, in his famous speech on 'Freedom at Midnight' committed the state to this objective, he was not being entirely rhetorical or metaphorical. Universal adult franchise was introduced in 1952 when both the non-democratic Left and the non-democratic Right were invited to compete equally with the Centre and the moderate Left and Right for political power through elections. From the outset, politics took precedence over economic or social reasoning. The basic parameters of the Indian model that took shape after Independence were political participation, the ability of the political system to give shape to many of the initiatives from below and ideas from above in the shape of new institutions or to reinforce existing institutions, and finally, the ability of the political actors of India to engage in 'two-track strategies' that combine normal political action with rational protest.[8]

Many of the strands of these empirically grounded theories are drawn from Kothari's pioneering contributions to the empirical study of politics and social change which provided both the groundwork for an analytical context and the methodology to juxtapose fragments of India's political discourse with political theory (1970). One can see further maturing of these methods in *Citizens and Parties* (Sheth 1975), which pioneered the concept of empirical verification of broad conjectures on change by drawing on empirical data, both ecological and attitudinal. By undertaking multivariate analyses of attitudinal and statistical data, Sheth and his co-authors made it possible to isolate the effects of social status from other aspects of the political universe such as education, age, gender, political networks and social class. In the second place, the regional focus made it possible to measure the variations within India's federal polity where regional and sub-regional identities have increasingly emerged as important influences on the voter.[9]

The latter theme has been further developed in subsequent texts such as Frankel and Rao (1989/90) which within a theoretical framework that represents the triangular relation of caste, class and dominance was able to show the variation across regions. In their efforts to generate a general explanation for the triangular relationship of caste, class and dominance within different regional arenas, Frankel and Rao and their co-authors drew deeply on political economy, as a consequence of which they did not relate collective outcomes to strategic choices of individuals. Mitra and Lewis (1996) have shown the impact of the strategic thinking of leaders and ordinary political actors on their alliances. The melange of noble rhetoric and unsentimental lucidity, when it comes to bargaining for sectional interests, constitutes a heuristic device to explain political behaviour. Political elites at the local, regional and national levels—always alert to an opportunity in the shifting landscape of Indian politics—have responded by taking policy initiatives that combine sanction and welfare with a fine recognition of custom and the imperative of cultural continuity.

The flow diagram (Figure 1.1) summaries the policies and institutions that link democracy and orderly rule in the Indian context. In Europe, the great transformation in agriculture induced by the industrial revolution initiated comprehensive structural changes in the pattern of landholding, agrarian relations, crops and migration from the countryside to the city because machines gradually replaced men. These structural changes, described in poignant detail by Charles Tilly, Barrington Moore, Hobsbawm and Rudé caused great social strife, food riots, machine breaking and forced migration to the newly growing industrial centres. The modern world that emerged from these upheavals reached a new social and

FIGURE 1.1
A Dynamic Neo-institutional Model of Democracy and Orderly Social Change

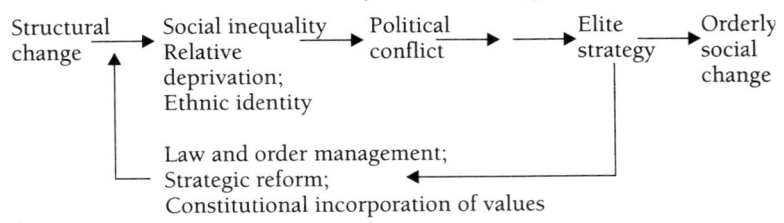

Structural change → Social inequality; Relative deprivation; Ethnic identity → Political conflict → Elite strategy → Orderly social change

Law and order management; Strategic reform; Constitutional incorporation of values

Source Mitra 2005: 16.

political equilibrium where the stakeholders in land and industry, whether as owners of capital or labour, were linked to political power through representative bodies such as parties, unions and civil associations. A similar transformation from the agricultural to the industrial world in contemporary changing societies generates comparable political strife, which, as we learn from Huntington (1968), if unchecked, can lead to the collapse of the political system. In the trade-off between the pace of extending participation and the pace of change, Huntington counsels caution, preferring to arrest the rate of social mobilisation through enfranchisement, lest the weak and non-yet-established institutions be overwhelmed by the new arrivals in the political arena. The Indian solution has been to permit the simultaneous expansion of both the reach of elections and the depth and breadth of social change because elite agency—intervening between conflict mobilisation and institutional collapse—has found an effective antidote in the form of a strategic combination of law and order management, necessary reform and institutional recognition of identity.

The perceptions of market niches by vote-maximising leaders and social groups in search of opportunities constitute the main template of politics in India. The previous model helps explain exactly where the opinions, attitudes and preferences of the mass public fit in within the larger architecture of institutions, processes and coalitions of political leaders. The diversity, complexity and contradictions of public opinion on the contentious aspects of social change are tapped into by survey research. (See Appendix 2 for the survey instruments.)

Bringing the Actor Back in Again: Public Opinion, Survey Research and Social Dynamics

The book departs from the experts' view of democracy and social change to that of the actor. In reality, specialists turn out to be keener to peddle their pet theories than to look for relevant evidence. As such, human agency gets replaced by large abstractions of caste, class, gender, race, nationality and the ubiquitous ethnicity. In our research design as in our method, we seek to bring the actor back in again by bridging the two worlds of modern institutions and 'the web of meanings that those actions have for the participant's (*Encyclopaedia* vol.16 1974). Accordingly, our research design brings together the neo-institutional model based on structural parameters of action and the logic of individual perceptions of values, choice and strategy.

Models do not make men, but given the right combination of attitudes and attributes in the mass public, a model might offer a satisfactory explanation. What kind of human base underpins the institutional arrangement of democracy and social change in India? Fortuitously, the availability of three major surveys of social and political attitudes in India from 1971, 1996 and 2004 provide the requisite information on the indicators of change and their subjective meanings to the actors.

Stakeholders in the system are crucial to our analysis. Two questions, related to efficacy and legitimacy, selected from the rich treasure trove of facts of democracy and social change, help identify these political anchors of democratic social change. The question '*Do you think your vote has effect on how things are run in this country, or, do you think your vote makes no difference?*', asked in all three surveys, to measure the sense of efficacy that people attach to their vote. In view of the right to universal adult franchise and the political culture that has grown around it, the normative perception of the vote gives us the most general measure of individual efficacy. The results are quite revealing in terms of the strength and reach of India's democracy at the level of individual perception, drawn in this case from his normative belief as well as empirical experience. A majority of people believe that their votes have an effect on the political state of affairs in the country. The percentage of such people has gone up from 48.5 per cent in 1971 to 67.5 per cent in 2004. A second revealing fact is the decline, over the past 25 years, of the number of those who could not answer this question (the 'don't know' response in this case is a sure sign of the lack of involvement with the political system, as well as lack of control over one's own life) from 35.3 per cent in 1971 to 15 per cent in 2004 (see Table 1.1).

TABLE 1.1
Efficacy of Vote (in per cent)

Do you think your vote has an effect?	1971	1996	1999	2004
Has effect	48.5	58.6	63.0	67.5
Makes no difference	16.2	21.3	17.4	17.5
Don't know	35.3	19.1	19.6	15.0

Source National Election Survey (NES), Centre for the Study of Developing Societies (CSDS) 1971, 1996, 1999, 2004.

As individual perceptions go, efficacy and legitimacy are the two faces of democracy. A question, designed to measure legitimacy, asked, *Suppose there were no parties or assemblies and elections were not held—do you think that the government in this country can be run better?* The question was deliberately phrased in the negative, requiring the interviewees to show their commitment to democracy by formulating the answer in the negative—not a simple thing to do, considering the radical difference in the status of the interviewer and the interviewee in the backdrop of a traditional society where social deference and a tendency to agree with those who represent superior power point in the same direction. Those who consider India's current institutional arrangement to be consistent with their own value preferences have steadily gone up from 43.4 to 72.2 (see Table 1.2).

TABLE 1.2
Legitimacy of the Institutional Arrangement (in per cent)

Better government without parties, assemblies and elections?	1971	1996	2004
Yes	14.2	11.4	9.0
No	43.4	68.8	72.2
Can't say or don't know	42.4	19.8	18.8

Source NES, CSDS 1971, 1996, 2004.

By combining efficacy and legitimacy, we can generate a measurement of involvement of the individual with the political system. Thus, 'stakeholders' in India's political system are people who consider themselves personally efficacious and who consider the institutional arrangement to be legitimate. Opposed to them are 'rebels', who consider themselves as people with political influence but who do not accept the legitimacy of the political system.

These rebels could be political loose cannons—free-wheeling between electoral democracy and its opposite—depending upon the local and regional opportunity structure, and the power of the ideology that colours their perception of the system. Between the two categories are people who do not have an opinion on either of the two questions, or who see themselves as people without any influence whatsoever.

The headcount of stakeholders over a 25-year period gives an insight into the deepening of the democratic social change in India. From Table 1.3, one can see that the percentage of stakeholders has grown from 29.7 per cent in 1971 to 53.4 per cent in 2004; the proportion of rebels has fallen from 9.1per cent to 6.1 per cent and 'others' have shrunk from a majority of India's population at 61.2 per cent to 40.5 per cent.

TABLE 1.3
Subjects into Citizens (in per cent)

Year of survey	Stakeholders	Others	Rebels
1971	29.7	61.2	9.1
1996	45.1	48.1	6.8
2004	53.4	40.5	6.1

Source NES, CSDS 1971, 1996, 2004.

The social profile of stakeholders (see Table 1.4) reveals further evidence of the broadening and deepening of the democratic social change in India. Besides the sheer growth in numbers, the gap in their social origin has increasingly narrowed. Thus, whereas in 1971, the stakeholders tended to be predominantly male, urban, relatively young and literate, upper-caste and affluent, in the span of a quarter of century, though the main trends generally hold, one begins to find stakeholders in almost all social categories. Stakeholders are not only numerous; they also seem to be almost everywhere! A second interesting fact that will be taken up for detailed analysis later in this book refers to the percentage of stakeholders among different religions. Compared to the base line figures of 1971 when Sikhs and Christians contributed to stakeholders in significantly higher numbers, by 2004, the percentage has evened out, reaching

TABLE 1.4
Social Base of Citizenship: Time Series, Cross-section Profile

	Stakeholders			Others			Rebels		
Social background	1971	1996	2004	1971	1996	2004	1971	1996	2004
All Groups	**29.7**	**45.1**	**53.4**	**61.2**	**48.1**	**40.5**	**9.1**	**6.8**	**6.1**
Gender									
Male	37.8	51.9	59.7	49.8	39.2	33.5	12.4	8.9	6.8
Female	19.5	38.1	46.3	75.5	57.2	48.4	5.0	4.7	5.3
Locality									
Rural	25.9	44.0	51.4	65.8	49.9	42.7	8.3	6.1	5.9
Urban	42.8	48.4	60.9	45.1	42.4	32.4	12.1	9.2	6.7
Age group									
Up to 25 years	36.0	47.8	54.3	54.1	45.8	39.3	9.9	6.4	6.4
26 to 35 years	31.5	47.0	56.0	60.3	45.4	37.7	8.2	7.6	6.3
36 to 45 years	29.2	47.0	54.1	60.4	46.8	39.6	10.4	6.2	6.3
46 to 55 years	28.2	41.1	51.7	63.3	51.6	42.4	8.5	7.3	5.9
56 years and above	21.6	37.6	48.0	69.3	55.9	46.7	9.1	6.5	5.3
Education									
Illiterate	17.4	34.0	39.0	76.1	60.9	56.3	6.5	5.1	4.7
Up to middle	40.3	47.5	52.7	47.0	48.0	40.4	12.7	4.5	6.9
College-No degree	58.8	54.2	62.3	27.3	37.1	30.9	13.9	8.7	5.8
Graduate and above	66.2	60.3	71.8	20.6	26.9	21.2	13.2	12.8	7.0
Caste									
Scheduled Tribe	22.5	35.7	45.0	76.4	62.0	50.5	1.1	2.3	4.5
Scheduled Caste	23.6	47.6	50.1	69.4	46.6	44.9	7.0	5.8	5.0
Other Backward Caste	28.3	41.3	52.5	61.4	50.5	40.2	10.5	8.2	7.3
Upper caste	41.4	50.1	59.2	47.1	41.8	35.0	11.5	8.1	5.8
Muslim	29.2	47.6	53.6	59.9	47.7	40.5	10.9	4.7	5.9
Others	42.2	48.9	54.9	44.5	42.1	39.7	13.3	9.0	5.4
Religion									
Hindu	29.0	44.4	53.5	62.5	48.5	40.3	8.5	7.1	6.2
Muslim	29.2	47.6	53.6	59.9	47.7	40.5	10.9	4.7	5.9
Christian	49.4	53.5	55.8	31.3	39.4	39.1	19.3	7.1	5.1
Sikh	42.4	45.2	53.0	40.7	45.3	41.0	16.9	9.5	6.0
Others	33.3	47.6	48.1	66.7	47.6	46.0	–	4.8	5.9
Economic class									
Very poor	–	37.3	44.0	–	57.5	50.3	–	5.2	5.7
Poor	–	45.9	53.3	–	47.6	40.9	–	6.5	5.8
Middle	–	50.4	60.2	–	41.9	32.9	–	7.7	6.9
Upper	–	53.4	66.7	–	35.7	27.5	–	10.9	5.8

Source NES, CSDS 1971, 1996, 2004.

almost uniformity across religions. Interestingly, however, the percentage of stakeholders has tended to be almost similar among Hindus and Muslims—a figure that has remained constant all the way from 1971 to 2004.

The Scheme of the Book

The introductory chapter has dwelt on the nature and course of the interaction of electoral politics and democratic social change in India. The indicators of social change such as the sense of efficacy and legitimacy of the system will be analysed further in juxtaposition with other factors such as involvement in the electoral process and the level of political information in subsequent chapters. India's particular pattern of decolonisation affected the nature of India's post-colonial state and the ruling elite. The exploration of the path-dependency and the context of democracy and social change are taken up in Chapter 2. This chapter also examines the all important role of the state. Independence came as a result of a transfer of power from the colonial rulers to the Congress elites rather than a revolutionary break from the past. Chapter 3 will measure the extent to which the ancien régime survived into the post-Independence era in the form of the attitudes and opinions of the pre-Independence generation.

The analysis of historical continuity is followed by the changing profile of the Indian society in Chapter 4. It undertakes a broad overview of the findings of the surveys to identify the limits to the consensus on all aspects of the state–society interaction in India. It also provides a very broad overview of the responses of individuals when queried about where they stand on these issues. The strands of the specific arguments are then elaborated into a deeper analysis of the contrast between the perceptions of the Indian 'mainstream' and those located at the margins of society.

Since the interaction of the traditional society and the post-colonial state takes place primarily in the electoral arena where political parties are the main actors, Chapter 5 focuses on an analysis of the social bases of parties and the transformation of the party system of India. Though electoral politics is conceptualised as the main instrument of democratic social change in this book, our understanding of the inner dynamic of this process would remain incomplete without an exploration of the organisational context in which electoral participation takes place. The nature of India's party system has changed radically since the days of the single-party-dominated system, with the hegemonic role of the Congress party as the fulcrum of the political organisation. Some of these ideas, presented in an embryonic form in the introduction, are further developed in this chapter. The transformation of the party system is analysed on the basis of the electoral statistics regarding partisan voting in national elections since Independence. The chapter then identifies the supporters of the main political parties and analyses their social bases. The intention here is to show as to what extent there is a resonance of the electoral rhetoric of leaders, be it Dalit power, class politics or cultural nationalism.

The results of the analyses of partisanship show that individual voters generally make the connections between their preferences and that of the leaders, and that electoral choice is influenced by this connection. An individual's abilities to establish these connections have important implications both for his/her own sense of efficacy as well as his/her evaluation of democratic politics as compared to the politics of movements, riots, terrorism and insurgency for achieving political demands. The chapter also shows how, at the level of party supporters, there exists a great measure of consensus on major national issues despite the fiery rhetoric of their leaders. That perhaps explains why, once the parties are voted into the legislature, they have little difficulty in jettisoning the more extreme elements of their electoral rhetoric, seeking out potential coalition partners in order to come up with legislation with far-reaching implications for social and economic change, while, at the same time, maintaining overall stability of policy and polity.

The issue of regionalism, which recalls the fear of *Balkanisation* that marked the early decades after Independence, is the main theme of Chapter 6. This chapter, devoted to the nature of 'nation and region in India', raises the question of the inclusive character of identity in India where the loyalties to the nation and the region are not seen as *conflicting* but rather as *converging* categories. The spatial boundaries of the political arena that define the limits of the political world of the individual and the relationship of his/her political universe to the larger bodies of which it is a part, are also an important aspect of social change in India. Does the insular individual, long confined to the limited world of the locality, simply reject it in favour of the world beyond the village, once he is given the knowledge of the potentials it holds for him and the opportunity to exercise a choice? Does locality simply dissolve itself in favour of the region and the region for the creation of the nation? Or, does the assertion of local and regional identities act to the detriment of the nation? We answer these questions in terms of the opinions and attitudes of 'regionalists' who are found to use their identification with the region more as a tool of transactional politics rather than as exclusive territorial categories, promoted as a necessary contradiction of the 'idea of India'.[10]

How inclusive is the robust economic growth that India, following the liberalisation of the economy, has been able to achieve? The issue is taken up in Chapter 7. The economy of independent India has remained an integral part of her politics from the outset, in striking contrast to that of the 'developmental states', where the authority to direct the course of growth and distribution was entrusted to an elite, immune to political control by the masses (Johnson 1983). Despite the ubiquitous bureaucracy and the Planning Commission which controlled the 'commanding heights of the economy', ultimate authority for regulating the direction of the economy always remained in the hands of the elected executive, ever sensitive to the political demands of the masses. Successive governments of India have sought, over the last few years, to change the role of government in regulating growth and redistribution through the policies of liberalisation and deregulation. The issue of popular perception of these policies, the overall perception of growth and welfare and the linkages between class and perception of economic change are examined in detail in this chapter which analyses the linkage of poverty, economic policy and social opportunity in India.

The analysis of class and economic development undertaken in Chapter 7 is followed by the relationship of social capital, region and trust in India, in Chapter 8. It focuses on socio-economic change and political conflict in India and illustrates the main argument by drawing on a regional comparison. Based on conventional theories of relative deprivation, the chapter first examines the links between the socio-economic status of the individual and his/her perception of his/her welfare and that of his/her children over the past, present and future. These findings provide useful insights into the existence of slow growth combined with stable democracy in India. This global picture, constructed on the basis of the full sample, is then further analysed at the level of regions.

The book offers two sets of conclusions. Chapter 9 examines the theme of the resilience of India's democratic political system. It moves in the direction of drawing some general inferences about the underlying strengths and vulnerabilities of democratic social change in India. Important in this respect are the survey findings regarding the high trust that individuals repose in the political system as a whole and their general distrust of the people who run them, particularly, politicians and the police. Chapter 10 seeks to draw the general lesson that one learns about the prospects of democracy in post-colonial societies from the Indian case. Finally, since many of the attitudes reported in this book are politically sensitive and difficult to measure in a consistent manner, a detailed methodological appendix provides some insights into the methods of sampling and conditions of the survey.

Conclusion

Six decades since Independence have brought about a social revolution that has seen people from the lower social strata come to the top of the ladder. Indians, thanks to the Gandhi–Nehru legacy of social justice and the foundational role of this rhetoric in the institutional arrangement of the state, have tended to take this great achievement for granted. The pace of the Indian revolution has been marked by a slow, steady and incremental growth which has none of the spectacular images of the Great Leap Forward, or the Cultural Revolution emanating from China. In consequence, India's dynamic social process is seen as static. Domestic observers, echoing the morbid curiosity of the international media, tend to focus on the breakdown of the process of democratic social change, as one can see from the obsessive interest of the media in the sensational cases of torture, rape, arson, rioting and suicides. The book seeks to redress this imbalance between image and reality with regard to the extent of Indian achievement.

We argue that the answer to the Indian puzzle of orderly social change lies not so much in the 'Indian culture' as in the unique combination of general factors such as the legacy of colonial rule, the diversity of primordial cultures, the flexibility of India's institutional arrangement, and the availability of elites who have mastered the art of negotiation and political compromise. These empirical facts have far reaching implications for the theories of social development. Echoes of these are to be found in the re-thinking of development in India as well as in the international scholarship on democratic social change. The field is marked by a growing scepticism of the cultural assumptions on which the earlier models of development, economic growth and modernisation were based. As the assumption of the nineteenth century European thinkers about the eventual spread of 'universal' rationality has come under critical examination, the demand has grown for the creation of 'theoretical frameworks that combine a demystified, rationalist world-view with an understanding of the phenomenology in societies where the gods have not yet died' (Rudolph and Rudolph 1987: 742). The next chapter will take up this general theme with specific reference to the Indian state, which, as the context of social change and the institutional arrangement of democracy, deeply affects attitudes, opinions and strategies of India's political actors.

Notes

1. Attempts at giving minor concessions to the minority Catholics in the eighteenth century Britain (Gilmour 1992) have provoked vicious riots on the part of the Protestants. In more recent times, minor changes in labour legislation have brought students and the youth to rampage in France. Closer home, in West Bengal, attempts at public procurement of agrarian land to pave way for industry have provoked violent clashes of the peasants and the police.
2. For a detailed discussion of Ayub's radio broadcast, see (Ali 2007).
3. Kohli's own position with regard to prospects of democratic transition in changing societies has shifted over time. This becomes evident when one contrasts the tone of his earlier depiction of the growing crisis of Indian society (Kohli 1990) with his recent work (Kohli 2001).

4. This is the result of the 73rd and the 74th amendment of the constitution, which has added over six hundred thousand village councils as the third tier of the federal system. Among these, one-third are women and about 22 per cent are Dalits and adivasis. See Peter de Souza (2007).
5. See S. E. Finer (1970) for the role of the military in developing societies. True, the controversial Armed Forces Act gives substantial powers and initiative to the military in Kashmir and the North-East, but political accountability of the state for lawful governance even in these areas remains with civilian authorities.
6. This complex issue has been analysed at length, for which a vast literature exists already (see Kohli 2001, Mitra 2005, Varshney 1989, Jayal and Pai 2001).
7. See Mitra (1999a and 1999b) for a detailed discussion of the theoretical and institutional implications of social change in the context of a post-colonial state. Though both volumes draw on the logic of competing paradigms and their convergence through competitive politics, the main arguments of the two volumes are expressed in different forms, drawing on case study and historical data in the former, survey data in the latter. The research findings based on analysis of the survey data in the former are complementary to the case studies presented in the former are complementary to the case studies presented in the latter.
8. For a preliminary discussion of this model, see Mitra (1997a). The parameters of the model are discussed in Mitra (1997a: 36–38).
9. Ahmed and Singh (1975: 165) refer to this as 'structural consolidation'.
10. See, for instance, Khilnani's (1997) interesting book with the same title.

2

The Context of Social Change: Interfacing Society and State in India

Context matters. The stimuli, originating from the world in which men and women are ensconced, deeply affect their attitudes, preferences and values. As such, variables like the historical path that connects the present to the past, memories of salient political events, the institutional arrangement, the economy and the social system are of great salience in the formation of political trust, institutional preferences and attitudes that individuals have towards the major issues of the day. The causality operates in the other direction as well. If 'form affects content', then reciprocally, collective political will can also transform the context in many ways. Even more radically—thanks particularly to advances in communication—an individual, located in the middle of nowhere, can seek out his/her context in a network of like-minded people—far away spatially—but in everyday contact over the net and its myriad equivalents.

This chapter analyses this reciprocal relation between the context of social change and the process of change. It prepares the stage for the analysis, in subsequent chapters, of how India's political attitudes have gone on to affect the context of Indian politics. We examine here how the state, first under the colonial rule and subsequently, as part of India's post-Independence regime, affected social transformation and what consequences this process of modernisation has had for trust, democracy and the pressing political issues (we focus on Kashmir as an example) that confront the Indian state today. We briefly examine the process of political mobilisation during the first decade after Independence, the introduction of universal adult franchise and how elite recruitment in the local arena has 'trickled up', in course of which the new entrants have become stakeholders of modern India.

Social Agenda of the Post-colonial State

Social change is a quintessentially political process. The state affects the structure, course and pace of the transformation of traditional society. For over a century now, every part of India has been affected by the process collectively referred to as modernisation, though the ferocity of the winds of change or, the tardiness of social transformation, has varied from one region to another, reflecting India's geographic diversity. Areas most affected by the British colonial rule and more recently, by the liberalisation of the economy have been opened up more effectively to modern communication networks, commercialisation of agriculture and penetration of commerce and industry. The late-comers to development have nevertheless been affected by the ubiquitous presence of the modern state. cellular telephone and the vote-seeking politician. Consequently, under the double impact of modernisation and political competition, new social elites have found their way to local and regional power everywhere in India.

The modern men and women, to whom the British transferred power in 1947, had their task cut out for them. Echoing the spirit of the times, Jawaharlal Nehru, every bit a Prometheus on the ramparts of Delhi's Red Fort, outlined his vision of the future of Indian state, society and the economy, in a famous oration that has since become a landmark comment on modern India.[1] Ensconced in the Constituent Assembly on the eve of the attainment of Independence, the recently anointed Prime Minister of India described his mission as the 'Tryst with Destiny'. In this speech, famously known as 'Freedom at Midnight', Nehru described the magical moment as one redolent with the spirit of independence, when one 'step[s] out from the old to the new, when an age ends and when the soul of a nation, long suppressed, finds utterance'. Nehru had gone on to exhort the nation to redeem the pledge of 'dedication to the service of India and to the larger cause of humanity ... the ending of poverty, ignorance and disease and inequality of opportunity' (Rushdie and West 1997).

Nehru, a quintessential renaissance man, had presented this modernist agenda against the background of the carnage that followed the Partition of British India into Pakistan, carved out as a homeland for India's Muslims and the Indian Republic that chose to remain a secular state. As India's first Prime Minister, Nehru, a social democrat by temperament, intensely aware of the urgency of a concerted effort to remove mass poverty and ignorance, sought legitimacy through the promotion of general welfare. Democracy, a sense of community and modernisation were values that were to lead the way into the promised future. The fact that these principles were of alien provenance did not matter at that moment of euphoria. India had already been exposed to some of them for the better part of the duration of colonial rule. The most radical of them, namely, universal adult franchise as the basic principle of legitimacy and popular accountability, was very much in the air, at least since the 1937 elections. The six decades that preceded Independence had witnessed a steady, incremental extension of the right to vote under the overall hegemony of the British colonial rule. While these limited experiments had already planted the seeds of mass democracy, the extension of franchise to the entire adult population in one fateful moment was a bold leap, particularly when one takes into consideration the fact that the Constituent Assembly which decided on this momentous step was itself the product of restricted franchise.

The reformist agenda of the colonial state has been a fortuitous legacy for the post-colonial state. The colonial state, partly inspired by events at home in England, partly under the influence of Utilitarian philosophy, but also acting with the interest of gaining popular support and to check the growing influence of India's national leadership, had initiated limited reforms during the first half of the nineteenth century. The momentum for reform had carried on despite the setback suffered by the reformers, thanks to the violent backlash of the Sepoy Mutiny of 1857. The leaders of the post-Independence regime continued in the same vein. As the political process of post-Independence India gained momentum under the aegis of universal adult franchise and a republican constitution, social change gathered a new dynamism with far reaching consequences for the federal, democratic institutional arrangement. In consequence, social change in India, which, in contrast to Europe, had begun as a top–down process, acquired the character of popular movements and agendas, trickling upwards through the 'two-track strategies' of protest and the normal political process, first used by Mahatma Gandhi against the colonial rule and subsequently adopted by India's vote-seeking politicians as an Indian political genre.

The Indian National Congress, carrying the aura of its proud record as the party of Independence, ruled everywhere in India during the formative decade of 1947–57. The gradual transformation of India's political process from the tutelage of one-party-dominance to the multi-party democracy that we have today corresponds to the steady demolition of social hierarchy through legislative measures aimed at strategic reform, political competition, land reform and commercialisation of agriculture. The final blow came in the fourth General Election of 1967 when anti-Congress coalitions threw it out of power in many Indian states, cut it down to size at the centre and turned it from India's hegemonic ruler into a normal political party. After this, the Congress started alternating with other political parties and coalitions, very much like any other political party. Under the leadership of Indira Gandhi, the party took the path of popular authoritarianism, which brought the party great electoral success in 1971 but led to the corrosion of its organisational links with the society. One consequence was the period of Emergency Rule 1975–77, which, ending in the General Election of 1977, saw the Congress party out of power in Delhi, at the Union level, for the first time. Since then, Indian politics has entered a period of broad-based coalitions. After the 12th General Election, an unprecedented coalition of the Bharatiya Janata Party (BJP) and several regional parties continued the task of democratic governance at the centre. Though the General Election of 2004 brought the Congress, as the head of the UPA coalition, into power at the centre—the change of the political complexion of the government, nevertheless, did not radically affect the core policies in the areas of liberalisation of the economy, nuclear weapons and continued rapprochements with Pakistan, signifying the overall stability of the Indian polity.

The Radical–Liberal Ideology of Indian Development

Nehru's was the foundational voice—radical in tone but liberal in content—synonymous in his time with modern state in India, which remains both a legacy and a reminder for his successor. However, though Nehru and his entourage were the main wielders of power and patronage, they were not alone as far as political ideas and strategies were concerned. Despite colonial rule and restricted franchise, by the time Independence came, India had already experienced over 60 years of vigorous, competitive politics, which had seen the growth of an ever-expanding political class with opinions ranging between the extreme Left to the advocates of liberal economic policies. There were the proponents of secularism and those wishing to see religion at the centre of politics; advocates of close political relationship with the democratic, capitalist West and opposed to them—those advocating an alliance with the Soviet bloc. All these voices found articulation in the first General Elections of India held in 1951–52. Underpinning them, there were very different and internally coherent ideas. A brief analysis of these is essential to the understanding of the subsequent development of the political space, which accommodated dissent without letting it upset the basic Indian consensus and its institutional arrangement (Figure 1.1, Chapter 1) that underpinned India's contentious political arena.

The process of accelerated interaction of politics and society, of which mass elections were the main instruments, is fraught with contradictions, appearing occasionally to run into the cul-de-sac of populist rhetoric and electoral consecration into political power of rogues and scoundrels. Democratisation can thus appear to gnaw at the roots of governance and civility and the quickening and deepening of the pace of politicisation, characteristically releasing into the political arena, social forces that are capable of destroying the very basis of stable government and norm-bound institutions. This fear of popular politics getting out of the elite control always underpinned the thinking of the Congress high command during the days of the freedom movement.[2] The spectre of India breaking apart under the cumulative weight of such politics became a refrain of the commentaries on Indian politics in the early years after Independence (Harrison 1960). The full fury of this phenomenon would, however, not be released until the 1980s, growing in its frenzy until it reached a climax in the terrorist violence, communal clashes and political disorder, poignantly symbolised by the destruction of the Babri Mosque in December 1992 and periodic repetitions of the outbreak of inter-community violence. The following section analyses how India managed to map a dynamic political process into a set of stable institutions.

Political Structure and Social Change in the Local Arena

Indian politics, on the wake of Independence, consisted of an enormously large, national, mass electorate, parts of which had not even experienced direct British rule and were stepping out of feudalism straight into popular democracy. The electorate comprised of a majority of Hindus, still recovering from the trauma of Partition, who were being asked to become citizens of a country which did not recognise any official religion; of poor marginal, land-hungry peasantry, who would be the eventual victims of the economy of scale; of manual labourers, who would have to choose between eventual redundancy and replacement through more productive, skilled and necessarily fewer workers. What should have followed is described by several specialists. One of the most cited is Harrison (1960), who spelt out a future of conflict, social disharmony and break up of the recently founded Republic.

The constitutional design and the structure of institutions that were intended to give concrete shape to the idealistic goals of the Republic, enshrined in the preamble, adopted methodological individualism as the cutting edge of social change. However, such principles as individual rights, representation, based, not on group identities but on individual interests and structured along the lines of political majority—seen in the context of a society based on hierarchy and tightly-knit social groups—could only lead to conflicts based on values and interests of everyday politics. Free and fair elections, universal adult franchise and extension of the electoral principle into all realms of social power were intended to articulate, aggregate and eventually incorporate indigenous political norms and alien political institutions within the structure of the political system of the post-colonial state.

Elections are necessary but not sufficient for social change. Though elections were intended to be a necessary feature of Indian politics after Independence, by the makers of the Constitution, the electoral process on its own could not have constituted a sufficient basis for its functioning. An effective electoral process requires a specific political culture and appropriate political institutions for its functioning. The existence of such cultural attributes and political structures could not be taken for granted at the outset. There was no unanimity about the objectives of social change at that time, as indeed there was no single hegemonic idea that dominated the national movement to the exclusion of other shades of ideology. The issue, therefore, is how India developed the high degree of instrumental attitude toward politics and a basic minimum of trust in institutions which facilitate the functioning of a democratic system.

Students of comparative electoral sociology, familiar with the history of the slow and unsteady development of franchise and participation in contemporary stable democracies, might wonder as to how the uncoupling of political dominance and the pre-modern social order came about in India. By drawing on the rational calculus of participation[3] which basically suggests that people vote because they consider it worthwhile for them, one can understand how this transition took place.

Voting behaviour in India, in the immediate aftermath of Independence, is often described in terms of 'vote banks'. A vote bank was a unique institution in the sense that unlike people voting as a group, in this situation, though the bulk of the voters in a particular village or locality might vote a particular way, the decision is not really a group decision. Members of a vote bank are guided towards the polling booth by the 'banker', possibly the head of a local family of high social status, owning land and wielding political influence. The Rudolphs have described this as *vertical mobilisation* which implies:

the marshalling of political support by traditional notables in local societies that are organised and integrated by rank, mutual dependence and the legitimacy of traditional authority. Notables reach vertically into such social systems by attaching dependants and socially inferior groups to themselves through their interests and deference. (Rudolph and Rudolph 1967: 24, also 1960: 5–22)

But even here, voting remains an individual decision except that the basis of the act is not grounded on the explorations of the limits of what is politically possible. Rather, it is the expression of a pre-existing social bond. The vote bank describes a cluster of exchange relations which runs parallel to the social system based on *Jajmani*. However, the hold of the *Jajmani*-vote bank system began to decline as people at the bottom of the social pyramid gradually dispensed with some of the intermediaries and started negotiating the terms of exchange directly with the politicians from outside seeking support. In the more successful cases of this transformation, new forms of mobilisation, described by the Rudolphs as *differential* and *horizontal* patterns of mobilisation, gradually replaced *vertical* mobilisation.

Horizontal mobilization involves the marshalling of popular political support by class or community leaders and their specialised organisations. Ignoring the leaders and members of natural associations or little platoons, they make direct ideological appeals to classes or communities. Horizontal mobilisation of solidarities among class or community equals introduces a new pattern of cleavage by challenging the vertical solidarities and structures of traditional societies. (Rudolph and Rudolph 1967: 25)

In a typical case of transition, however, both horizontal and differential mobilisations are likely to take place within the same political arena, creating what the Rudolphs have described as differential mobilisation, which involves:

the marshalling of direct and indirect political support by political parties (and other integrative structures) from viable, but internally differentiated communities through parallel appeals to ideology, sentiment and interest. The agent of mobilization in this case is the political party rather than the local notable or community association and its strategies of mobilisation vary. (Rudolph and Rudolph 1967: 26)

This transition from social hierarchy to egalitarianism can be presented in terms of two diagrams. We shall define the baseline in terms of the reciprocal bonds of obligation known as the *Jajmani* system (Srinivas 1987) and the political implications arising out of it as a 'pyramid of dominance' (Frankel and Rao 1989; see Figures 2.1 and 2.2).

The circle depicting the *Jajmani* system describes the reciprocal relations between the centre where the groups owning land and disposing of higher status, are located and the periphery where the service groups are situated. In the ideal type situation, at the centre are groups, which derive their dominant status from their control over force and the means of production. Politically, these groups and families form the local elite. Once again, since the bond that binds the 'elite' and the 'non-elite' is deeply ingrained, the social pyramid looks like a natural rather than a political construction.

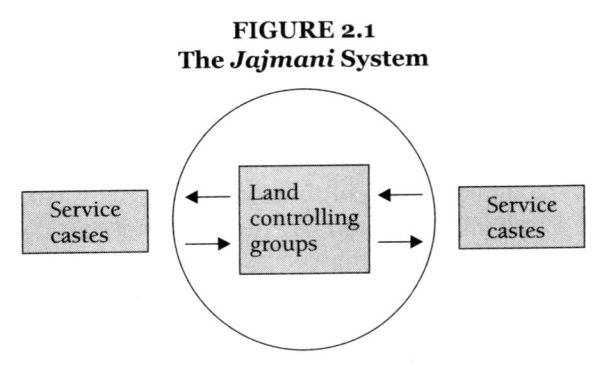

FIGURE 2.1
The *Jajmani* System

Source Authors.

The representation of the *Jajmani* system in Figure 2.1 follows the patterns of domination that one considers natural from within the framework of the caste system. The bonds behind the members of this system are reciprocal, though neither the obligations nor the rights are by any means equal. The land owning groups, around which the system is organised, possess the bulk of the means of production, in most cases land, which forms the main source of economic activity in the village. The others, with their specialised

FIGURE 2.2
The Breakdown of the Pyramid of Social Dominance

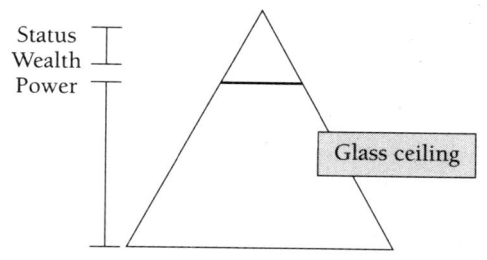

Source Authors.

occupations that form part of the process of cultivation, or of the other functions necessary for the purposes of ritual or social interaction, form the large and unspecified group of service castes.

The complex social relationship with their political and economic linkages constitutes the *Jajmani* system in its ideal form. All this, however, changes with the coming of political consciousness and organisation, creating political tension and conflict. The process is depicted in Figure 2.2. Thus, in the ideal world of the *Jajmani* system, which can be presented as a pyramid of dominance, based on status, power and wealth, which accumulate in the families of the socially notables, a form of social closure creates a low upper-threshold which defines the limits of social aspirations on the part of the peripheral groups in the village.

The convergence of the different forms of power in society gives a certain stability and rigidity to the system. However, the extension of franchise brings an additional political resource. Since the constitutional right to vote does not respect status, power, or wealth, their conglomeration at the lower levels of the pyramid upsets the pattern of dominance inherent in the traditional social structure. Metaphorically, the pyramid breaks as the bottom is empowered through elections. Since the literature (particularly Huntington 1968) warns against the ensuing disorder, the question that we need to raise here is why did the social pyramid not break chaotically.

The tensions that are implicit within any form of social domination become explicit; legislation and economic change bring about a sense of empowerment to the peripheral social groups. The pyramid in Figure 2.2 depicts the convergence of different sources of power in the form of an ideal type. It shows how status and wealth might continue to inhere in the socially notables, whose dominance is visible through the glass ceiling to the non-elites but who are kept off power through various means of social closure. Strategic reform in the form of voters' registration and incentives to vote, combined with competitive electoral campaigns under the watchful eyes of the Election Commission, breaks this glass ceiling and causes 'differential mobilisation' of the electorate to set in. Thus, the enfranchisement and political mobilisation of the erstwhile peripheral social groups, generally more numerous than the socially notables, reverse the direction of power, where the tiny base of the pyramid is dominated by the poor and low-status groups who vastly outnumber them. When these divergent forms of power are superimposed on one another, the result is the fracturing of the cohesive life of the *Jajmani* system, which now splits into several factions. Once factions intersect the established class patterns of the village, with some members of each social group of the village finding themselves within every faction, short-term electoral coalitions form and in the atmosphere of political promiscuity, tiny but well organised groups in a pivotal position start throwing their weight about.

The empowerment of the lower social orders through elections has been described by the Rudolphs as the transformation of *vertical* mobilisation into *differential* and *horizontal* mobilisation. Typically, as the social groups, located at the periphery, discovered the negotiable value of the vote, they started participating directly in the political trade that matches electoral power to material resources. Established *Jajmani* systems break down to create new groupings, based more directly on initiative from below, formation of coalitions among disparate interests and, finally, creation of caste associations among groups with horizontal social and economic interests (see Figure 2.3).

The state structure in India has institutionalised these ideological and social changes from below in the form of institutional innovations. Federalism, consociationalism and elite policy initiatives, linking social power to political and economic change, have created in the hands of national, regional and local elites a useful 'room to manoeuvre in the middle'.[4]

FIGURE 2.3
Local Elites and the Regional Policy Environment

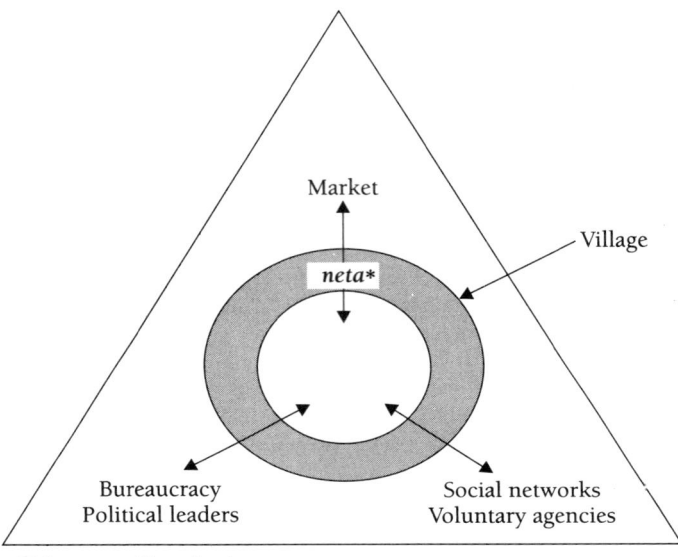

[Figure: Triangle with vertices labeled "Market" (top), "Bureaucracy / Political leaders" (bottom left), "Social networks / Voluntary agencies" (bottom right); "Village" labeled on the right side; a ring inside the triangle with "neta*" at the center, with arrows pointing from the ring to each vertex.]

Note *Netas are village leaders.

These innovations have been possible in India because of four factors. (*a*) The Gandhian legacy which gave the first formal shape to a 'two-track' strategy where political actors seek to use the tactics of conventional political participation and recourse to protest movements as part of the same strategy.[5] Politics after Independence gave formal acknowledgement to this development. (*b*) The ability of the national and regional elites to transfer knowledge from one arena to another; Panchayati Raj is a good example. (*c*) The availability of the Congress system and the elite consensus that defined it during the formative years after Independence. (*d*). Though India, unlike the stable Western democracies, lacked a tradition of liberal political movements or institutions, its feudal past did not lead to re-emergence of authoritarian tendencies, as in post-Meiji Japan. Contrary to the Japanese case, the princes and zamindars of India were creatures of British rule and as such, did not enjoy the same depth of traditional legitimacy that made them, in the post-Independence political arena, a source of political competition. They were not, in any sense, natural political leaders whose support came from outside the democratic political system. As such, they could not provide a social basis, equivalent to the military-authoritarian tendencies of the Tokugawa Japan (1603–1868) which resurfaced and subverted the democratic experiments of the 1920s and 1930s.

We have seen in this section how politics at the micro level moved from the *Jajmani* and vote bank-based vertical mobilisation to unstable, short-term coalitions, sustained by differential mobilisation, enhancing the sense of power on the part of small but well organised groups, capable of playing a balancing role among other, larger groups. Political entrepreneurship of this kind led the transition of India from one-party-dominance to a multi-party democracy.

To sum up, the successful transition of a traditional society based on hierarchy to one which is egalitarian and participatory, requires, first and foremost, the institutional basis for a participatory democracy. But these institutions would not be effective if they were not underpinned by an electorate that is conscious of its rights and, in consequence, feels efficacious. However, while efficacy is a necessary condition, it is not sufficient by itself because without the restraint of institutions, a sense of empowerment deriving out of efficacy can quickly degenerate into anarchy, inviting non-democratic forces to intervene and take over in the name of public interest. Thus, the best conditions of transition are provided by a situation where a conscious, participatory mass electorate is ensconced within the context of an elite consensus about the core values of the political system and a basic commitment to the political institutions.

Subjects into Citizens: From Colonial Rule to a Stakeholders' Democracy

However, as the record shows, elections and democracy have kept pace with one another (see Table A3.1 in Appendix 3). On all aggregate indicators, as the data show, India has kept up steady progress. True, the level of electoral participation has not reached the level of national elections in Europe, but the national average of

India certainly compares favourably with that of the United States. Statistical data on the participation of women, former untouchables, tribals do not lag far behind that of the national average. Finally, the levels of electoral participation in some regions of India are as high as in continental Europe.

The relatively modest rate of participation in the first General Election should be seen in the context of its relative novelty to the Indian electorate, for this was the first ever General Election where universal adult franchise became the norm. This was applied to the whole of India, including former princely states which had not known the incremental growth in representation and was introduced in steady degrees in those parts of India that were ruled directly by the British. Added to this was the problem of the relative lack of political linkages between voters and candidates, normally mediated by party machines which were not yet effectively organised at the constituency level. But, as the figures show, the level of participation has grown over the years, occasionally declining in the mid-1950s, but generally hovering around 60 per cent. Unlike the United States, where the responsibility of registration with the electoral authorities lies with the voter, in India, the state takes the necessary steps. A number of measures, such as, close proximity of the polling booth (of which, there is more than one, on the average, for each of India's five hundred thousand villages), their location in schools and such public places where access is relatively free for people of all walks of life and an electoral machinery specially mobilised for the occasion to make sure that voters can exercise their franchise without fear and without an inordinate delay—have been taken.

If the level of participation in the national elections, on the average, is respectable by world standards, then participation in the regional Assembly Elections is truly remarkable (see Table A3.2 in Appendix 3). The level of participation has not only kept pace with the national figures, but in some instances, has even been at a higher level.

Finally, the levels of voting vary greatly in India at the State level (see Table A3.3 in Appendix 3). In states with high education and political consciousness, participation has reached levels one normally finds in national elections in continental Europe. Kerala is an outstanding example of this. But equally significant is the very high level of participation in the small hill states, long thought to be outside the pale of national democratic politics. The figures from 1993–95, with Arunachal Pradesh at 81.4 per cent, Manipur at 88.8 per cent Mizoram at 80.8 per cent and Sikkim at 81 per cent, show how important political participation has become even for regions that are normally so far removed from the mainstream of India's high politics (see Table A3.3 in Appendix 3).

Trust in Democracy: Interfacing Institutions and Politics in India

Trust in institutions is both a cause and consequence of democratic politics. We shall now discuss the survey findings with regard to trust in institutions from 1996 and its equivalent data from 2004 (see Tables 2.1, 2.2 and 2.3).

TABLE 2.1
Trust in Institutions 1996

Question: I would like to seek your opinion about different institutions of India in which you may have a good deal of trust, some trust or no trust at all.

Great deal of trust/confidence in …	Stakeholders	Others	Rebels	Total (sample average)
The Central Government	41.8	28.4	38.8	35.1
The state government	42.5	29.3	39.2	37.1
The local government/panchayat/ municipality	43.7	34.5	39.1	39.0
The judiciary	50.1	34	37.5	41.5
The Election Commission	57.1	34.1	54.7	45.8
Political parties	21.2	13.7	17.8	17.3
Government officials	20.7	13.6	19.6	17.2
Elected representatives	25.7	14.7	18.4	19.9
The police	15.2	10.5	15	12.9

Source NES, CSDS 1996.

The trust question was not repeated in 2004. Instead, we have a more direct question on the form of government.

TABLE 2.2
Normative Evaluation of Democracy 2004

Question: People have different opinions about democracy. Some people believe that democracy is better than any form of government. Others believe that dictatorship is better than democracy in certain conditions. And, others believe that it makes no real difference between a democratic or any other form of government. What is your opinion about it?

Opinion	Stakeholders	Others	Rebels	Total (sample average)
Democracy is better	84.6	52.5	68.5	70.6
Dictatorship is better	3.0	3.6	10.5	3.7
Makes no difference	3.8	10.5	7.6	6.0
DK	8.6	35.7	13.5	19.9

Source NES, CSDS 2004.

TABLE 2.3
Kashmir: Challenge to India's Statehood

Question: People's opinions are divided on the issue of Kashmir problem—some people say that the government should suppress the agitation by any means while others say that this problem should be resolved by negotiation. What would you say—should the agitation be suppressed or resolved by negotiation?

Opinion	1996 (All)	1996 (Stakeholders)	2004 (All)	2004 Stakeholders
Negotiation	33.5	43.6	59.2	70.3
Cannot say	31.9	21.9	21.2	11.7
Suppression	11.1	13.8	8.8	9.9
Other	1.9	1.4	1.4	1.2
Not heard	21.6	19.4	9.3	6.9
Total	100	100	100	100

Source NES, CSDS 1996 and 2004.

Conclusion

We have examined in this chapter how, starting from an electorate largely organised as vote banks in the aftermath of Independence, India has gone on to become a stakeholders' democracy and the role that the context has played in the process of this transformation. Of course, not all have joined in. Some have continued to resist the power of the Indian state though not the modern idioms of politics or methods of political manipulation, going even to the extent of using parts of the state against the rest. But, more often than not, India's two-track political process that combines institutional participation with rational protest has succeeded in turning rebels into statesmen, just as the amorphous group of people not directly involved with the political process, ensconced between the stakeholders and the rebels, has shrunk, earning extra bonus points for democratic social change.

All of this is a far cry from the pessimistic prognosis of 'peaceful paralysis' by Barrington Moore who thought '... a strong element of coercion remains necessary if a change is to be made' (Moore 1966). The findings about the steady rise in the proportion of the Indian electorate that can be seen as 'stakeholders', their broad social base and robust political attitudes—all point in the direction of a robust and vibrant democratic political process. These findings, which would be reinforced by others in subsequent chapters, should put the apprehensions of scholars who had anticipated a difficult transition from the 'single-party-dominated' phase of Indian politics. Early pointers to these developments had already caught the critical eye of Rajni Kothari:

> In India, the legacy of a long tradition, the integrity of a historical culture and the great solidarities that were built through religious and social movements that were characteristically Indian had for long acted as buffers against an inherently fissiparous situation. The social system provided a key to political stability. Now this very social system is undergoing profound changes and has entered a process of continuous fluidity and fragmentation.
> (Kothari 1970: 3)

The robustness and resilience of the Indian 'model', replete with modern institutions and institutional trust, should provide a measure of security to these apprehensions. The developments discussed here indicate a certain degree of resilience of the political system which has been able to strike a dynamic balance between the perils of mass participation with all its potentials for exorbitant political demands and the rewards of popular legitimacy which alone can sustain long-term trends of nation and state formation, growth of citizenship and the growth of regional identity in the context of a co-operative federation.

Notes

1. See Jawaharlal Nehru, 'Tryst with Destiny', speech as reported by *The Hindu* in the issue of 15 August 1947. Reprinted in *The Hindu*, 15 August 2007. Though Shashi Tharoor does not use the metaphor, his depiction of Nehru's spirited oration is evocative of the myth of the Greek hero, both for the courage underpinning his modernist agenda and the subsequent ordeal it was to go through in the face of resistance by the unyielding forces of tradition. See Tharoor (1997 [2000], p. 15).
2. Nanda (1995) reports faction fights and rowdy behaviour in the national sessions of the Congress party long before the party got into real power, indicative of more recent happenings.
3. This follows theories of utility maximisation as proposed by Downs (1957) and Riker and Ordeshook (1973).
4. See Lijphart (1996) for an application of the logic of consociational type power working as a corrective to Indian federalism and as a general explanation of the stability and legitimacy of India's democracy. The 'room to manoeuvre in the middle' applies to the tendency of India's political elites to interpose themselves between the traditional society and the modern state.
5. See Mitra (1992) for a detailed discussion of this argument.

3
Continuity and Change in Indian Politics: An Inter-generational Analysis

Unlike many post-colonial states, India has been able to avert the crisis of succession. This crisis occurs when the ruling group is unable or unwilling to pass power on to the next generation. This is the case with many post-colonial states that start their independent careers with a brave programme of social change but fail to sustain it beyond the founding generation. More often than not, this is caused by the lack of inter-generational continuity in commitment to values vital to the system. Many factors such as population transfer, inter-generational mobility and patterns of social control account for this. The institutional arrangement of the political system itself plays a crucial role in this context. A robust political system is one which produces a consensus between generations at a given point of time, anticipates future demands and straddles between the generation currently in power and future generations.

We examine the issue of inter-generational continuity in India in this chapter. The social basis of power has changed considerably over the past six decades since Independence. However, the continuity of commitment to the core values of the system between the two age cohorts, roughly corresponding to those born at or after the end of colonial rule and those born during the colonial rule and the ones born after it ended, remains strong. Even as the political system recruits new social forces into positions of power and leadership, it subtly transforms them, recasting their initial attitudes into a mould that conforms to the democratic character of the system. As a preliminary step to the analysis of the transformative capacity of India's political system, going to be taken up in the subsequent chapters, this chapter analyses inter-generational continuity in terms of the political attitudes and values of the two main age cohorts of the Indian electorate in order to establish an empirical argument with regard to the sustainability of the Indian 'model' (see Figure 1.1).

Plus ça Change? The Conservative Dynamism of Indian Politics

Debates about the nature and pace of social change deeply divide the people in the post-colonial states. The political articulation of these divisions and their further transformation into violent conflict, hold the potential for disastrous consequences for the state. The main reason for singling out the issue of the generational conflict for detailed analysis is derived from the fact that, unlike gender, caste and class—generation, particularly in a post-colonial context—often represents a radical break with history. The generation that came to maturity after Independence in many post-colonial states—the younger cohort in the population, whether it is in the form of angry students or younger officers and soldiers in the armed forces—is often the main source of challenge to the basic values and institutions that the generation to which power was transferred at Independence stands for. However, while there has been plenty of debate in post-Independence India relating both to politics *within* the system as well as the politics *of* the system, the ferocity of the controversies has been more in rhetoric than in action. Age, except perhaps in the North-East, has not appeared in the form of a social cleavage underpinning political competition.

Generation-based conflict is different from other cleavages because of the radical rupture it leads to in terms of the modes of conviviality and social discourse. In a situation where the competing parties in the conflict break off all contact with one another, or, systematically talk past one another, violence and civil war are the most likely outcomes. When normative conflicts give rise to an intergenerational debate and the electoral process becomes a means through which it is articulated, the hiatus between generations can precipitate a crisis. On the other hand, some differences between generations, with regard to the key issues of the system, can induct new energy to the system and keep it in tune with the changing political environment. Generational balance is the key to stability and renewal.

The survey data analysed in this book are intended to help identify the linkage between the resilience of India's modern institutions and the inner world of the citizens. These voices—which are assertive, discordant, self-contradictory, but, as we argue here, ultimately convergent within the framework of India's democracy—have long historical trails. In many post-colonial states, the failure to gain acceptance for the political system by the post-Independence generation hinders a smooth succession of power. In the light of these examples, India's ability to sustain the main structure of its parliamentary democracy and federal state, in spite of the passing away of the generation of Independence, makes inter-generational difference an important area of inquiry. We take this up in this chapter by comparing the attitudes of the two generations of Indians on a grid of issues, crucial to the system. By comparing the attitudes and values of the generation that was born after Independence with the ones of those born before, the chapter asks if a distinctive political idiom has evolved in India and, it draws on survey data to understand the challenges of politics and social change.

Age Cohorts and Salient Elements of Political Culture

Indian political discourse refers to the generational conflict in terms of the values and attitudes of the 'Midnight's Children', a concept that has gained popular currency after Salman Rushdie's work of fiction with the same title.[1] The method that we shall follow in this chapter in order to evaluate the generational attitudes towards the achievements of India during the six decades since Independence will draw on these usages and operationalise them by dividing the sample of our survey into two groups. Those who are about 45 years of age in case of the 1996 survey and 55 years for the

2004 survey would be treated as the representatives of the post-Independence generation, who would then be compared to those who are older.

The attitudes we analyse here have evolved in response to the issues which serve as reference points for two generations of India's voting population. However, the listing of the main components of India's political culture for the purpose of this comparison is not easy, partly because, being a relatively open society, the debate on India and within India is vast and also because the very nature of India's political discourse, while generating a rich body of ideas, never shies away from casting doubts on those very ideas themselves.[2] Since the research on India, carried out over the past five decades, has produced a rich body of information on these questions, the following list is necessarily selective.

Institutionalisation of authority is one of the most important criteria to measure the success that a post-colonial society has in achieving and sustaining statehood, one where India has been relatively more successful than the majority of post-colonial societies. Political power is wielded by democratically elected governments. In the beginning, the Indian National Congress, which had functioned as an umbrella organisation for the co-ordination of the anti-colonial movement against British colonial rule, won power at the federal as well as the regional level all across India. That hegemonic role of the Congress party was over within 20 years of the founding of the Republic. Opposition parties of the Left and Right as well as Centre started coming to power, first at the level of regions and eventually, at the federal level. However, in spite of this change, the major institutions of the state have survived. Even before the French put the concept of cohabitation into the language of politics, Indians started practising it in terms of the sharing of power by elected governments of the Right, Left and Centre at the regional level, with the Central Government being controlled by the Indian National Congress. The territorial division has seen many changes, particularly at the level of the regions. New regions have been created to give more salience to regional identity, language and economic needs. But, unlike in neighbouring Pakistan, which, mainly as a result of regional imbalance, split into two in 1971, the territorial integrity of India continues to be stable.

India's institutions are not mere artificial constructions, devoid of essence. For proof, we need only look at the Supreme Court of India, which, at its own initiative, ordered the Central Bureau of Investigation (a government agency), to speed up the investigations into illegal money changing and other forms of corruption by highly placed politicians and civil servants. Thanks to a watchful judiciary and media, trust in institutions has emerged as one of the crucial foundations of the Indian Republic.

Mass political participation as the basis of legitimacy is the second crucial value of India's political system. The perception of participation, particularly of voting as the basis of a sense of efficacy on the part of the political actor, is an important corollary of this systemic value. Political power in India originates through the consent of the governed, expressed through regular elections at the level of the federal parliament, regional assemblies, or Gram Panchayats (village councils).[3] Elections are supervised by an independent body called the Election Commission, which is guaranteed autonomy by constitutional design and which maintains fairness and efficiency. Participation in elections was in the region of 40 per cent of those eligible to vote in the first elections after Independence, but that has gone up to about 60 per cent. Elections are crucial to the exercise of power in legislative bodies at all levels of the system; they are essential to the functioning of any public or private body which receives public money.[4] Microstudies in Indian villages show how deep the roots of the electoral principle are. Electoral campaigns are conducted routinely not only for elections to the Parliament, State Assembly and Gram Panchayat—the three legislative layers of the country—but also elections to the co-operative society, the youth group, the women's association, the committees of the high school, the minor school and the primary school as well as to the associations for the welfare of the former untouchables and tribals.

Universal adult franchise was introduced in India in 1952 and both the non-democratic Left and the non-democratic Right were authorised to compete equally with the centre and the moderate

Left and Right for political power through elections. Participating in the first General Elections after Independence were the Communist Party of India which only three years earlier had risen in a violent peasant revolution against the nascent Indian state, as well as the Hindu Right-wing party Jan Sangh, joining the electoral fray with the background of the assassination of Mahatma Gandhi by a member of the Rashtriya Swayamsevak Sangh, a Hindu extremist group closely allied to the Hindu nationalist party. This bold gamble on the part of Jawaharlal Nehru appears to have paid rich dividends, by encouraging attitudes favourable to multi-party democracy within these extremist groups.

India's record, with regard to electoral participation at the Central and regional levels, is comparable to stable western democracies. Elected governments have taken major policy initiatives. Parties have alternated in power as a result of elections. On all aggregate indicators of participation, India has kept up steady progress. The level of electoral participation has gone up steadily, reaching the levels of continental European voting in some parts of the country. Participation is widely spread. We learn from survey data that there is no significant variation in participation along gender, age, occupation, caste, religion and residence.

A sense of common citizenship is the third most important norm that one can attribute to the political system. Using the Constitution as the main instrument, the Republic of India sought to establish individual rights to equality—irrespective of religion, race, caste, creed, gender, age, or place of birth—as the cornerstone of the political and the social process. In a country where the society was traditionally organised on the principle of hierarchy of gender and status, the introduction of the principle of equality was nothing short of a revolution. The effect of this radical juxtaposition of social inequality and legal equality first manifested itself, in a public way, in the 1960s, when political parties, set up by the backward castes, who had traditionally worked for landowners from the upper-castes as tenants or as small and marginal farmers, started exercising power in their own right. The 1980s saw the next wave of this revolutionary process when the former untouchables—beneficiaries of legislative quotas and other methods of affirmative social action—reached independent political status as key components of national and regional political formations. The stories of great political mobility in spite of social disadvantages are many, but none so impressive as among the new breed of assertive political leaders, who have, in the span of one generation, overcome the disadvantages of gender, class, caste and minority religious status.

The subsequent chapters of this book will provide further evidence of the growth of citizenship in India. It is useful at this stage to refer to the historical context in which this has occurred. Since the recent prominence of the Bharatiya Janata Party (BJP), which many identify with Hindu Nationalism, has drawn worldwide attention to the conditions of Muslims in India, our discussion of the condition of Muslims and other non-Hindus, who form about 18 per cent of the population, is an important part of the understanding of the growth of equal citizenship in India. At Independence, when British India was partitioned and Pakistan was created as a homeland for the Muslims of the subcontinent, about a third of India's Muslims nevertheless chose to stay on in the country of their birth. Rather than following the politics of separation, the electoral choice of India's Muslims follows multiple considerations, more like their other non-Hindu neighbours. This should reassure those who always see the polarisation of India's political community on the lines of religion. The point is also proved from the presence of a large number of Muslims in India's legislatures. Except for the former untouchables and tribals who get guaranteed representation in India's legislatures, simple majority rather than proportional representation is the general rule in Indian election. However, the total percentage of Muslims in India's legislatures is not very different from their share of the population. In addition, Muslims are found in such high offices as India's President, the Supreme Court and the High Courts in the States, the Bureaucracy and the Military, even in the arena of competitive sports.

A joint emphasis on growth and redistribution is our fourth important criterion, because the founders of the political system held public welfare as the foundation of legitimacy. Despite the controversy over the exact nature of poverty reduction, one can safely assert that the percentage of the population below the poverty line has been reduced significantly over the past decades. Thanks to the rise in food production and a competent public distribution system based on a network of food reserves linked to a system of fair price shops, famines have become a thing of the past. During the 150 years of the colonial rule, India's GNP per capita hardly registered any growth at all. After the steady but slow growth over several decades since Independence, Indian economy has gathered momentum since 1991 when India started liberalising the economy, accelerating the pace of the integration of India's economy with the international market. This has, on the whole, improved the international confidence in India's economic potential. The chapter analyses the perception of the economic scene by the two age cohorts.

Finally, the perception of the state of law and order is crucial to the legitimacy and stability of a political system. Compared to many anti-colonial movements, India's struggle for Independence was largely peaceful in character. Politics after Independence has continued this trend. The alternative of violent class struggle has had its advocates. Following the split of the Communist Party of India (Marxist), the Maoist CPI (M-L) had briefly emerged as a powerful challenger to the state and had enjoyed a period of intense support from sections of students. However, the movement remained geographically limited to pockets of strength and has not been seen as a party specific to the youth. While the violent mass insurgencies of Punjab, Kashmir and the North-East have attracted worldwide attention, on the whole, India continues to be relatively orderly. Rather than violent conflict, a widely dispersed belief in the rationality of protest movements and their acceptance as a legitimate political resource is an integral part of India's political culture.

Despite the aura of Gandhi and Nehru that still underpins political rhetoric of India's leaders, violent, bitter inter-community riots such as those in Ayodhya (1992), Gujarat (2002) and Orissa (2008) have drawn international attention. However, the debate, mostly condemnatory in its tone in the English press, provides a contrast to the vernacular press of India, which is more ambivalent. This gives us a new dimension on such conflicts. Clearly, democracy, which has brought power in the hands of ordinary people, has also revived historical memories of Islamic invasion, forced mass conversion, loot and violence on women. The fear and anxiety translate themselves, through the political mobilisation, into social and communal conflict.

The coexistence of a main framework of cultural traits, integral to stable democracies and an undercurrent of social attitudes that indicate their negation, resulting in violent riots and occasional collapse of democratic rule, must come across as confusing to the observer. The issue is: Why do the structures of representative democracy function, in spite of the contradictions that underpin the political discourse? The survey data provide an opportunity to dissect these apparent contradictions and move in the direction of identifying their inter-connection. The contradiction of civic virtues and uncivil attitudes is caused by social cleavages, such as caste, class, gender, religion and in many post-colonial societies, the political incompatibility of generations. The analysis we are going to take up in this chapter will concentrate on the generational conflict of attitudes and values.

Inter-generational Attitudes Towards Efficacy and Trust

The survey data on the main components of India's political culture and the doubts that underpin them, provide some concrete issues where we can compare the views of the generations. In this section we shall present some statistical information on these issues.

Level of Education

There are interesting differences between the two generations in terms of formal education. While the number of illiterates among the Midnight's Children is still disconcertingly high, it is significantly lower than their elders, where about half of them are illiterate (see Table 3.1). At the upper level, however, about 50 per cent have formal education at the level of middle school or above, a figure that is twice as high as that of the elders.

TABLE 3.1
Level of Education by Generation (in per cent) 2004

Generation	Illiterate	Up primary	Middle school	Higher secondary	College and above
Post-Independence	29.9	22.0	13.8	24.1	10.2
Pre-Independence	49.0	25.3	8.4	12.0	5.3
All	**35.4**	**22.9**	**12.3**	**20.6**	**8.8**

Source NES, CSDS 2004.

Institutionalisation and Participation

Now that we have established that the Midnight's Children are better educated than their elders, one could expect political attitudes and a sense of their own worth at variance with the pre-Independence generation. Astoundingly, that does not appear to be the case. There is a process of levelling that is built into India's political discourse, so much so that when it comes to the crucial question of efficacy, the generational differences do not appear to be radically at variance.

As answer to the question: *Do you think your vote has an effect on how things are run in this country, or, do you think your vote makes no difference?*, about 70 per cent of the post-Independence generation consider their vote to have effect, compared to about 64 per cent of the pre-Independence generation (see Table 3.2). While the score for the younger generation is several points higher with regard to the sense of efficacy, it should be noted here that even though a majority of them are illiterate, the majority of the older generation *does* think of its participation as both meaningful and efficacious.

TABLE 3.2
Effect of Vote by Generation (in per cent) 2004

Generation	No difference	Don't know	Has effect
Post-Independence	16.7	14.4	68.9
Pre-Independence	19.3	16.5	64.2
All	**17.5**	**15.0**	**67.5**

Source NES, CSDS 2004.

When asked about the instrumental efficacy of political parties: *How much in your opinion do political parties help to make government pay attention to the people—good deal, somewhat or not much?*, no great difference emerged between the two generations (see Table 3.3). It is interesting to note that when we aggregate the 'somewhat' and 'great deal' scores, more people of both generations find parties instrumentally efficacious than the opposite. The close to 40 per cent score of 'not at all', indicating very low level of trust in political parties (where the two generations draw level), however, gives indications of an underlying fragility within the political system.

TABLE 3.3
Parties' Attention to People by Generation (in per cent) 1996

Generation	Not at all	Somewhat	Great deal
Post-Independence	38.5	43.8	17.1
Pre-Independence	38.5	42.5	18.3
All	**38.5**	**43.5**	**17.4**

Source NES, CSDS 1996.

In the same vein, when asked, *How much does having elections from time to time make the government pay attention to the people—good deal, somewhat or not much?*—we find a quarter, in both generations, having rather a low opinion of the instrumental efficacy of the electoral process in terms of its impact on the policies of the government (see Table 3.4). The aggregate of the moderate to highly positive evaluation of the efficacy of the electoral process indicates a higher score for the younger generation than the older, pointing towards a more optimistic and positive view of the capacity of the electoral process in influencing government.

TABLE 3.4
Importance of Election by Generation (in per cent) 1996

Generation	Not much	Somewhat	Good deal
Post-Independence	25.6	35.3	12.2
Pre-Independence	25.3	30.8	10.9
All	**25.5**	**34.0**	**11.9**

Source NES, CSDS 1996.

The process of political participation and the sense of efficacy both assume the government as the main reference point, because influencing the government is the overall objective of both. In order to measure the perception of the government in its various institutional expressions, including the two institutions whose function is to ensure fair and legal government, we have developed a general indicator by aggregating a number of measures of trust. The responses to the various measures of trust have been added up to produce a composite index. The items included in this battery are as follows—trust in the Central Government, state government, local government, judiciary and trust in the Election Commission.

The results, presented in Table 3.5, show over three-quarters of the post-Independence generation exhibiting medium or high trust in institutions, slightly more than the generation born before Independence. This is significant in view of the fact that the institutions are the very ones with which the Republic of India started its career. Manifestly, contrary to the impression created in the media, trust in institutions stays reasonably high, actually higher among the Midnight's Children than the generation that witnessed the birth of the Republic.

TABLE 3.5
Trust in Institutions by Generations (in per cent) 1996

Generation	Low	Medium	High
Post-Independence	24.9	45.3	29.7
Pre-Independence	26.7	42.6	30.7
All	**25.4**	**44.6**	**30.0**

Source NES, CSDS 1996.

We next take up the attitudes towards the main political, religious and moral issues of the day. It will be noticed from the data presented in the subsequent tables that in practically all cases, the post-Independence generation is more sure about its attitudes (that is, there are fewer of them who do not profess an opinion); and, their opinion is polarised, that is, there is more support for the syncretic, multi-cultural, accommodative position, but also, marginally more support for the hard, cultural-nationalist position.

Attitudes Towards Social Conflict and Discrimination

The demolition of the Babri Mosque on 6 December 1992 marks a watershed in Indian politics. In one powerful and poignant move, this single incident reopened the confessional character of the state in India as an open issue, challenging those who were, so far, contended to leave the ambiguous character of the Constitution with regard to religion relatively undisturbed. It simultaneously showed the high price of non-action in terms of direct, anarchic, mass outbursts. It also indicated the need for concerted action by those who consider tolerance and minority rights to be important elements of Indian politics, making it imperative for mainstream Hindu nationalism to moderate its tone and to seek electoral allies outside the BJP and its partners.

The data presented in Table 3.6 capture the political consequences of the incident at Ayodhya four years after it took place. About two-fifth of the national electorate disapproves of the demolition; the level of disapproval among the younger generation is significantly higher than among the older generation. Interestingly, however, while only a small minority of about a fifth of the electorate approves of the demolition, the percentage is marginally higher among the younger people. The question was formulated in the following way: *Some people say that the demolition [of the disputed building in Ayodhya (Babri Masjid)] was justified while others say it was not justified. What would you say, was it justified or not justified?*

TABLE 3.6
Attitudes Towards Ayodhya Incident by Generation (in per cent) 1996

Generation	Unjustified	Can't say	Justified
Post-Independence	39.2	10.2	23.0
Pre-Independence	34.5	9.9	22.4
All	**37.9**	**10.1**	**22.8**

Source NES, CSDS 1996.

54   When Rebels Become Stakeholders

The attitude of accommodation and tolerance towards minorities that the largest number of respondents in Table 3.6 expresses, finds an echo in further questions that tap the same dimension. On the issue of an approach of accommodation towards Pakistan, we notice, in Table 3.7, a greater agreement towards accommodation from both generations. This position, which became the accepted Indian policy in the years after the survey, indicated a departure from the line developed by Indira Gandhi, first in the late 1960s and put to practice in the 1980s through a number of tactical moves, particularly against Pakistan. However, responses to the question, *India should make more efforts to develop friendly relations with Pakistan. Do you agree or disagree?* do reveal some support for the continuation of a policy of domination of the smaller neighbours by India. Significantly, support for this policy is higher among the younger generation than the older people.

TABLE 3.7
Policy Towards Pakistan by Generation (in per cent) 1996

Generation	Disagree	Can't say	Agree
Post-Independence	18.3	36.1	45.2
Pre-Independence	15.3	41.7	42.6
All	**17.5**	**37.7**	**44.5**

Source   NES, CSDS 1996.

The policy options towards the militant insurgency in Kashmir evokes a comparable picture, with generally more people opting for negotiation than suppression of the insurgency by force. The lower 'can't say' indicates a comparably higher readiness of the younger generation to pronounce itself—and they do tend to express stronger views on both options (see Table 3.8). *People's opinions are divided on the issue of the Kashmir problem—some people say that government should suppress the agitation by any means, while others say that this problem should be resolved by negotiations. What would you say, should the agitation be suppressed or should it be resolved by negotiation?*

On the issue of nuclear weapons, however, we have greater willingness from both generations to keep that option open.

TABLE 3.8
Resolution of Kashmir Issue by Generation (in per cent) 2004

Generation	Negotiation	Can't say	Suppression
Post-Independence	60.6	28.6	9.4
Pre-Independence	55.7	35.3	7.4
Total	**59.2**	**30.6**	**8.8**

Source NES, CSDS 2004.

We asked: *There is no need for India to make atomic bomb. Do you agree or disagree with this?* Here the younger leads the older, just as in the other option of foreclosing the nuclear option. The higher responses on both options among the post-Independence generation apparently come from the fact that the rate of the 'can't say' option is about 7 per cent lower among them than is the case with the older generation (see Table 3.9).

TABLE 3.9
No Need of Atomic Bomb by Generation (in per cent) 2004

Generation	Agree	No opinion	Disagree
Post-Independence	32.2	33.4	34.4
Pre-Independence	29.3	41.0	29.7
All	**31.4**	**35.6**	**33.0**

Source NES, CSDS 2004.

The problem of personal law has been an emotive issue since the Shah Bano incident[5] where an attempt to equalise the law of divorce and alimony for all women (regardless of religion) through judicial interpretation was defeated by an amendment of the constitution which retained the status quo in favour of the practice of polygamy among Muslims. Responses to the question '*Every community should be allowed to have its own laws to govern marriage and property rights. Do you agree or disagree?*' show a greater degree of tolerance for different personal laws in the country than the opposition to such plurality, among the younger generation than the older people (see Table 3.10).

Setting up quotas for the underprivileged sections of the population in public services and admissions to educational institutions

TABLE 3.10
Separate Civil Code by Generation (in per cent) 1996

Generation	Disagree	Don't know	Agree
Post-Independence	31.4	23.7	44.5
Pre-Independence	26.9	28.5	44.3
All	**30.1**	**25.0**	**44.5**

Source NES, CSDS 1996.

is one of the instruments with which the state in India has sought to combat the historical weight of social discrimination. In this vein, the reservation of 30 per cent of all elected places in village councils has already been written into the basic law of the land through the 73rd Amendment to the Constitution in 1993.[6] The extension of similar reservations for women in legislatures at higher levels has been suggested as the next logical step forward. The responses to this question have been overwhelmingly in favour throughout the electorate as a whole, with three-quarters of the post-Independence generation supporting the measure, about 5 per cent higher than the older people (see Table 3.11). The posited question was—*Like Gram Panchayats, there should be reservations for women in assemblies and Parliament. Do you agree or disagree?*

TABLE 3.11
Reservation for Women by Generation (in per cent) 2004

Generation	Disagree	Don't know	Agree
Post-Independence	13.8	13.7	72.5
Pre-Independence	12.9	19.6	67.5
All	**13.6**	**15.3**	**71.1**

Source NES, CSDS 2004.

Unlike women, lower classes, former untouchables and backward castes, there is no provision in the Constitution for quotas for religious minorities. Should the practice of reservations be further extended to Muslims? The issue remains implicit, but deeply divisive. To the extent that the Muslim electorate is perceived to vote as a bloc, political parties see the logic of conceptualising their interests in terms of their religious character as a minority rather than according to the conventional categories of caste, class, gender and age. Since the Constitution prohibits discrimination on the basis of religion and the Election Commission has stringent rules against the use of religion for electoral purposes, explicit statements of this strategy would be possibly against the law of the country/ land. Parties, therefore, often resort to informal quotas for Muslim candidates, just as the government often appoints Muslims to high positions in the government as a token of its commitment to the welfare of the minorities. The practice has been vigorously criticised by the Hindu nationalists as 'pseudo-secularism', which actually traps a part of the population into vote banks—conveniently designed political boxes which are deftly manipulated by vote-hungry politicians at election times. The controversial character of the issue can be seen from the responses in Table 3.12, where less than a fifth of the electorate agrees with the assertion than the needs of Muslims have been neglected. Of particular interest to us is the difference between the responses of the generations; the older generation which has lived through the trauma of Partition has a greater rate of non-response compared to the younger, who are more polarised than the older people, with more of them perceiving Muslims as a neglected minority but also more of the post-Independence generation suggesting that the needs of Muslims have not been neglected. The question, in this case, was: *The needs and problems of Muslims have been neglected in India. Do you agree or disagree?*

TABLE 3.12
Needs of Muslims Neglected
by Generation (in per cent) 2004

Generation	Disagree	No opinion	Agree
Post-Independence	43.6	29.4	27.0
Pre-Independence	39.3	35.3	25.4
All	**42.3**	**31.1**	**26.5**

Source NES, CSDS 2004.

Age Cohorts and the Economy

When it comes to the attitudes towards the economy, the post-Independence generation distinguishes itself with a robust and buoyant attitude. Three questions were asked to measure the level of satisfaction with the economy in the past and present, as well as the expectations about the economic future. The answers to these are reported in Table 3.13.[7]

TABLE 3.13
Economic Satisfaction by Generation (in per cent) 2004

Generation	Past	Present	Future	Average
Post-Independence	28.1	64.9	52.0	48.3
Pre-Independence	23.3	60.9	43.4	42.5
All	**26.7**	**63.7**	**49.5**	**46.6**

Source NES, CSDS 2004.

On each score, the post-Independence generation is ahead of its seniors. Even though figures reported under 'future will get better' category are lower than those satisfied with their present, the fact that the future expectation is much higher than the experience of the past, indicates a sense of generalised confidence in the system as a whole.

Age Cohorts and Liberalisation of the Economy

When it comes to the specific issue of liberalisation, for which two questions have been asked, the first point to note is the large extent of non-response, much larger among older respondents than among the post-Independence generation (see Tables 3.14 and 3.15).

TABLE 3.14
Privatisation by Generation (in per cent) 2004

Generation	Disagree	No opinion	Agree
Post-Independence	47.2	28.4	24.4
Pre-Independence	43.5	35.1	21.4
All	**46.2**	**30.2**	**23.6**

Source NES, CSDS 2004.

However, with regard to the evaluation of the measures being undertaken to liberalise the economy, whether through privatisation of public sector undertakings or through closer integration with the world market, opinions of both the generations tend to be polarised, that is, some are more enthusiastic and others are more sceptical. The first question was: *Government companies should be given in private hands. Do you agree or disagree?*

The second question was: *Foreign companies should not be allowed free trade in India. Do you agree or disagree?*

TABLE 3.15
No Free Trade to Foreign Companies by Generation (in per cent) 2004

Generation	Disagree	Don't know	Agree
Post-Independence	31.2	29.1	39.7
Pre-Independence	27.5	36.2	36.3
All	**30.1**	**31.1**	**38.8**

Source NES, CSDS 2004.

The opinions and attitudes towards liberalisation should be seen in the context of a relatively strong commitment to egalitarianism, which, thanks to the democratic ethos propagated by India's leaders since Independence, has become a part of the core values of the system. This can be seen from the answers to the question regarding the legitimate upper limits to wealth (see Table 3.16). *Some people say that the government should pass legislation so that people are not allowed to own and possess a large amount of land and property. Others say that people should be allowed to own as much property and land as they can make/acquire. What would you say?*

TABLE 3.16
Limited Ownership by Generation (in per cent) 2004

Generation	No ceiling	Don't know	Ceiling
Post-Independence	17.7	13.9	68.4
Pre-Independence	16.2	17.6	66.2
All	**17.3**	**14.9**	**67.8**

Source NES, CSDS 2004.

Participation and Partisanship

Similarly, the necessity of parties and elections for the viability of the political system is a deeply held value. So strong is the belief, indeed, that their hypothetical abolition, advocated from time to time and practised for a period of 19 months during the Emergency regime of Indira Gandhi (1975–77), is seen as a solution that is unlikely to lead to better government. While this opinion is advocated by a vast majority of over 72 per cent of the population as a whole (see Table 3.17), the proportion is even higher among the Midnight's Children. *Suppose there were no parties or assemblies and elections were not held—do you think that the government in this country can [then] be run better?*

TABLE 3.17
Government Better Without Parties by Generation (in per cent) 2004

Generation	No	Yes	Can't Say
Post-Independence	73.3	9.1	17.6
Pre-Independence	69.7	8.7	21.6
All	**72.3**	**9.0**	**18.7**

Source NES, CSDS 2004.

Finally, the data on partisan preferences give us an explanation of the tendency of the political and social attitudes of the Midnight's Children to polarise at the extremes. Table 3.18 shows that, while the UPA, led by the Congress party enjoys an equal support from both the generations, the NDA led by the BJP gets slightly more support among the post-Independence generation. However, in the case of other parties, they are, more or less, equally divided.

TABLE 3.18
Party Support by Generation (in per cent) 2004

Generation	UPA	NDA	Left	BSP	SP+	Others
Post-Independence	21.4	21.6	3.1	2.9	3.0	3.3
Pre-Independence	21.3	18.5	3.4	2.4	2.7	3.3
Total	**21.4**	**20.7**	**3.2**	**2.7**	**2.9**	**3.3**

Source NES, CSDS 2004.

Conclusion: The Convergence of India's *Million Mutinies*

Looking at contemporary India five decades after Independence, one can argue that the bold vision of Nehru has found concrete shape, albeit in ways that might have surprised him somewhat. There are new kids on the bloc and many of them hail from social origins that are very different from what the case used to be during Nehru's watch. However, the main idiom of the political class remains very much unchanged. The available indications strongly suggest that the post-Independence generation remains committed to the legacy of constitutional democracy, rather like the one that had fought for independence from the colonial rule. The recently mobilised social groups have found the necessary space to explore the pre-colonial roots of Indian nationalism and to induct those sections of Indian society that have stayed outside the pale of India's political mainstream. This theme of continuity and change would be analysed at greater length and across a broader spectrum of issues in the next chapter.

Notes

1. References to the concept are many. See, for example, Sen Gupta (1996), where he raises the issue of the continuity in basic values between the Midnight's Children and their elders as a main parameter of the legitimacy of the post-colonial state.
2. For the writings of an early doubter, see Krishna (1979).
3. For a detailed discussion of the successful implementation of local-level democracy, see Bhattacharyya (1998).
4. The electoral principle, which was already being institutionalised as the most dependable basis of legitimacy in India, came bouncing back following the lifting of the Emergency.
5. The Shah Bano case, filed in the Supreme Court, became one of the main political issues in the 1980s. The judgement in this case, which sought to establish the rights of the divorced Muslim women as comparable to those of Hindu women under similar conditions, was ultimately overturned by an amendment of the Constitution. The measure, brought about by Rajiv Gandhi, who hoped, perhaps through this gesture, to retain the loyalty of the Indian Muslims, also created a major point for mobilisation in the hands of the BJP.

The Muslim Women (Protection of Rights on Divorce) Bill, passed on 5 May 1986 'only by dint of stringent three-line whip to enforce Congress Party discipline' provided a temporary reprieve, but indicated a deeper political crisis on the issue. See Rudolph and Rudolph (1987: 45).
6. For more details in the 73rd amendment, see Bhattacharyya (1997: 106, 138).
7. The questions asked and the abbreviation used for reporting the answers are as follows.
   (a) *During the past few years, has your financial situation improved, worsened, or has it stayed the same?* (Past—improved.)
   (b) *In whatever financial condition you are placed today, on the whole, are you satisfied with your present financial situation, somehow satisfied or not satisfied?* (Present—satisfied.)
   (c) *Now looking ahead and thinking about the next few years, do you expect that your financial situation will stay the way it is now, get better or get worse?* (Future—get better.)

4
The Elements of Political Agency and the Limits of Consensus

Social conflict and bickering, leavened with a deep political consensus, is a distinctive feature of contemporary Indian politics. The Indian Republic had set off on its perilous journey with the legacy of the Partition and the communist uprising in Telengana. However, while each left a trail of bitter memories, neither resulted in permanent political cleavages. Despite continuing, the Maoist insurgency over the past four decades and the intermittent outbreak of violent inter-community riots, the basic parameters of the Indian political system have remained intact. This Indian genre of conflict, which mobilises new social groups without breaking up the foundations of the political system, is crucial to the functioning of the neo-institutional model of orderly and democratic social change (Figure 1.1). India, in this respect, stands apart from many other transitional societies, which share with India the pre-Independence history of colonial rule but not the peculiar combination of the politicisation of social differences and their ruthless negotiation within the ever-expanding political arena.

We argue in this chapter that the stable equilibrium around the basic consensus has been possible, despite the passing of the Congress hegemony and the generation that was associated with the transfer of power, because of some elements of political agency that have helped India continuously replenish the stock of political capital. These factors that reinforce the dynamic model of orderly and democratic social change comprise of the vigorous and boisterous Indian electoral campaigns, political information and communication that contribute to the relative transparency of the system, perception of individual mobility and a certain abhorrence of political violence.

Political Aggregation in the Context of Social Diversity

India's daunting diversity is a challenge for the process of democratisation and modernisation to which Nehru was committed. The social choice, in order to be legitimate, needs to emerge out of the summation of a bewildering range of arenas, communities and social cleavages. At the same time, in order to be effective, it needs to be reasonably rapid and cohesive. Long-term partisanship and effective communication in the course of the campaign, that make this possible in the older democracies of the West, are not present in the same manner in India. But, economic inequality and its resultant effects—an even greater hurdle than social diversities—constitute a greater cause of concern for the legitimacy of the system. To sum up, problems of relative deprivation, regional imbalances, poor transport and communication links, mass poverty and illiteracy inhibit the growth of civil attitudes that Lipset and his generation of democracy theorists held as indispensable to the working of democratic institutions.[1] However, belying all popular myths about adverse conditions, India has succeeded in bringing a large swathe of its population into the democratic processes and the Indian electorate, as we have already seen in the previous chapter, has already established its credentials as a rational and discriminating body.

Voting Decision

One of the first questions that arise in connection with the electoral process is to what extent the campaign has an impact on electoral choice. We see from the data presented in Table 4.1 that the percentage of people who make up their minds once the election campaign starts is far more than those who had decided their

TABLE 4.1
Timing of Voting Preference (in per cent)

	1971	1996	1998	1999	2004
On polling day	26.3	19.6	16.0	14.1	13.9
During the campaign	23.0	38.6	44.6	38.6	26.5
Before the campaign	27.3	22.2	26.8	32.4	43.8
Can't say	1.8	7.0	4.1	4.5	3.1
Not applicable (did not vote)	21.7	12.7	8.5	10.4	12.7

Source NES, CSDS 1971, 1996, 1998, 1999, 2004.

partisan choice before the process of campaign began. Clearly, campaigns play a crucial role in influencing voters' choices. Having come to a considered decision, people have more of a tendency to remain stable (that is, fewer people make up their minds on the polling day now) than in 1971. Those who make their electoral choice on the polling day have declined from 26.3 per cent to only 13.9 per cent in 2004 (see Figure 4.1). Those making up their mind about whom to vote for in course of the campaign have also declined from 38.6 per cent in 1996 to 26.5 per cent in 2004. Most interestingly, those who have made up their mind before the campaign starts used to be about one-fourth of the total electorate in the past (22.2 per cent in 1996); this has now gone up significantly (43.8 per cent). This indicates a greater stability of the structure of electoral preferences and a consequent reduction of floating voters in the Indian electorate. Part of the explanation for this comes from the emergence in the 1990s of regional parties and electoral formations with binding contracts with specific social segments.

Those who settle their electoral choice on the polling day largely belong to the group of people who are less informed, which includes primarily women, older people, rural people and the illiterate. Contrary to this, people belonging to urban areas, highly educated and male, tend to take decisions at quite an early stage, that is, before the campaign starts (see Table 4.2). Interestingly, quite a few Muslims and Scheduled Castes have also taken their voting decisions before the start of the campaign. Interestingly,

FIGURE 4.1
Timing of Voting Preference

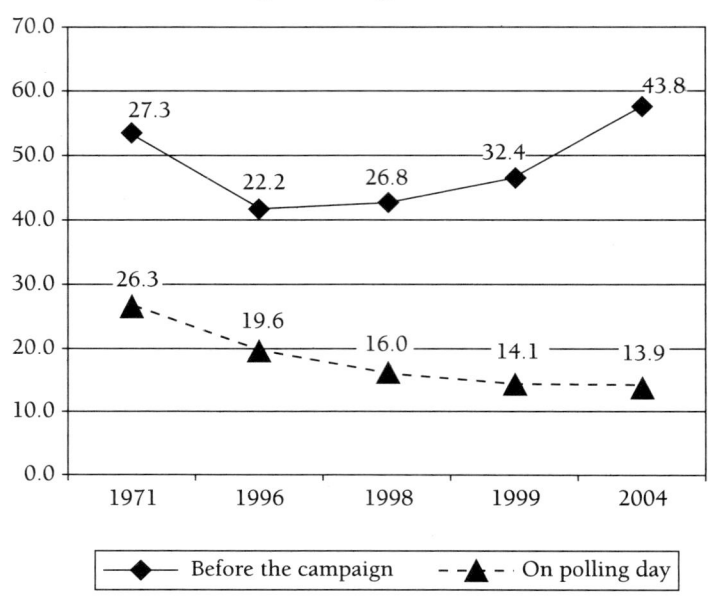

```
        1971    1996    1998    1999    2004
Before   27.3   22.2    26.8    32.4    43.8
On poll  26.3   19.6    16.0    14.1    13.9
```

♦ Before the campaign   ▲ On polling day

Source NES, CSDS 1971, 1996, 1998, 1999, 2004.

their proportions have almost doubled in 2004. Both these groups are known for their group voting in the past (Singh 1974b, Mitra and Chiriyankandath 1992). Characterised as traditional Congress voters their shift away from the Congress was largely caused by two factors, specially in the Hindi heartland. While the Scheduled Castes (Dalits) gradually moved towards Bahujan Samaj Party (BSP) after its formation in the late 1980s, the Muslims, after the 1992 Ayodhya episode, felt more confident with Mulayam Singh Yadav's and Lalu Prasad's Samajwadi Party and the Janata Dal respectively. This kind of group affinity seems to have affected these communities and their leaders to take a position quite in advance. That is why, despite belonging to group of less informed and low educated people half of them have been able to make up their mind about their voting choice prior to the actual campaign process.

TABLE 4.2
Timing of Voting Decision by Sub-categories:
Comparing 1996 and 2004

Timing of voting decision	1996 Polling day (%)	1996 Before the campaign (%)	2004 Polling day (%)	2004 Before the campaign (%)
College and above	7.0	27.2	8.8	51.6
Urban	13.6	25.4	12.1	45.6
Upper caste	15.3	27.1	12.4	46.2
Male	15.6	25.9	11.8	47.9
Upper class	16.9	23.1	9.4	50.6
Muslims	17.5	24.6	12.7	41.4
Scheduled Caste	18.2	23.5	14.3	44.5
All India	**19.6**	**22.2**	**13.9**	**43.8**
Aged less than 25 years	19.9	20.2	12.9	41.6
Hindu	20.1	21.8	14.3	43.5
Aged more than 56 years	21.2	22.6	15.1	44.2
OBC	21.3	18.6	14.8	42.3
Rural	21.4	21.2	14.4	43.3
Female	23.6	18.3	16.4	39.0
Very poor	24.9	20.5	16.8	40.9
Illiterate	26.2	17.9	18.0	38.6
Scheduled Tribe	31.3	15.4	14.5	40.0

Source NES, CSDS 1996, 2004.

Interest in the Campaign

Contrary to popular belief that frequent elections produce voter-fatigue and apathy, our data suggest otherwise. The percentage of people interested in the campaign has gone up from 27.9 per cent in 1971 to 36.6 per cent in 2004 (see Figure 4.2). But roughly two-thirds of electors do not take any interest in the campaign. When it comes to the disadvantaged sections of society, such as women, illiterates and Scheduled Tribes, the proportion of non-interested people crosses three-quarters, compared to two-thirds for the population as a whole. Similarly, the older people, rural voters, the poor and the Scheduled Castes also have the larger

FIGURE 4.2
Interest in Election Campaign

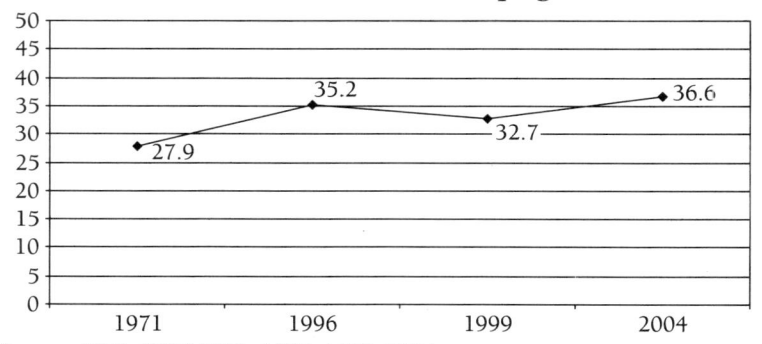

Year	Value
1971	27.9
1996	35.2
1999	32.7
2004	36.6

Source NES, CSDS 1971, 1996, 1999, 2004.

shares of the non-interested people among them. The reverse is true as well. Educated people belong to the highly interested group. Further calculations show that the Muslims and the Christians both show above the average level of interest in the campaign. The distribution of cases in 'interested' and 'not interested' categories and its relationship with different social groups clearly indicates that people belonging to informed groups tend to take greater interest in campaigns (see Table 4.3). Moreover, the interest in the campaign is not merely determined by knowledge: it is also influenced by one's level of partisanship (Sheth: 1975: 111–33).

Attending Election Meetings

Related to above findings, greater interest in the campaign has led to greater participation in election meetings, going up from about 12 per cent in 1971 to over 16 per cent in 1996. Participation in meetings went still higher in 1998 elections. It crossed 25 per cent mark and declined in 1999 and, subsequently, in 2004 elections. This may be due to increase in proportion of people who makes up their minds prior to the campaign starts. Women, along with illiterates form part of the least exposed groups. The poor, Scheduled Tribes and older people do not seem to have any interest in attending political meetings. However, the Muslims and the Scheduled Castes join the group of young, educated and well-to-do people who form the larger contingent of those attending election meetings.

TABLE 4.3
Interest in Election Campaign (in per cent)

	1971	1996	1999	2004
Interested in Election Campaign	27.9	35.2	32.7	36.6
No Interest	71.5	64.8	67.3	63.4
Took Interest in Campaign		**1996**		**2004**
Illiterate		21.8		25.1
Scheduled Tribe		22.3		32.4
Female		25.2		25.6
Very poor		30.3		31.0
56 years or above		32.0		31.3
Rural		34.1		36.8
Scheduled Caste		34.8		34.7
Hindu		35.2		36.3
All India		**35.2**		**36.6**
Muslims		35.9		37.3
OBC		36.5		38.1
Upper caste		37.7		36.9
25 years or less		37.9		37.1
Urban		38.9		35.9
Upper class		40.2		44.7
Male		45.0		46.2
College and above		52.3		47.8

Source NES, CSDS 1971, 1996, 1999, 2004.

We do not have comparable data from 1971, but the 1996 and 2004 data show that participation in meetings is not just passive. About 9 per cent of all those who have been interviewed admit having taken an active part in organising election meetings, joining processions, raising funds, etc., to help parties and candidates during the election campaign.

Participation in election campaigns presupposes a minimum level of involvement or motivation in politics for one reason or the other. Since very few people have any such motivation, we find such a low level of participation in campaign activities. Women, older people, the illiterates along with the Scheduled Tribes form the group of non-participants. In the male-dominated society of India, one is not surprised to find that about 80 per cent of campaign participants are men, which is roughly four times the rate for women (see Table 4.4). Participation in campaign positively correlates with income and level of education, but then those struggling hard for their livelihood would hardly find time to campaign for any party or candidate.

TABLE 4.4
Attendance of Election Meetings during Campaign (in per cent)

	1971	1996	1998	1999	2004
Yes	12.1	16.2	25.1	22.9	19.9
No	87.9	83.8	74.9	77.1	80.1
Election Meetings Attended, by Sub-categories		**1996**			**2004**
Female		7.7			9.3
Illiterate		9.5			12.0
Scheduled Tribe		9.9			20.8
Very poor		12.8			16.6
56 years or above		13.1			15.5
Rural		15.9			19.9
All India		**16.2**			**19.9**
Hindu		16.4			19.9
Upper caste		16.6			20.3
Upper class		16.7			25.2
OBC		16.8			19.7
Muslims		16.9			20.5
Urban		17.4			19.8
Scheduled Caste		17.7			18.9
25 years or less		18.3			19.2
College and above		20.2			27.1
Male		24.6			29.0

Source NES, CSDS 1971, 1996, 1998, 1999, 2004.

Index of Campaign Exposure

Peoples' orientation in election politics can be judged better by combining together the individual responses about one's interest in the campaign, attendance in political meetings and participation in campaign activities to construct a composite index of *Campaign Exposure*. The distribution of cases on the scale thus constructed and its relationship with different socio-demographic groups are presented in Table 4.5.

**TABLE 4.5
Campaign Exposure (in per cent)**

Campaign exposure	1996	1999	2004
No exposure	60.3	62.5	58.0
Low exposure	24.9	17.2	22.7
High exposure	14.8	20.3	19.3

Campaign Exposure, by Sub-categories	1996		2004	
	No exposure	High exposure	No exposure	High exposure
College and above	42.2	19.1	46.1	26.5
Male	49.5	23.0	46.9	28.5
Upper class	55.6	15.5	50.7	25.3
Urban	56.1	16.2	58.7	18.8
Upper caste	57.7	15.5	58.0	19.8
25 years or less	58.2	17.3	57.8	19.7
OBC	59.0	15.0	57.0	19.3
Muslims	59.7	14.9	57.0	19.6
Hindu	60.3	15.0	58.4	19.3
All India	**60.3**	**14.8**	**58.0**	**19.3**
Scheduled Caste	60.4	16.8	59.2	18.7
Rural	61.7	14.4	57.8	19.4
56 years or above	64.3	11.6	63.6	15.2
Very poor	65.4	10.9	63.2	15.7
Female	71.4	6.4	70.9	8.7
Illiterate	74.7	7.6	70.4	11.9
Scheduled Tribe	74.8	7.8	60.3	18.6

Source NES, CSDS 1996, 1999, 2004.

The detailed figures in Table 4.5 need to be seen relative to the column averages. Thus, whereas about 60 per cent of the sample in both the surveys had no campaign exposure at all, the figure was lower among particular sub-populations, for example, 42.2 per cent among college graduates and 49.5 per cent for men. Three-fourths of the Scheduled Tribes (74.8 per cent), illiterates (74.7 per cent) and the women (71.4 per cent) belong to the category of little exposure. Similarly, about two-thirds of the aged people (64.3) do not have any exposure of campaign. Contrary to this, while males dominate the group of highly exposed (78.5 per cent of the highly exposed are men) the educated people, the majority of whom belong to younger age group have greater exposure to campaign. The Scheduled Castes and the Muslims both belong to the above-average group. Interestingly, the former, with above the average exposure shows the importance they have begun to attach to politics, particularly the elections, through which, they feel, they might hasten the process of overcoming their other disabilities. To most of them, the fight for a share in political power appears to be easier than empowering themselves in other spheres of socio-economic life. Similarly, the Scheduled Tribes, who lag far behind all other social groups on this indicator in 1996, also show a sign of improvement, from 74.8 percent in 1996 to 60.3 per cent in 2004 elections.

House to House Contact

Finally, we have the obverse aspect of campaigns where, instead of the voter seeking out the candidates, they themselves are contacted by party workers in the course of an election campaign. An impressive number of electors are contacted by party workers. Despite the fact that mobility of campaign workers was restricted in 1996 and 2004 because of strict implementation of 'model code of conducts for the candidates', especially in number of four-wheel motorised vehicles being used in the campaign as compared to the 1971 elections, the percentage of electors contacted by the campaigner has not declined. On the contrary it has increased from 40.6 per cent in 1971 to 42.4 per cent in 1996 and to 51.8 per cent in 2004 (see Table 4.6). We asked the following question: *Did any candidate, party worker or canvasser come to your house during the campaign to ask for your vote?*

Scheduled Tribes, whose integration with the mainstream of national political life is far from complete, are subject to utter neglect from political leaders and party activists. Leave aside the period between two elections no special measures are taken to mobilise them during the election campaign as well. As the data suggest, they are the least exposed group insofar as campaign coverage is

TABLE 4.6
Visits by Candidate, Party Worker and Canvasser (in per cent)

	1971	1996	1998	1999	2004
Yes	40.6	42.4	41.5	48.5	51.8
No	59.4	57.6	58.5	51.5	48.2
Visits by Candidate, Party Worker, Canvasser		**1996**			**2004**
Scheduled Tribe		16.2			40.7
Illiterate		34.2			46.4
Female		38.7			48.9
Rural		40.7			51.5
Very poor		41.0			46.5
Hindu		41.6			51.6
All India		**42.4**			**51.8**
Upper caste		43.2			53.3
Upper class		44.0			60.2
Male		46.1			54.4
OBC		46.4			53.1
Scheduled Caste		46.5			51.7
Urban		47.9			53.1
Muslim		48.5			52.1
College and above		48.8			59.2

Source NES, CSDS 1971, 1996, 1998, 1999, 2004.

concerned. Neither do they have an interest in the campaign as one can see in Table 4.5 (74.8 per cent in 1996), nor do they take part in election meetings (9.9 per cent in 1996) (Table 4.4). Over and above these, they have not been approached by the party workers and canvassers either. Only 16.2 per cent of them (compared to 42.4 per cent for the total population as a whole) have been contacted by any party worker in 1996. However, the situation seems to have improved in 2004 when we notice that 40.7 per cent of them have been approached. Interestingly, the Muslims and the Scheduled Castes along with highly educated people form parts of the chosen few who have been contacted by the campaigners most. Considering greater propensity of group voting among the Muslims and the Scheduled Castes special attention have always been paid to them by respective parties and candidates to mobilise their support. However, the highly educated people enjoying special status in their respective communities and, by and large, performing the role of opinion makers in the society turn out to be the most favoured lot to be contacted first, not merely for their vote, but for general support.

Advice on the Vote

Notwithstanding the lack of exposure to campaign activities, for a large part of ordinary voters, the period of election campaign provides occasion for political discussion and mutual consultation leading to formation of opinion on various socio-political issues. Even people having no interest whatsoever in politics, suddenly become receptive and curious to know, at least, about the major contestants in their area. From dictating one's own political preference on others, to seeking advice to arrive at a decision all activities go side by side during the campaign to influence voters' choice.

To what extent is the voting decision made by the voter himself, as compared to the decision made by others on his behalf? An astoundingly high percentage of three-quarters of the population claim that the decision was an individual one, when they were asked: *In deciding whom to vote for, were you guided by anyone*? As for those who sought advice or in any case, were advised by others, the interesting point here is that the bulk of such people were advised by the members of their family and *not by people from outside*—a finding which strongly questions the existence of vote banks and those who engage in the buying and selling of votes.

Table 4.7 shows that proportion of people seeking advice has gone up from 25.3 per cent in 1996 to 40.5 per cent in 2004, indicating thereby the complexities of contests that have taken place in 2004 due to formation of two major alliances, led, respectively, by the BJP and the Congress. As expected, women top the list in seeking advice from others. More than one-third of them in 1996 and above 50 per cent in 2004 admit to have been advised, as against only 16.2 per cent and 32 per cent for men respectively. Similarly, illiterates, Scheduled Castes, Muslims and the very poor section of the society turn out to be advice-seekers more than the population as a whole. Not surprisingly, the highly educated have a markedly lower tendency to seek advice.

Table 4.7
Guided in Voting Decision (in per cent)

	1996	2004
Yes	25.3	40.5
No	74.7	59.5
'…were guided in the voting decision'		
College and above	13.2	29.8
Male	16.2	32.0
Scheduled Tribe	16.3	46.7
Upper class	23.4	39.3
Upper caste	24.1	39.2
All India	**25.3**	**40.5**
OBC	26.9	39.9
Muslims	28.2	45.6
Scheduled Caste	29.2	41.4
Very poor	29.5	40.9
Illiterate	31.2	49.2
Female	34.7	50.3

Source NES, CSDS 1996, 2004.

As regards the information for the sources of such advice, one may be surprised to note that the majority of people restricted their consultations to the family only. More than two-thirds of the total advice seekers have admitted to have received advice from family members. Interestingly, as further analysis of the data shows only 7.2 per cent of the advice seekers have sought advice from the caste and community leaders as against 69.7 per cent from the family. Negating the vote bank theory, generally construed to explain voting behaviour in India, our data suggest that voting decisions are made by and large by the voters themselves. Since this observation appears to fly directly in the face of what one observes in everyday life of the politics of the nation, this finding needs to be explained at some length.

A simple perusal of politics from India's local and regional arenas shows how powerful leaders are constantly pandering to their own constituencies where political coalitions based on caste and community constitute the main component of politics and where caste and religion dominate the discourse on politics. Does this not signify that electoral logic is group-oriented and that the political calculations of the voters as well as candidates are based on group affiliations rather than 'rational' individual maximisation of expected utility? Two points need to be noted here. In the first place, while the rhetoric of caste and community is the consequence of voters' strategic thinking, the process of reasoning is nevertheless based on the individual's perception of where his interests lie. Caste affiliation, in this mode of thinking, is a convenient tool with which to pool one's political resources. The mapping of caste or religion into political support is thus 'sophisticated', rather than mechanical and manipulated by the elite. Caste is thus an important consideration in the voters' choice but is a good predictor of partisanship only if the party is perceived by the community to be representing its collective interest. Setting up a candidate from a given caste is, therefore, no guarantee that s/he would be able to deliver the votes of the caste in question. The second important point here is that the articulation of individual interest in the rhetoric of the caste or community has long-term consequences for the idiom of politics, because the salience of the categories of discourse becomes important fixtures of the political process. As such, the expectation that with growing politicisation caste and community would lose their relevance as instruments of political mobilisation and would be superseded by class and ideological polarisation can turn out to be a neo-socialist utopia.

Seen in the light of the above, the data reported in Table 4.7 appear to suggest a complex process. It is possible to argue that the college educated and above might make up their mind on the basis of the information that they have and their heightened perception of the instrumentality of the vote compared to the illiterate. Similarly, men are less likely to be guided by someone as compared to women, or, the upper classes as compared to the very poor. However, the Other Backward Classes, Muslims and Scheduled Castes, given to a track record for pooling their votes in collective interest admit having been guided by someone in their voting preference. That the Scheduled Tribes do not appear to require external prompting for voting is not necessarily indicative of greater individual political consciousness, but to less political mobilisation, indicative of their late incorporation into the rough and tumble of competitive politics.

Further analysis of the data shows that caste and community leaders enjoy a greater credibility among the Muslims and the Scheduled Castes, where 14.2 per cent and 12.2 per cent respectively of the advice seekers followed their advice. Considering the rather closely-knit character of these communities on the one hand and special emphasis on sectional appeal by the parties and candidates to win over their support on the other, the hold of caste and community leaders, even in these groups, seems to be inconsequential as far as obedience to their advice on vote preference is concerned.

Who Governs? Political Information and the Rational Voter

Electoral choice is crucially contingent on political information. But here, as in life in general, the flow of this important resource follows Biblical wisdom: 'to those that have shall be added!' Findings based on an index of political information, constituted on the basis of four questions, namely, the names of the Prime Minister, the Chief Minister, the Member of the Lok Sabha from the respondent's constituency, both the recently elected one and the outgoing, from the 1996 survey (see Tables 4.8 and 4.8a) bear this out. Women, Tribals, the very poor and the illiterate are at the lower extreme, as opposed to college graduates and male, urban and upper-caste voters. Still, *ceteris paribus*, politically salient groups such as the Scheduled Castes and Muslims come up close to the national average, which shows to what extent politically relevant attributes can still compensate for the normal coordinates of information such as class and education.

TABLE 4.8
Index of Political Information (in per cent) 1996

	1996
No information	28.5
Low information	31.5
High information	40.0

Source NES, CSDS 1996.

TABLE 4.8a
Index of Political Information Per Social Group (in per cent) 1996

	No information (%)	High information (%)
College and above	1.4	84.3
Male	14.8	57.1
Urban	16.3	54.8
Upper caste	18.8	52.3
Upper class	20.5	50.6
25 years or less	24.7	42.6
Muslim	27.5	39.1
All India Average	**28.5**	**40.0**
Hindu	28.7	40.1
Scheduled Caste	29.8	33.7
OBC	31.9	36.8
Rural	32.3	35.4
56 years or above	38.3	31.7
Female	42.5	22.5
Very poor	44.6	20.6
Scheduled Tribe	48.4	19.9
Illiterate	51.1	14.8

Source NES, CSDS 1996.

Perception of Economic Conditions

One of the most important conditions determining prospect of any democratic system is its economic condition. A relatively prosperous nation, with an equitable distribution of societal resources, provides the best milieu for democracy. Studies on the subject show that 'the more well-to-do nations have a greater chance of sustaining democratic governments than those with widespread poverty' (Thorson 1962: 143). Any reservation expressed against the sustainability of Indian democracy is largely guided by such considerations only. Those who put forth this viewpoint perhaps have little knowledge of Indian culture, which derives its strength from theory of rebirth, wherein, for most of their sufferings people blame themselves (*karma* of previous birth) and not the system. Moreover, they have a tendency to judge their present in comparison to their own recent pasts. Rather than material conditions it is generally subjective feelings of a person with regard to his own economic condition, which shapes his view and/or attitude towards the system.

A battery of four questions measuring voters' perception of their own economic conditions was asked in order to investigate into the associated aspects of the financial question. Since the issues would be analysed in detail later in this book, we shall confine ourselves into the main themes here.

Improvement in Financial Situation

First of all, voters were asked to tell whether their financial situation has improved during the last few years. Data presented in Table 4.9 suggest an improvement. Compared to 1971, more people report an improvement in their financial situation, going up from 20.2 per cent to 29.2 per cent in 1996, but declining to 26.5 per cent in 2004. Nevertheless, it is more than 6 per cent higher than in 1971. Similarly, the percentage of those who feel that their financial situation has worsened also has gone down from 39.7 per cent to 17 per cent in 1996 and 19 per cent in 2004 (see Table 4.9).

TABLE 4.9
Financial Situation during the Last Few Years (in per cent)

	1971	1996	2004
Improved	20.2	29.2	26.5
Same	40.1	53.8	51.1
Worsened	39.7	17.0	19.0
No opinion	–	–	3.4

Source NES, CSDS 1971, 1996, 2004.

Since the perception of improvement in one's financial situation largely depends on one's own satisfaction in life, people having done well would automatically feel an improvement. This may well be the reason why people belonging to upper-income groups, upper castes, higher occupations and, of course, the urban dwellers, constitute larger shares of those who report an improvement in their conditions. Contrary to them, the Scheduled Tribes along with the

Scheduled Castes, OBCs and the Muslims constitute lesser shares of those perceiving improvement. Further calculations show that the illiterates are the worst placed people in this respect, accounting for the bulk of those who feel that their financial situation has worsened.

Satisfaction with Present Financial Situation

Similarly, when it comes to sense of satisfaction with one's present financial conditions we find a remarkable improvement between 1971 and 1996 but a drastic decline in 2004 (see Table 4.10). From merely 10.7 per cent in 1971, the share of satisfied people has gone up to 28.4 per cent which again declined to 16 per cent in 2004. This provides an interesting insight to the defeat of the NDA in 2004 when the focus of the campaign on the prowess of the government in redressing the economic situation of the country as the 'India Shining' campaign manifestly claimed.

TABLE 4.10
Present Financial Situation (in per cent)

	1971	1996	2004
Satisfied	10.7	28.4	16.0
Somewhat satisfied	28.6	41.2	47.4
Not satisfied	60.7	30.4	33.4
No opinion	–	–	3.2

Source NES, CSDS 1971, 1996, 2004.

A sharp decline in proportion of 'not satisfied' people (from 60.7 per cent in 1971 to 30.4 per cent in 1996 and 33.4 per cent in 2004) is quite revealing. Two-thirds of Indian population in 1996 and 2004 reported feeling satisfied or somewhat satisfied with their present financial situation, which may appear unrealistic at the first glance but the element of subjectivity that this observation embodies conveys an important message about politics in India. One learns from this subjective assessment that, in whatever situations they are placed today, to most of people, their present looks better than the past; hence, the satisfaction. Since behavioural manifestations are largely guided by one's subjective feelings, it is this state of mind which prevents people from directing their resentment against others, specially the system, for their own sufferings and/or failures. Thus, it acts as shock absorber not for the toiling masses alone, but also provides sustenance to Indian democracy by containing resentment against the system.

Like perception of improvement in financial condition, satisfaction with one's own present financial situation also reflects similar relationships. The Scheduled Castes, Scheduled Tribes, the illiterates and, of course, the people belonging to 'very poor class' have the smallest proportions of satisfied people among them. Women (as usual) have shown reservation vis-à-vis the men, the proportion of satisfied among them is about 5 per cent less than their counterparts.

Financial Prospects

The assessment of the present is a function of relative judgement wherein people place their present vis-à-vis their immediate past and promise for the future. Even if the improvement over their recent past is not very satisfactory, a strong optimism about the future acts as solace to moderate their feelings about the present hardships. Moved by this, peoples' perception about their future prospects was also ascertained; relevant data are presented in Table 4.11.

TABLE 4.11
Future Financial Situation (in per cent)

	1971	1996	2004
Get better	38.6	47.9	49.2
Remain the same	20.9	27.0	19.4
Get worse	18.8	8.9	6.2
Don't know	21.7	16.2	25.2

Source NES, CSDS 1971, 1996, 2004.

Following the pattern as already seen in two preceding tables, responses presented here, too, show noticeable improvement over the 1971 situations. The percentage of those who think that their financial situation would get better has gone up from 38.6 per cent in 1971 to 47.9 per cent in 1996 and 49.2 per cent in 2004. If one excludes the 'don't know' cases, the proportion of optimist people goes still higher. Compared to this, the proportion of those who apprehend worsening of their future financial situation has gone down from 18.8 per cent in 1971 to merely 8.9 per cent in 1996 and 6.2 per cent in 2004. In India, where about one-third of its population still falls below the poverty line, from the point of view of the state, there cannot be a better situation than this as far as containing the grievances against the system for one's own economic hardship is concerned.

Further analysis of the 1996 survey shows women are marginally more apprehensive about the future. Compared to men, 50.5 per cent of whom expect better promises for future, only 45.3 per cent of women have similar expectations. Those educated (college and above), distinguish themselves with as high as 69.4 per cent, who foresee better prospects for themselves. Similarly, the urbanites (56.9 per cent), white collar and professionals (59.2 per cent), upper class (54.1 per cent), Christians (59.1 per cent) and, of course, the younger people below 25 years of age (52.5 per cent) also show larger share of people who perceive the future to be more promising. The pitiable conditions of the poor (36.9 per cent), illiterates (39.5 per cent) and older people (40.1 per cent) have once again been reflected when the majority of them fail to visualise a better future.

Index of Financial Satisfaction

Individually, these questions have shed light on three different aspects of one's economic life, such as, improvement over the past, satisfaction with present and prospects for the future. However, a composite picture is possible only if we construct a scale by using responses to all these questions together. An index, 'Financial satisfaction' is accordingly constructed and the distribution of responses in different categories of level of satisfaction and identification of 'high satisfaction' and 'low satisfaction' in terms of socio-demographic groups are presented for both the surveys of 1996 and 2004 in Table 4.12.

TABLE 4.12

Financial Satisfaction (in per cent)

	1996		2004	
Low satisfaction	22.0		23.5	
Medium satisfaction	44.0		48.0	
High satisfaction	34.0		28.5	
	1996		**2004**	
Social Groups	Low satisfaction	High satisfaction	Low satisfaction	High satisfaction
College and above	11.2	51.4	14.4	38.8
Christian	16.9	38.5	27.0	22.4
Sikh	10.6	52.1	19.0	39.3
Urban	14.7	43.2	20.4	31.7
Upper class	9.0	55.8	11.3	45.7
Upper caste	16.7	43.4	19.1	33.8
Male	19.7	36.2	22.4	30.8
25 years and above	19.9	38.0	19.6	32.6
All India	**22.0**	**34.0**	**23.5**	**28.5**
Hindu	22.5	33.9	23.0	29.1
OBC	23.8	30.9	25.2	27.3
Female	24.5	31.6	24.9	25.8
Scheduled Tribe	21.9	29.4	21.8	25.1
Muslims	21.5	32.3	26.8	23.6
Rural	24.5	30.9	24.5	27.5
56 years and above	27.0	29.4	28.6	24.8
Scheduled Caste	28.4	25.8	29.1	22.6
Illiterate	28.8	25.4	30.3	21.4
Very poor	33.3	21.1	32.5	18.5

Source NES, CSDS 1996, 2004.

The distribution of cases on the satisfaction scale presents more or less a balancing picture where half of the population falls in the middle, that is, medium level of satisfaction. The low satisfaction group also includes cases who fail to perceive any improvement/ satisfaction on any of the three indicators measuring financial satisfaction. It is a matter of some comfort that there are very few cases in this category.[2] Placed in a broader context they present a cause for serious concern. Notwithstanding their size it is the degree of frustration, which may result problematic both for the society and its order and the system in the long run.

Except these rather extreme cases, the data presented in the Table 4.12 weigh quite heavily in favour of satisfaction. That is about three-quarters of the respondents, except 1.7 per cent, all others show some level of material satisfaction. The category of 'medium satisfaction' includes cases of people who are satisfied at least on two indicators and have no negative response on the third. Similarly the 'high satisfaction' includes only those who are satisfied on all the three indicators or, at least, on two but none from the dissatisfied on any of the three indicators. Both these categories put together account for over 70 per cent of Indian population who are moderately or highly satisfied with their financial conditions. Since one of the three indicators focuses on future prospects (that is, will financial situation get better, worse or remain the same), the moderately and highly satisfied categories also tell us about the confidence and hope people generally repose in the system. Such a feeling, while saving people from getting frustrated in their personal and family life, it also minimises dissent against the system. However, while *karma* might sustain democracy, the punishment for poor performance is meted out ruthlessly to the party in power as was reflected in the 2004 General Elections.

Seen in this perspective the positive relationship between socio-economic status and the satisfaction sends signals in two directions. First, the well-to-do sections of the society having larger proportions of satisfied people among them may, with their opinion making abilities, be able to provide sustenance to the system and contain natural growth of dissatisfaction germinating out of the material conditions of the toiling masses. Second, the concentration of the less satisfied in select group of people like, illiterates, Scheduled Castes, Scheduled Tribes, Muslims and the very poor may pose a threat to the party in power and also to the system. Short-term disturbances combined with a long-term tendency towards stability are one of the likely consequences.

Conclusion

We learn from our survey findings that there are hardly any sections of the Indian population, which remain entirely untouched by elections. The overall picture questions the images of vote banks and political passivity with which the Indian electorate has been described in the past. Far from being the victim of manipulation by social notables, the electorate is politically conscious and engages actively in campaigns. Despite the occurrence of militant violence and caste conflict in parts of India with a regularity that challenges India's democratic image, the rhetoric of its leaders presents the legitimacy of the process of institution-building and democratic transition as the main facts of political life in India. The fact that the bitterness that inevitably follows every outbreak of inter-community violence does not drive a permanent wedge between the parties to the conflict marks India apart from other divided societies seeking a common political destiny. The resolve to present a consensual view of Indian society has some pre-Independence precedents. At the height of India's freedom movement, just as 'divide and rule' had become the main political basis of colonial rule, 'unite and oppose' was the main strategy through which the Congress party sought to channel the energy of the Indian people in its efforts to accelerate the achievement of Independence. The mantle of united struggle under the banner of a few core values and the organisational framework of a national movement has been the main political capital of the Congress party after Independence. However, as the memory of the hegemonic rule of the Congress rapidly recedes into past history and India enters the politics of coalition politics, it becomes increasingly important to ask how deep is the support for the core values and institutional norms that constitute the Indian political system and the process of democratic transition. Are conflict and consensus complementary? What role do institutions play in weaving them together an inclusive political culture?

The impact of social disadvantages on political agency paves the way for a discussion of the role of political parties. Since political parties in a democracy are the main agents of the articulation and aggregation of demands and in their capacity as watchdogs of democracy, are responsible for disciplining the government, the next chapter will put the party system in the context of pclitical competition and social mobility in India.

Notes

1. See Lipset (1959). For new research that reverses the historical sequence of social change and political democracy, see Varshney (2007).
2. Further analysis shows that only 1.7 per cent belong to this extreme group who have not perceived any improvement during the last few years: they are not satisfied with their present condition: nor do they find their future any better.

5
Political Competition, Social Cleavages and Institutionalisation of the Party System

The renewal of the political capital is a crucial challenge for every political system. This problem takes an extreme form in the changing societies where the political aura, surrounding the founding generation, provides the requisite legitimacy for the system to operate smoothly. Not surprisingly, the political systems of many changing societies do not survive their founders. In this chapter, we shall analyse the macro-foundations of the sustainability of the political capital, in order to supplement the discussion of the microfoundations of the political capital, offered in the previous chapter. Drawing on the aggregate electoral statistics as well as survey data, we will focus on the competitiveness of India's elections, the party-cleavage linkage, the perception of efficacy and legitimacy and the cross-cutting value conflicts as the main contributory factors to the sustainability of India's multi-party democracy.

Competitive Elections and the *Indigenisation* of the Party System in India

Political parties are among the most important institutions that play a crucial role in the modernisation and democratisation of the post-colonial societies. Whether explicitly political or with implicit political functions, they are the interface of society and the state.[1]

88 When Rebels Become Stakeholders

As such, parties, pressure groups and elections, which underpin the process of interest articulation and aggregation, become the agent, as well as the site of social change. A democratic political community, in this vein, becomes institutionalised when its key institutions, such as parties and elections, achieve the requisite autonomy from the actual holders of power and are self-sustaining.

The process of transition from traditional to democratic order can challenge the very existence of new states. The practical problem of eliciting consent through regular elections makes it necessary for the 'old' elites to keep the door of entry for the new social forces sufficiently open, while making sure that they do not lose their own authority altogether. Political parties have this delicate task of balancing 'new blood' and old authority. The failure to perform this vital function can cause political institutions to collapse under the cross-pressures of the conservative and the obdurate, locked in battle against the radical and the impatient.

Unlike the western party systems, which rose from below, the party system of India is a creation from above. But, fortuitously as well as by acts of deliberate design, the party system, since its modest start in 1885, has become a part of the indigenous idiom of politics.[2] The party system and the elections in India are based on single-member constituencies, 'first–past–the post' system of plurality voting and a bicameral legislature at the centre. The leader of the majority party or coalition in the lower house forms the government. The President of the Republic normally plays the ceremonial role of a formal head of the state. With minor differences, these rules resemble the British system of parliamentary democracy. However, the British party system is the product of the great economic and social changes that rocked society and the state in the nineteenth century Europe and produced the political basis for the extension of franchise. India did not go through a similar historical experience. The familiar sequence of the early stirring of the industrial revolution, the radical changes in agriculture, migration and the evolution of the working class movement for the extension of suffrage did not occur in India prior to the institutionalisation of universal adult franchise and a competitive party system. Hence the puzzle: why did multi-party democracy appear in India and how do her people cope with western style political parties and elections?

An important part of the explanation of this puzzle lies in the history of the political development in India during the last six decades prior to Independence in 1947. A brief perusal of the interaction of the British Raj and the Indian resistance to it during this crucial period reveals that conditions for the emergence of political parties were steadily growing. Partly under the impact of Utilitarianism, but mostly as a matter of expediency, the British had started experimenting with limited self-rule in issues of minor importance, such as the municipal administration by the 1880s. This formed part of the British strategy of ruling India with the help of the Indian intermediaries, in this case, selected by a very restricted electorate of urban, rich and loyal subjects. The Indian National Congress was set up in 1885 by Sir Alan Octavian Hume, a retired British civil servant, in order to present the Indian interests to the British Crown in a systematic and organised manner. It soon became the leading voice of the Indian middle classes, constantly clamouring for more jobs under the colonial government and for greater political participation. The successive Acts of the British Parliament in 1909, 1919 and 1935 extended the franchise and brought increasingly greater number of Indians into the scope of party politics, based on restricted participation.

The process was neither as effortlessly incremental nor as linear as it may sound. Periods of the extension of franchise and cooperation between the colonial rulers and the elected representatives were interspersed with ruthless suppression and imprisonment of Indian leaders. The Congress party itself was often divided in its opinion between collaboration with colonial rule and radical resistance to it. Gandhi brought these two strands together in his strategy of non-violent non-cooperation and built a powerful mass movement that united the peasantry and the national bourgeoisie under the banner of the Congress party. By the 1930s, however, the national movement was split once again, this time on the issue of religion. The majority of the Muslims, under the banner of the Muslim League, had started agitating for an independent homeland for the Muslims of the subcontinent. As a result, when Independence finally arrived in 1947, British India was partitioned into India and Pakistan. The Congress party, under Nehru, inherited power in a smaller but politically and religiously more homogeneous country, with its links to the constituents intact. This was not the case in Pakistan where the Muslim League, victorious at last, took power, but only at the cost of abandoning its political hinterland in Northern India, which blighted the growth of a competitive party system in Pakistan.

This brief historical background partly explains the relative ease with which India developed electoral democracy and a competitive party system, in contrast with Pakistan. Universal adult franchise was introduced in 1952 and both the non-democratic Left and the non-democratic Right were permitted to compete against the Centre and the moderate Left and Right for political power, through elections without any legal or political obstacles. At Independence, the electorate consisted of large numbers of voters who had not experienced direct British rule and were stepping out of feudalism straight into popular democracy. The Hindus, still recovering from the trauma of Partition, became citizens of a 'secular' state, which did not recognise any religion as its official religion. Millions of poor, marginal, land-hungry peasantry, radicalised through communist agitations and unorganised manual labourers and unionised industrial workers, were all being asked to repose their faith in multi-party democracy as the most effective method of social change.

What should have followed is described by several specialists. One of the most cited is Harrison's *India: The Most Dangerous Decades* (1960) spelt out a future of communal conflict, disharmony and Balkanisation.[3] Huntington's *Political Order in Changing Societies* (1968) predicted structural discontinuity in the face of popular mobilisation.[4] State theorists like Myrdal, in his *Asian Drama: An Inquiry into the Poverty of Nations* (1968), came up with the formulation of the 'soft state', based on popular consent, that would necessarily be lacking in the authority with which to tackle the basic problems of structural change. Weaving all these strands into a unified and comparative theory, Moore in his *Social Origins of Dictatorship and Democracy: Lord and Peasant in the Making of the*

Modern World (1966), predicted a state of peaceful paralysis for India in the years following Independence.

But, as the record shows, the elections have been held regularly. Major policy initiatives have been taken by the governments and the parties have alternated in power as a result of elections. On all aggregate indicators of participation, as discussed earlier, India has kept up steady progress. The level of electoral participation has steadily gone up, reaching the levels of continental European voting, in some parts of the country. Participation in elections has been widely spread across all social strata and in urban areas as well as villages. The level of electoral participation of women, former untouchables and tribals does not lag far behind that of the national average.

The elections and party competition in India have played a double role. Rather than inhibiting the growth of party competition, social conflict (which has got interwoven with political conflict) helps deepen political partisanship. As beneficiaries of the process of political reform, introduced by the British towards the end of colonial rule, elections with limited franchise facilitated political transition by acting as the institutional context, in which power was transferred by the British rulers to the elected Indian leaders. After Independence, the same process accelerated the pace of social change, leading to a second phase of political change, when the social class and generation that was identified with the freedom movement was replaced by younger leaders, many of whom came from the upwardly mobile, newly enfranchised, lower social classes.[5]

The Indian experience shows how the pace of social change has been accelerated through social reform legislation, recruitment of new social elites into the political arena and political mobilisation through electoral participation. Their overall impact on the stability of the political system has been moderated by the existence of political intermediaries and parties, at the regional and local levels. The established *Jajmani* systems—reciprocal social bonds based on the exchange of service and occupational specialisation—broke down to create new groupings. Finally, caste associations, based on horizontal social and economic interests, emerged as links between the parties and society.[6] These processes, that facilitate social and political mobility and multi-party competition have taken the form of federalism, consociationalism and elite policy initiatives.[7] This has created a useful room to manoeuvre in the middle in the hands of the national, regional and local elites.[8]

These innovations have been possible in India because of three factors. First, the Gandhian legacy, which gave the first formal shape to the two-track strategy that combines institutional politics—such as voting, lobbying and other forms of participation, based on party politics—and protest movements, undertaken as a rational device to this development.[9] The second factor is the ability of the national and regional elites to transfer knowledge from one arena to another.[10] The third was the availability of the 'Congress system' and the elite consensus that defined it during the formative years after Independence, helping India to build up a valuable stock of institutional capital.[11]

A number of strategic reforms in the electoral laws and the efforts of the Election Commission to hold free and fair elections at all levels of the system have greatly increased the competitiveness of politics in India. A competitive party system provides the crucial backdrop to the political articulation of competing interests. As such, it is an important indicator of a functioning civil society. Party competition creates the political spaces in which social groups come together, in order to engage in competition for the allocation of the scarce public resources and for the assertion of their collective identity and values in the public space. A non-competitive party system denotes the existence of social closure, a restricted public sphere and of elite values and interests that are hegemonic in nature, in the sense that they are treated as if they were above politics. The absence of a party system altogether denotes the absence of an effective and enduring basis of dialogue and transaction between social interests and the state.

The party system of contemporary India, as discussed earlier, is the result of the six decades of growth under the British rule, prior to Independence, considerably reinforced with the political mobilisation of all sections of society. It is a fairly complex system which, specialists of comparative party systems find hard to characterise because of the continuous and influential presence of the Congress party in the national political arena, the emergence of a powerful Hindu nationalist movement, the world's longest elected communist government at the regional level and the occasional lapse into authoritarian rule. The picture becomes much clearer if we divide the post-Independence period in terms of a single-party-dominated period (1952–71) transforming into a period of multi-party system (1977–2004) (see Tables A3.4 and A3.5 in Appendix 3). The growing competitiveness of India's elections can be seen from the changing gap between the vote shares of the Congress party and its nearest rival. The gap between the vote share of the Congress and that of the largest non-Congress party or coalition has steadily narrowed following the election of 1984, which, in view of the sympathy wave in favour of the Congress, led by Rajiv Gandhi, following the assassination of Indira Gandhi, has been thought of as a deviant election, temporarily obscuring the decline of the secular credentials of the Congress (see Figure 5.1).

The challenge to the dominance of the Congress party had already become clear in the fourth General Election of 1967, when the first coalitions of the Left and the Right took place at the regional level, leading to the breakdown of the dominance of the Congress party in several states. These opposition coalitions were successful in some states like in Kerala and West Bengal and became the basis of the beginning of a multi-party system, with the Congress alternating with other political parties and coalitions very much like a normal political party. At the national level, however, the Congress party continued to rule, albeit with a reduced majority. The situation changed radically after the split of the Congress party in 1969 into the Congress (Requisionist) and the Congress (Organisation). The faction led by Indira Gandhi, referred to as Congress (R), brought about radical changes in the programme of the centrist Congress party. A number of new, Left-leaning policies, like the nationalisation of banks, abolition of the special privileges of the Indian princes and closer ties with the communists, were reinforced with a more forceful populist leadership style. These policies brought the party great electoral success in 1971 but led to the corrosion of its organisational links with the electorate.

FIGURE 5.1
Per cent of Votes of the Congress, Relative to the Largest Non-Congress Party or Coalition

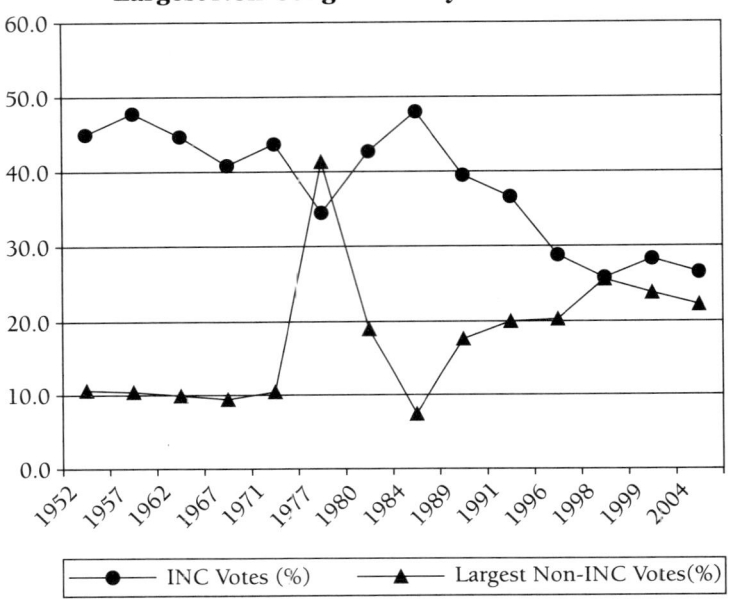

	Largest non-INC parties (votes)	
1952	SOC	16.4
1957	SOC	10.4
1962	CPI	9.9
1967	BJS/BJP	9.4
1971	INC (2)	10.4
1977	JP/JD	41.3
1980	JP/JD	19.0
1984	BJS/BJP	7.4
1989	JP/JD	17.7
1991	BJS/BJP	20.0
1996	BJS/BJP	20.3
1998	BJS/BJP	25.6
1999	BJS/BJP	23.8
2004	BJS/BJP	22.2

Source Tables A3.4 and A3.5.
Notes Election years.

In retrospect, the period 1967–77 can be thought of as a period of transition from one-party-dominance to multi-party democracy. The setback suffered by the Congress party in the election of 1967 demonstrated the vulnerability of the centrist Congress to the broad electoral coalitions of the Left and the Right. After its initial setback, however, the Congress, under Indira Gandhi's forceful leadership, turned its new policy of radical, populist leadership into its main asset. Its initial success in the 1971 election was further reinforced in the Assembly Elections of 1972, when Indira Gandhi transformed India's successful intervention in the Liberation War in East Pakistan, leading to the birth of Bangladesh, into the electoral platform of the Congress. However, the radical rhetoric rebounded on the party when a number of interest groups, including the industrial workers, railway employees and students, started political agitations. The culmination to this period of unrest was the authoritarian interlude of 1975–77.

Competitive Elections and Interest Articulation: Political Parties and Social Cleavages

So far, we have seen, how the Indian party system originated under the British rule as part of the deliberate policy to rule India effectively, chiefly through native intermediaries, whose character gradually changed, in keeping with the pace of rising political consciousness. This core was greatly reinforced after Independence, when social change and political conflict got interwoven within the fabric of a democratic state. The ultimate expression of the plural character of the Indian society was a multi-party system. The issue that we need to address now is, what keeps the party system socially anchored and reasonably stable.

A stable multi-party democracy is based on an effective linkage between the social cleavages and the political parties. The nature of the party system typically follows the complexity of the social cleavages. Political systems with 'first–past–the post' system, where social class constitutes the main cleavage tend to develop two-party systems. Those with other cleavages, such as religion, language and region, in addition to social class, produce more complex, multi-party systems. India's multi-party system, as we shall see in Table 5.1, exhibits the effects of multiple cleavages. The Congress party, occupying the ideological centre of Indian politics still continues to be a catch-all party, cutting into all the social cleavages (Kirchheimer 1966). Parties of the Left, such as the Communists and the Social Democratic Left, such as the National Front in 1996, tend to get more support from the lower social classes, whereas parties of the Right, such as the BJP, get more support from the upper social groups. However, religion, at the heart of the controversy about the secular credentials of the state in India, divides the electorate into those who are for a closer relationship between Hinduism and the state and others, who wish to retain the wall of separation between religion and the state that Jawaharlal Nehru, at the head of the Congress party, had drawn on as the basis of India's institutions, during the first phase of the party system. On this issue, the BJP finds itself closely identified with a strong 'Hindu' position as compared to the National Front and the Left Front, who have allied themselves on a 'secular' agenda. One faction of the Congress party would like to count itself as a member of the secular front, but, keeping to its centrist character, the party itself tends to be ambiguous on the issue. Some of these observations would be illustrated later with reference to particular political parties.

The 1996 elections to the Lok Sabha produced the best results for the BJP, considered to be the main symbol of Hindu nationalism, in recent electoral history. The data presented in Table 5.1 reveal the strong support it enjoys among the more educated, urban, affluent and younger voters. However, its vote remains confined to particular regions of India. Moreover, within these regions, the party is identified with particular sub-populations. Thus, while on the one hand, the BJP has the most efficient vote to seat ratio, it might have already exploited the support among its 'natural' clientele to saturation. Against its national average of 24.9 per cent votes, in 1996, the BJP, along with its allies, polled much less from the Scheduled Castes (14.4 per cent), the Scheduled Tribes (19.0 per cent), the illiterates (21.1 per cent), the unskilled workers (17.0 per cent) and from the very poor (16.0 per cent).

TABLE 5.1
Social Bases of Political Parties (1996–2004) (in per cent)

Background characteristics	1996 INC+	BJP+	NF	LF	BSP	1998 INC	BJP+	UF	BSP	1999 INC+	BJP+	LF	BSP	SP	2004 UPA	NDA	LF	BSP	SP+
All India Average	**27.5**	**24.9**	**10.1**	**7.5**	**3.4**	**27.3**	**32.9**	**19.2**	**2.9**	**36.5**	**38.9**	**7.8**	**3.0**	**2.5**	**39.5**	**37.9**	**6.4**	**5.0**	**5.4**
Gender																			
Female	27.6	23.0	9.4	7.6	3.1	28.0	29.5	19.6	2.8	39.3	36.7	8.3	2.5	2.0	40.4	37.1	7.0	5.0	5.1
Male	27.4	26.8	10.8	7.4	3.6	26.5	36.3	18.7	3.0	34.0	40.9	7.4	3.6	2.9	38.8	38.5	5.9	5.0	5.7
Locality																			
Rural	28.1	22.6	10.6	8.8	3.8	27.0	31.8	19.6	3.1	36.1	37.6	9.2	3.4	2.3	39.2	37.3	6.2	5.5	5.8
Urban	25.6	32.2	8.7	3.4	2.0	28.2	36.3	17.7	2.4	38.2	44.0	2.8	1.5	3.3	40.7	40.2	7.1	3.1	3.9
Age group																			
Up to 25 years	25.7	27.0	10.2	6.9	3.8	24.4	35.0	17.8	4.3	35.7	40.4	7.0	3.3	3.3	38.3	38.3	5.9	5.5	6.0
26–35 years	27.1	25.5	9.9	7.7	3.5	27.5	33.9	18.6	2.6	35.6	39.1	8.0	3.5	2.4	40.5	37.7	6.4	4.3	5.6
36–45 years	28.8	25.1	9.7	8.1	2.9	27.4	32.4	20.5	2.6	35.3	38.1	8.9	2.8	2.7	39.5	38.6	6.0	5.1	5.0
46–55 years	27.0	23.6	10.2	8.4	3.5	28.2	32.0	21.5	2.2	40.5	37.5	7.5	2.2	2.2	37.8	38.2	7.2	4.6	6.3
56 years and above	30.0	21.3	10.9	6.4	2.9	29.7	29.9	18.2	2.6	37.0	39.4	7.2	3.0	1.9	40.6	36.3	6.9	5.8	4.2
Education																			
Illiterate	28.6	21.1	12.3	6.6	5.0	29.1	28.9	18.3	4.0	41.6	33.6	5.9	4.1	2.8	40.6	34.3	5.1	7.8	6.5
Up to middle	28.4	23.8	9.2	8.9	2.8	26.9	34.3	20.8	2.4	36.8	37.8	10.2	2.1	2.1	42.9	35.6	8.6	3.5	4.3
College, without degree	25.8	31.3	8.0	7.7	1.6	25.7	36.5	19.1	1.8	32.1	43.4	9.0	2.8	2.5	37.8	38.6	6.9	4.1	5.9

(*Table 5.1 continued*)

(Table 5.1 continued)

Background characteristics	1996					1998					1999					2004				
	INC+	BJP+	NF	LF	BSP	INC	BJP+	UF	BSP	INC+	BJP+	LF	BSP	SP	UPA	NDA	LF	BSP	SP+
Graduate and above	21.1	36.7	6.1	6.0	0.9	21.5	42.5	16.6	1.6	27.6	50.8	7.0	1.9	2.4	34.9	46.7	5.0	2.8	4.4
Occupation																			
Unskilled worker	30.6	17.0	9.9	10.8	5.2	34.6	23.0	21.4	4.1	42.7	23.5	10.9	5.6	3.8	42.6	27.4	8.0	9.8	6.0
Agricultural and allied worker	28.4	17.8	11.5	8.9	5.2	26.2	26.2	24.5	4.5	36.7	34.4	11.2	3.6	2.1	43.4	36.6	6.8	4.8	3.8
Artisan and skilled worker	27.3	24.1	9.3	7.7	3.0	26.9	30.6	23.1	2.1	40.8	35.5	7.2	3.2	2.7	43.9	34.8	6.8	3.9	5.3
Cultivator (Less than five acres)	26.1	26.2	14.0	6.4	4.9	21.7	32.8	18.3	3.1	35.0	41.5	4.8	3.8	2.5	35.4	37.3	4.0	7.6	8.9
Cultivator five acres and more)	29.7	34.6	8.2	1.6	2.5	31.1	41.9	10.8	2.0	36.7	47.4	1.8	0.6	2.0	35.8	44.5	3.0	3.0	8.0
Business	23.3	33.0	10.1	7.6	0.7	26.2	37.9	21.5	1.5	33.4	44.0	8.2	2.1	3.1	37.0	42.7	7.1	3.0	4.5
White collar and professional	26.2	30.8	5.6	8.0	0.3	24.3	39.6	15.7	1.0	33.8	45.9	8.4	1.1	1.7	37.4	42.3	9.0	2.5	2.2
Caste																			
Scheduled Caste	31.6	14.4	5.6	11.0	12.1	29.6	20.9	22.2	11.2	40.2	25.0	10.5	11.8	0.8	39.7	25.9	8.8	18.4	2.9
Scheduled Tribe	39.2	19.0	6.2	6.5	1.0	41.9	25.6	11.6	0.4	48.2	31.8	7.1	0.1	0.3	46.2	34.3	7.0	0.6	0.6
Other Backward Caste	21.7	23.6	16.3	5.9	2.3	22.5	34.6	21.0	1.6	38.2	39.6	6.2	1.6	4.4	40.7	38.7	4.4	2.8	7.6
Upper caste	28.4	33.6	7.1	7.3	0.4	28.1	38.5	17.4	1.1	30.0	47.3	7.9	0.7	1.8	36.0	44.6	7.3	1.5	5.5

Religion															
Hindu	26.2	28.9	8.4	7.4	3.7	25.6	37.4	17.4	3.0	33.2	42.8	7.7	3.4	2.0	36.8	42.3	5.9	5.3	4.4
Muslim	35.3	3.1	25.3	10.1	1.2	35.1	6.8	34.4	1.3	57.1	14.3	10.1	1.6	7.2	54.8	11.8	6.9	2.9	16.4
Christian	39.9	3.0	2.0	5.6	–	42.1	9.1	18.6	0.4	55.0	20.1	8.6	–	0.4	60.5	21.1	8.6	0.9	0.4
Sikh	18.3	14.3	16.7	2.4	5.6	21.9	39.8	18.0	10.2	23.9	44.3	–	1.1	–	30.4	48.2	6.9	4.9	2.7
Other	26.5	6.0	12.0	2.4	4.8	39.5	19.7	3.9	10.5	38.2	40.0	1.8	3.6	–	41.7	21.3	15.9	10.4	2.4
Economic Class															
Very poor	29.6	16.0	10.7	11.3	4.4	27.3	27.1	23.7	2.7	39.4	29.8	10.9	4.5	2.0	42.9	32.8	7.5	7.0	4.3
Poor	28.3	23.1	10.5	6.7	4.7	27.4	31.8	19.0	3.3	37.3	38.2	6.5	3.8	3.3	39.6	37.3	5.8	5.7	5.8
Middle	26.1	31.1	10.9	5.6	2.2	26.9	37.3	16.6	2.7	35.8	44.7	5.8	1.5	2.5	37.6	40.9	5.8	2.8	6.9
Upper	22.4	40.1	7.9	3.4	0.4	28.3	38.9	14.3	1.9	31.0	50.0	6.4	1.0	2.4	32.8	49.3	3.7	2.4	5.6

Source NES, CSDS 1996, 1998, 1999, 2004.

Notes Parties here represent pre-poll alliances.

1996: *INC+*: INC + AIADMK; *BJP+*: BJP + Samata + Shiv Sena + Haryana Vikas Party; *NF*: JD + Samajwadi Party; *LF*: CPI(M) + CPI + RSP + FBL

1998: *BJP+*: BJP+ Samata + Shiv Sena + Haryana Vikas Party + AIADMK + Akali Dal + Trinamul Congress + Lok Shakti + Biju Janata Dal + TDP (NTR); *UF*: Janata Dal + SP (Mulayam) + TDP (N) + AGP + TMC + DMK + MGP + CPI + CPI(M) + RSP + FBL

1999: *INC+*: INC + RJD (Lalu) + IUML + RPI (Prakash) + Kerala Congress + AIADMK; *BJP+*: BJP + Shiv Sena + JD(U) + Haryana Vikas Party + Akali Dal + HVC (Sukhram) + Trinamul Congress + MGP/MGRADMK + DMK + MDMK + PMK + TRC (Ramamurthy) + TDP (Naidu); *LF*: CPI(M) + CPI + RSP + FBL

2004: *UPA*: INC + TRS + RJD (Lalu) + LJNS(Paswan) + NCP + JMM + PDP + MUL + Kerala Congress (M) + JD(S) + RPI + RPI (Athawale) + PRBP + DMK + MDMK + PMK + PDS + Arunachal Congress;

NDA: BJP + TDP + JD(U) + IFDP + Shiv Sena + Biju Janata Dal + Akali Dal + AIADMK + Trinamul Congress + MNF + SDF + NPF; *LF*: CPI(M) + CPI + RSP + FBL + Kerala Congress;

SP+: SP + Lok Dal

The same pattern of support continued in 1998. Notwithstanding an overall increase in the vote share of the BJP alliance in 1998, the gap between the national average and the voters polled from these groups remained more or less the same. Thus, the lesser share of votes from the lower segments of society clearly indicates an upper-class and caste image of the party. A close look on the same data, however, may provide some solace to BJP and to its sympathisers. That is, its above-average support among the younger age group, among the white collar and professionals and among those educated to the level of graduation and above, put the party at an advantage.

In spite of a net fall in the votes cast in its favour, the Congress appears to have retained the broadly dispersed character of its social base. The image of the Congress as a 'coalition of minorities' lingers on. Its support among the Muslims is about eight percentage point above its national average. Roughly one-third of the Scheduled Castes (31.6 per cent, according to the 1996 data) and a slightly over one-third of the Muslims, the Christians and the Scheduled Tribes have lent their support to the Congress. It is a remarkable feat indeed. If there appears any desertion from the party, it is in fact the OBCs, who have gone to various regional formations, to the National Front and to the BJP. Similarly, its support among the Scheduled Castes (from 47.8 to 31.6 per cent), Muslims (from 58.5 to 35.1 per cent) and among the Scheduled Tribes (from 41.2 to 39.2 per cent) registered a heavy loss in 1998.[12] Be it religion or caste, the Congress is still a broad-based party—much broader than any of its main competitors in the fray. Both the 1996 and the 1998 data confirm the heterogeneous social base of the Congress party, but also demonstrates, as we will see later, the presence of other contenders (National Front for the Muslim vote and the BSP for the Scheduled Caste vote) for the support from these groups and their increasing ability to lure the support away from the Congress. It should be noted, that the support for the Congress is proportionately low among the educated and the young, which represents the mirror opposite of the BJP.

The Left Front appears as a 'rural' party, with its support confined to 3.4 per cent of the urban population compared to 8.8 per cent among the rural voters (in the 1996 data). This is explained by the regionally localised character of the Left movement, which from its beginning in the urban electorate has moved to the countryside, as the example of West Bengal shows. Its support is marginally higher at both the extremes of the social scale, with more than average support among both the Scheduled Castes and the upper castes. The picture appears to resemble that of the Congress party. But unlike the Congress, the Left Front draws less support among the illiterate. Its main support comes from the low/middle-educated and middle-aged people.

The Bahujan Samaj Party—the 'joker in the pack' of Indian politics today—is very much the party of the Scheduled Castes. Two-thirds of its voters belong to this group, whose members come largely from the rural areas and are mostly illiterate, manual workers and the poor. Its strong support among the poorest section of the Indian population is further reinforced by the data on education, as the level of education is negatively related to the support for the party. The picture resembles a mirror opposite to that of the profile of the BJP.

The relationship between voters' preferences and their social status, as reflected by caste, education and occupational classification, is amplified when we examine the same by one's ranking in the economic class. The BJP's capacity to attract voters from the upper economic strata was demonstrated by the data presented in Table 5.1. The higher the status one occupies on the class variable, the greater the possibility of her/his being a supporter of the BJP, the opposite being the case for the non-BJP-parties. The Congress and the BJP have marked differences in terms of drawing the support from different social groups. Comparing the patterns of support for the Indian National Congress and its allies with the BJP and its allies, over the figures for 1999 and 2004, gives us a clear idea of their respective social bases as well as the shift in partisan support. Thus, in 1999, the Congress and its allies came across as a party with slightly more support among women as compared to men, older and less educated voters, drawing support from the lower social orders, the Scheduled Castes and Tribes and more likely to get support among the non-Hindu voters than the BJP, its arch rival. The BJP and its allies, on the other hand, came across as a party drawing support largely from a male, younger, higher educated electorate; a party which was more likely to draw support from the Hindus. The 2004 figures confirm this trend, but there are major shifts. The UPA in 2004 has more than made up for its relative lack of support among the urban voters, while, retaining its rural base. It has made important forays into the 26 to 35 age cohort, without compromising its hold over the older voters. But most important of all, the UPA, under the leadership of Sonia Gandhi, in 2004, managed to turn the 'India Shining' campaign theme of the NDA on its head by drawing attention to both the issues of farmers' suicides and the inter-community conflict of 2002 in Gujarat. The result, as one can see from Table 5.1, caused the coalition's support among the urban, educated and affluent Hindu voters to surge as compared to the past, while retaining its traditional base among the religious minorities and the lower social orders.

Broadly-based Sense of Political Efficacy

Established patterns of party-cleavage linkages would be meaningful only if individuals, who constitute those social cleavages, perceive political parties as efficient instruments for the articulation of their interests. The survey data, as we can see from Table 5.2, provide adequate evidence that such a sense of efficacy is present in large sections of the Indian electorate.

The question: *Do you think your vote has effect on how things are run in this country, or, do you think your vote makes no difference?* was asked to measure the voters' sense of efficacy in their vote. A majority of the people believe that their vote has an effect on the political state of affairs in the country. The percentage of such people has gone up from 48.5 per cent in 1971 to 67.5 per cent in 2004 (see Table 5.2). Interestingly, though it is very much a minority phenomenon, the number of those who do not believe that their vote has any effect has also gone up, from 16.2 per cent in 1971 to 21.3 per cent in 1996 but has again declined to 17.5 per cent in 2004. Over the past 35 years, there has been a steady growth in consciousness of the efficacy of vote as well a sense of relative inefficacy. As a consequence, the percentage of those who could not answer this question one way or another has gone down from 35.3 per cent in 1971 to 15 per cent in 2004.

TABLE 5.2
Efficacy of Vote (in per cent)

	1971	1996	1999	2004
Has effect	48.5	58.6	63.0	67.5
Makes no difference	16.2	21.3	17.4	17.5
Don't know	35.3	19.1	19.6	15.0
Vote has effect		**1996**		**2004**
Illiterate		47.0		54.9
Scheduled Tribe		47.8		58.4
Very poor		50.4		59.2
Female		50.8		61.3
Aged 56 years or above		51.9		62.6
Rural		56.9		66.2
OBC		58.0		67.8
Hindu		58.0		67.7
All India		**58.6**		**67.5**
Scheduled Caste		60.0		65.1
Muslim		60.3		66.6
Aged 25 years or less		60.8		68.1
Upper caste		61.5		70.9
Upper class		62.1		78.7
Urban		64.1		72.3
Male		66.2		73.0
Christian		66.4		69.6
College and above		79.6		82.4

Source NES, CSDS 1971, 1996, 1999, 2004.

Like participation in different electoral activities, here too, we find that the lower social orders have less confidence in their votes. The women and the older people also belong, more or less, to this group. The highly efficacious groups in 2004 are the well educated (82.4 per cent), the Christians (69.6 per cent) and people from the higher income groups/class (78.7 per cent). It is important to note here, that even at its lowest; the sense of efficacy is still respectably high. Even among the illiterates, the proportion of voters feeling efficacious rises, from 47 per cent in 1996 to 54.9 per cent in 2004. The Scheduled Castes and the Muslims as a group are not far too behind, indicating thereby their above-average sense of political efficacy. Most important for us, among the 'partisans', that is, those who say that they have voted for one of the major parties, the figure for 'vote has effect' is higher than the national average.

Another interesting feature of the sense of efficacy, when seen in the context of party competition, is the symmetry across the political parties. As Table 5.2a shows this is true in 1996 and when the levels of efficacy go up in 2004 that too is reflected across all the political parties.

Political Legitimacy

While the existence of a sense of efficacy at the micro-level is a necessary condition for the effectiveness of a multi-party system, the perception of the system of competing parties and elections as legitimate, constitutes a sufficient condition. The larger implications for the relationship between efficacy and legitimacy should be clear by now: an efficacious electorate which does not hold the party system as legitimate would look for other institutions to articulate and aggregate their interests. Worldwide comparison makes it quickly obvious that the candidates for selection as the representatives of popular interest, against the background of a failing party system, are indeed many. The political parties are one of the main agencies available to people to articulate and aggregate their demands, censor errant officials and seek to influence public policy. But they are not the only ones. The same arguments have been made for the justification of military intervention, for the political role of the church, *mullahs, sadhus, bhikhus* (religious leaders active in politics), students and all manners of Left radicals.

The survey asked two main questions to measure the legitimacy of the system of parties and elections. The first question, *How much, in your opinion, do political parties help to make the government pay attention to the people—good deal, somewhat or not much?* provides answer to the usefulness of parties (see Table 5.3). In 1996 as well as in 1971, only a minority of the people was prepared to describe the instrumentality of the political parties in positive terms. It is important, however, to make the point that the positive evaluation of the parties has grown relatively, from 32.6 per cent to over 42.5 per cent (calculated number 'somewhat + good deal' in 1971, see Table 5.3) Opinion is more sharply polarised now, which is why the 'don't know' category has shrunk from 41.7 per cent to 30.3 per cent.

TABLE 5.2a
Efficacy of Vote by Party

Efficacy	1996						2004							
	INC+	BJP+	NF	LF	BSP	Others	Total	UPA	NDA	Left	BSP	SP+	Others	Total
Has no effect	22.6	20.6	15.6	19.6	19.2	24.7	**21.3**	17.6	14.9	13.9	20.7	16.5	16.7	**17.5**
Has effect	59.1	61.3	61.5	68.0	55.6	58.2	**58.6**	67.4	71.8	72.6	65.7	69.1	70.8	**67.5**
Don't know	18.3	18.1	22.9	12.4	25.2	17.1	**19.1**	15.0	13.3	13.5	13.6	14.4	12.5	**15.0**
Total	**32.0**	**28.8**	**11.7**	**8.7**	**3.9**	**14.9**	**100**	**39.5**	**37.9**	**6.4**	**5.0**	**5.4**	**5.8**	**100**

Source NES, CSDS 1996, 2004.

TABLE 5.3
Usefulness of Political Parties (in per cent)

Response	1971	1996
Good deal	10.9	9.5
Somewhat	21.6	33.0
Not much	25.7	27.2
Don't know	41.7	30.3
Usefulness of Political parties—Somewhat and good deal (%)		**1996**
Illiterate		27.7
Female		32.5
Scheduled Tribe		33.0
Very poor		35.1
56 years or above		37.1
Rural		41.1
Scheduled Caste		41.4
OBC		41.4
Hindu		41.9
All India Average		**42.5**
25 years or less		44.8
Muslim		45.4
Upper caste		46.9
Urban		47.0
Upper class		47.8
Male		52.2
College and above		65.6

Source NES, CSDS 1971, 1996.

It is good to find that the highly educated, with a great deal of ambivalence, still belong to the group having maximum faith in the political parties, with 65.6 per cent of the graduate and above perceiving the usefulness of the parties. Similarly, people belonging to the opinionated sections of society like, the urbanites, the younger age group, the upper-castes and the upper class, have larger shares of people who feel that the political parties play useful role in drawing attention to peoples' problems. Interestingly, the Muslims also belong to this group and the Scheduled Caste and the OBCs are not far behind the more efficacious sections of society. However, the Scheduled Tribes, along with the women, represent the lowest shares of such people. It is largely because; they constitute maximum number of 'don't know' types who lack awareness of and exposure to the political world.

The second question (a more direct measurement of the legitimacy of the system) asked, *Suppose there were no parties or assemblies and elections were not held—do you think that the government in this country can be run better?* The responses show how much significance do people attach to the system, which provides basis for their direct participation in it (see Table 5.4).

TABLE 5.4
Legitimacy (in per cent)

Can govt. be run better without parties, assemblies, etc.?	1971	1996	2004
Yes	14.2	11.4	9.0
No	43.4	68.8	72.2
Can't say or don't know	42.4	19.8	18.8
Not better government without parties, etc.		**1996**	**2004**
Very poor		61.5	65.9
Illiterate		61.6	61.1
Sikh		62.7	66.2
56 years or above		63.2	68.4
Female		64.0	67.1
OBC		65.4	72.1
Scheduled Tribe		66.3	68.0
Scheduled Caste		67.3	69.0
Urban		68.1	79.6
Hindu		68.2	72.6
All India		**68.8**	**72.2**
Rural		69.0	70.3
25 years or less		71.3	73.2
Upper class		71.6	81.8
Muslim		72.1	72.9
Male		73.4	76.8
Christian		73.4	72.8
Upper caste		73.9	75.5
College and above		74.1	85.0

Source NES,CSDS 1971, 1996, 2004

When asked to conjecture on a situation where no elections are available (this question was deliberately asked in a manner that highlights the absence of elections rather than their presence), the general electorate overwhelmingly reject a future without parties and elections. An impressively large 72.2 per cent of the sample, in 2004, disagrees with the proposition that the country could be run better without elections. Significantly, this percentage has gone up from the relative low of 43.4 per cent in 1971 and 68.8 per cent in 1996. In retrospect, the high voting for Indira Gandhi's Congress in the 1971 election did not have the backing of deep trust in the institution of elections which, perhaps, facilitated the imposition of authoritarian rule in a matter of years following the resounding electoral victory of her party. Perhaps, as a lasting legacy, particularly in view of the high trust we see in the 1996 and 2004 data, a repetition of the 1975–77 type of Emergency regime is less likely today. The confidence that the voter exudes in the process of voting is the consequence of the successful removal of Indira Gandhi's Congress from power, in the parliamentary election of 1977.

The younger people (73.2 per cent), the educated (85 per cent), the upper castes and upper-class people, constituting the group called 'opinion-makers', have come out overwhelmingly in favour of sustaining the present system in the 2004 data. More importantly, they are also joined, at least on this indicator, by the Muslims (72.9 per cent) and the Christians (72.8 per cent), but interestingly, not by the Sikhs, who, at 66.2 per cent, are 6 per cent lower than the national average.

The positive evaluation of the political system, based on parties and elections, by the better informed and the minority Muslims, reinforces the picture of steady empowerment of the electorate through participation in electoral politics. Against this background, the less than average support that elections and parties receive from the Sikhs can perhaps be understood in terms of the failure of the system, based on parties and elections, during the long years of political unrest in Punjab, which led to one of the longest stretches of direct rule from the centre. The most encouraging feature, reflected from this data (see Table 5.4), is that it cut across all social groups, as there is very little gap between the different sections of society, at least on this indicator. In both the elections, 1996 and 2004, whether informed or uninformed, rich or poor, male or female and so on, all of them feel, more or less, alike.

TABLE 5.4a
Legitimacy by Party

Legitimacy	1996 INC+	BJP+	NF	LF	BSP	Others	Total	2004 UPA	NDA	Left	BSP	SP+	Others	Total
No	70.0	72.4	70.6	71.4	67.4	61.1	**68.8**	73.4	75.5	69.8	65.7	69.2	75.1	**72.2**
Yes	10.6	10.2	10.9	8.6	14.6	16.0	**11.4**	9.2	9.0	8.6	7.7	8.0	7.9	**9.0**
Don't know	19.4	17.4	18.5	20.0	18.0	22.9	**19.8**	17.4	15.5	21.6	26.6	22.8	17.0	**18.8**
Total	**32.0**	**28.8**	**11.7**	**8.7**	**3.9**	**14.9**	**100**	**39.5**	**37.9**	**6.4**	**5.0**	**5.4**	**5.8**	**100**

Source NES, CSDS 1996, 2004.

Once again, similar to efficacy, with regard to the legitimacy of the system, there are no radical differences across political formations, whether in 1996 or in 2004 (see Table 5.4a).

Cross-cutting Value Conflict and Partisan Competition

The demolition of the Babri Mosque, at Ayodhya, on 6 December 1992, was one of the most important landmarks in Indian politics after Independence. The world media and the Indian press have consistently focused on it as a key issue in Indian politics and a key indicator of the civil society in India. The interesting point to note here is that, contrary to the speculations in the media, Indian opinion is neither as homogeneous nor as hostile to the Muslims as one is led to believe. Of all those who express an opinion on it, 63 per cent do not believe that the demolition was justified.

Babri Mosque in Ayodhya has been used as the bone of contention by the religious extremists on both sides for ages, but what happened in 1992 rocked the nation. The Mosque was demolished by the *kar sevaks* (voluntary workers)—activists of the Vishwa Hindu Parishad and the Bajrang Dal—supposedly with the connivance of the BJP, which headed the state government of Uttar Pradesh at that time. Many places in the country witnessed the worst communal riots of their kind; people got divided, albeit temporarily and the BJP was isolated by almost all the political parties of the country.

Interest in the data on the attitudes towards the destruction of the Babri Mosque arises from the fact that, in view of the propagation in the media of the spectre of Hindu fundamentalism. one would expect an internally undifferentiated phalanx of the Hindus (and the Muslims), taking radically opposite stances. However, when the electorate was asked to pass a judgement on whether they considered the demolition justified or unjustified, it largely condemned the act as unjustified. Only 22.7 per cent of Indian electorate have found the act (demolition) justified. Against this, 38.1 per cent termed it as unjustified (see Table 5.5). A large section (39.2 per cent) either have not heard about this episode, or failed to take definite position on it. When one recalculates by excluding the 'non-opinion' cases, share of those condemning the act goes up to 62.6 per cent, as compared to 37.4 per cent who justifies the demolition. Considering the opinion holders only, (those who say either justified or not justified) only while 86.3 per cent of the Muslims have found the act unjustified, a majority of the Hindus (31.6 per cent) have also expressed the same opinion (Table 5.5).

A closer look at the Table 5.5 suggests, that people with greater information and exposure constitute larger shares of those who have found the act unjustified. For example, people belonging to urban areas—highly educated, upper caste and upper class—do not

TABLE 5.5
Partisan Response to the Demolition of Babri Mosque (in per cent) 1996

Response	INC	BJP+	NF	LF	BSP	Total
Unjustified	42.9	25.7	48.2	54.9	26.7	38.1
Don't know	8.0	11.4	7.6	9.2	19.9	10.2
Justified	16.5	40.7	24.1	9.1	27.3	22.7
Not heard about demolition	32.6	22.2	20.0	26.9	26.1	29.0
Demolition was not justified (%)						
Scheduled tribe						18.6
Illiterate						23.8
Very poor						29.3
Hindu						31.6
Female						32.0
Scheduled caste						33.3
56 years or above						33.7
Rural						34.2
OBC						37.5
25 years or less						37.9
All India Average						**38.1**
Upper class						40.7
Male						44.0
Upper caste						46.6
Urban						50.3
College and above						59.6
Muslim						86.3

Source NES, CSDS 1996.

approve of the demolition. Similarly, party-wise analysis of justified and unjustified responses also does not show much polarisation on this line. Except the Left Front (9.1 per cent), all the other parties have significant shares of those who justified demolition. For example, as against 40.7 per cent of the BJP voters, 16.5 per cent of the Congress, 24.1 per cent of the NF and 27.3 per cent of the BSP voters come from those who happened to have justified the act. More importantly, as much as one-fourth (25.7 per cent) of the BJP supporters have condemned the act of demolition. If the 'don't know' and 'not-heard' cases are excluded, all the parties have sizeable proportions of support from both the groups. While larger share of the 'justified' category in the BJP support reflects its north Indian bias, a sizeable support from amongst those condemning the act shows a limit beyond which the BJP cannot go on to capitalise on its *Hindutva* stand.

Responses to the question, *People's opinion are divided on the issue of the Kashmir problem—some people say that government should suppress the agitation by any means, while others say that this problem should be resolved by negotiations. What would you say, should the agitation be suppressed or resolved by negotiations?* are presented in Table 5.6.

People's responses to an emotive issue like Kashmir also do not show any communal bias. Giving credence to their secular values, 33.4 per cent of Indian electors, in 1996, have rejected the option of suppressing the agitation by any means. (The figure goes up to 59 per cent in 2004.) On recalculation of the opinion holders (those who say either negotiation or suppression) as many as 75.6 per cent in 1996 and 87.1 per cent in 2004 have suggested, that the problem of Kashmir cannot be solved by using suppressive but by negotiations only.

The suggestion to resolve the Kashmir problem through negotiations receives support from almost all the relevant segments of society. That is, roughly half of the urban population, the upper castes and the upper class are in favour of negotiation. Obviously the Muslims have slightly higher percentage of such people, but it receives maximum support from the highly educated people (79.5 per cent), followed by the urban dwellers, indicating thereby a greater scope for a peaceful solution of the problem.

TABLE 5.6
Partisan Opinion on Resolution of Kashmir Problem (in per cent)

	1996						2004					
	INC	BJP+	NF	LF	BSP	Total	UPA	NDA	LF	BSP	SP	Total
Negotiation	33.8	34.7	32.6	32.9	25.5	**33.4**	58.8	61.7	63.0	46.4	57.8	**59.0**
Can't say	32.8	26.4	30.7	28.7	28.9	**32.0**	21.0	18.2	18.1	33.9	28.2	**21.4**
Should be suppressed	9.7	17.5	11.0	4.9	14.3	**11.1**	8.2	10.1	9.4	8.3	7.5	**8.8**
Not heard of Kashmir	21.2	19.8	23.3	32.2	30.7	**21.6**	12.1	10.0	9.5	11.3	6.5	**10.8**

Kashmir Problem to be Solved by Negotiation	1996	2004
Illiterate	15.3	39.9
Very poor	18.3	46.4
Scheduled Tribe	20.5	47.8
Female	24.7	50.9
Scheduled Caste	25.4	51.8
Rural	28.7	55.5
56 years or above	29.6	51.9
Hindu	31.3	57.4
OBC	33.0	59.0
All India	**33.4**	**59.0**
25 years or less	37.5	61.5
Upper class	39.2	75.2
Upper caste	41.7	66.6
Male	41.9	66.4
Muslim	45.7	71.0
Urban	48.5	73.0
College and above	62.1	79.5

Source NES, CSDS 1996, 2004.

Like the views on the demolition issue, except the Left Front, all other parties have, more or less, equal shares in those, who support the suppression of the Kashmir problem by force. Of course, the BJP accounts for slightly above the average and the Congress falls slightly below it. But the fact that, all the parties have received one-third of their support from those advocating resolution through negotiations, puts the problem in Right perspective. This finding is a dissuading factor indeed, for the parties as well as their leaders, to take any unpopular stand on it.

The same positive attitude of religious regional reconciliation within India is also reflected in attitudes towards Pakistan. Those, who suggest that India should make more efforts to develop friendly relations with Pakistan outnumber those, who suggest the opposite, or do not have an opinion on the issue. If we consider only those who are either for friendly relations or its opposite, the percentage of those in favour of friendly relations goes up to 72.

People's views on the Indo–Pak relations are positively in favour of negotiation. The people of India, by and large, want, that the government should make more efforts to develop friendly relations with Pakistan. Not only do 44.5 per cent of the total sample or 71.7 per cent of the opinion holders (those who either agree or disagree) support the development of friendly relations, but the people who matter in building a national opinion have come forward to lend more support than the non-opinionated sections of the society. For example, against the all India average of 44.5 per cent, the urban dwellers (59.3 per cent), the well-educated (68.2 per cent), the rich (49.8 per cent) and the upper castes (51.9 per cent) agreed to the proposition that India should make more efforts to develop friendly relations with Pakistan. The Muslims, the worst sufferers from the hostility between the two governments, have supported this viewpoint overwhelmingly: 72.5 per cent of them want friendly relations with Pakistan, compared to 40.8 per cent for the Hindus and 44.5 per cent for the population as a whole.

A certain congruence of opinion across the parties, at least on the national issues, is once again reflected by the data presented in Table 5.7. There is hardly any major variation in the proportions of votes that different political parties have received from those advocating friendly relations with Pakistan or opposing it. The National Front and the BSP with 51.8 per cent and 50.0 per cent respectively, have received majority of their support from the pro-friendship group, but then it reflects their above the average appeal among the Muslims. The Congress and the Left Front represent the national average, while the BJP accounts for slightly above the average from among those who disagree with this proposition.

TABLE 5.7
India should Develop Friendly Relations with Pakistan (in per cent)

Response	INC	BJP+	NF	LF	BSP	Total
Disagree	17.1	23.4	11.6	17.4	12.4	17.6
Don't know /No opinion	37.0	34.5	36.6	37.3	37.6	37.9
Agree	45.8	42.1	51.8	45.3	50.0	44.5

Develop friendly relations with Pakistan (%)

Illiterate	30.4
Scheduled Tribe	32.5
Very poor	33.0
Female	36.5
Scheduled Caste	39.4
Rural	39.8
Hindu	40.8
56 years or above	43.2
OBC	43.2
All India Average	**44.5**
25 years or less	46.8
Upper class	49.8
Upper caste	51.9
Male	52.2
Urban	59.3
College and above	68.2
Muslim	72.5

Source NES, CSDS 1996.

The issue of a common personal law for all Indians is one of the most important issues facing the country today. In this context, it is interesting to note here that a significant percentage of Indians are willing to concede to each community the right to retain its own personal law, in the areas of marriage and property rights. In order to measure attitudes towards personal law, the survey asked: *Every community should be allowed to have its own laws to govern marriage and property rights. Do you agree or disagree?* The responses are presented in Table 5.8.

Judging from the data of Table 5.8, there is considerable support within the electorate for a civil society in India. Of course, there is greater sensitivity within the Muslims for their own community to have the right to define the scope of their social institutions, similar to other minority communities, also concerned about their personal law. However, this position is supported by a considerable section within the majority community, as well as across the broad spectrum of India's political parties, including the supporters of the Hindu Nationalist BJP (see Tables 5.9 and 5.10).

Conclusion

The continuing strength and legitimacy of institutions, or, their fragmentation. are important indicators of democratisation, particularly in the context of a post-colonial state. While all institutions are, in a way, affected by social change, it is the party system which is, properly speaking, 'in the eye of the storm'. The parties are the first line of contact between the individual and the state and, as such, they are the first to register the change in the tone and content of social demands. Of course, other institutions of the state, such as the bureaucracy, judiciary, or the army and police, are also important institutions that deserve close study. But, considering the breadth and complexity of the institutions in a diverse state of continental proportions, the party system is perhaps the most effective instrument to measure the nature and course of social change in India.

The chapter has drawn on the survey data on partisanship in India to shed light on the core question—why did India succeed in making the transition from colonial rule to multi-party democracy. To the extent that multi-party democracy and civil society are effectively present, India, along with a few other poor,

TABLE 5.8
Need for Separate Civil Code for Every Community by Party Support (in per cent)

	1996					2004				
	INC	BJP+	NF	LF	BSP	Total	UPA	NDA	LF	BSP	SP	Total
Disagree	29.9	36.5	29.4	22.1	30.4	**30.4**	27.4	29.7	22.4	20.2	22.3	**27.1**
Don't know	23.8	22.9	28.5	18.2	24.8	**25.1**	19.0	17.4	15.0	26.3	23.5	**19.2**
Agree	46.3	40.6	42.2	59.6	44.7	**44.4**	53.6	52.9	62.6	53.5	54.2	**53.8**

Support for Separate Civil Code	1996	2004
Hindu	41.5	52.1
All India	**44.4**	**53.8**
Christian	50.2	61.2
Sikh	51.6	48.5
Muslim	67.1	66.0

Source NES,CSDS 1996, 2004.

TABLE 5.9
Issue Positions: Rebels, Stakeholders and Others

		Year	Stakeholders	Others	Rebels	Total
a.	Demolition of Babri Mosque was not justified	1996	46.5	28.9	47.9	**38.2**
b.	Kashmir problem to be resolved by negotiation	1996	43.6	22.3	46.2	**33.5**
		2004	70.3	43.5	66.4	**59.2**
c.	Develop friendly relation with Pakistan	1996	54.0	34.0	56.5	**44.6**
d.	Support for separate Civil Code	1996	46.7	42.2	46.4	**44.5**
		2004	57.6	48.2	57.3	**53.8**

Source NES, CSDS 1996, 2004.

TABLE 5.10
Party Support: Rebels, Stakeholders and Others

	1996						2004					
	INC+	BJP+	NF	LF	BSP	Others	Total	UPA	NDA	Left	BSP	SP	Others	Total
Stakeholders	31.8	30.1	11.8	9.9	3.4	12.9	**46.6**	38.0	39.8	6.5	4.3	5.3	6.1	**55.4**
Others	32.7	27.8	11.6	7.6	4.2	16.2	**46.5**	41.6	34.8	6.3	6.0	5.6	5.7	**38.4**
Rebels	30.3	26.8	11.5	7.5	5.0	19.0	**6.9**	40.2	40.0	5.9	4.5	5.3	4.2	**6.2**
Total	**32.1**	**28.8**	**11.7**	**8.7**	**3.9**	**14.9**	**100.0**	**39.5**	**37.9**	**6.4**	**5.0**	**5.4**	**5.8**	**100.0**

Source NES, CSDS 1996, 2004.

non-western societies as Barbados, Botswana, Costa Rica, Jamaica, Malta, Mauritius and Papua New Guinea, appears as a counter-example against widely held beliefs that link stable democracies with high levels of social and economic development (Dahl 1989: 253). Ensconced within the first puzzle is a second one: how does a poor society, with no democratic tradition of its own, manage to maintain, not only democratic institutions, but a competitive, multi-party democracy as well, successfully warding off the challenges of non-party, plebiscitary democracy and strong executive leadership based on popular authoritarianism, deemed by many non-Western societies as a more appropriate form of government?

The analysis undertaken in this chapter has shown how well established political parties and elections have become the preferred methods of political and social change in India. However, while the institutional legitimacy and efficacy of political parties are clearly borne out by the evidence presented here, the same cannot be said about the politicians who actually run these institutions. To that extent, the survey data closely resembles the sordid picture of scandals, corruption and illegal transactions on the part of politicians, high and low, that are routinely reported by the media.

This creates a paradoxical situation, where people routinely turn out for the elections, participate enthusiastically in the voting and witness the swearing in of the elected governments, while the low trust in the politicians leads to disenchantment at the first indication of wrong-doing. As any number of reports from the obsessive interest of the media in post-election revelations of the corrupt regional and national ministers would indicate, the combination of high trust in the elections but low trust in the politicians leads to a situation where efforts to establish trust replace the real business of the government, which is to govern through the enactment and implementation of public policy. The systemic implications of this phenomenon would be examined in detail later in the text. We shall next turn to another interesting characteristic of the politics of social change in India, namely, the juxtaposition of the assertion of regional identity in the context of the efforts to promote national unity.

Notes

1. North (1990: 3) defines the role of the institutions in the political process as follows:

    Institutions are the rules of the games in a society or, more formally, are the humanly devised constraints that shape human interaction. In consequence they structure incentives in human exchange, whether political, social, or economic. Institutional change shapes the way societies evolve through time and hence is the way to understanding historical change.

2. The process is delineated at length in, *Political Parties in South Asia* (2004), edited by Subrata Mitra, Mike Enskat and Clemens Spiess. Taking a position against the exclusive reliance on the cleavage theory, the authors argue,

    The emphasis on the role of agency rather than social cleavage in party foundation, evolution and adaptation to their environment explains the general and idiosyncratic aspects of specific party systems. Indigenisation, a general factor that provides a common agenda for an inter-region comparison through the analysis of parties in their national or regional contexts helps explain the variation in the success of South Asian political parties.

3. Harrison (1960) was one of the earliest to warn against the dangers of disintegration in India.
4. Huntington (1968) reflects upon the strong commitment to orderly change, if needed, at the cost of political coercion, characteristic of the modernisation approach.
5. The issue has been debated by a number of authors. See in particular, Rudolph and Rudolph (1967), Frankel and Rao (1989/1990), Kothari (1970). For detailed analysis of the electoral process, see Mitra and Chiriyankandath (1992). Sheth (1975) is an excellent source for the political sociology of the electoral process. Hardgrave and Kochanek (2008) is a very good source for the manifestos and background information. See especially chapter 6, 'Parties and Politics'.
6. For the formulation of these ideas in terms of an analytical framework on elections and social change in India, based on a model of electoral norms and organisational structure corresponding to them, see Mitra (1994b).
7. See Lijphart (1996) for a discussion of the efficacy of federalism and consociationalism in promoting democracy and social change.
8. For an application of this concept as a framework for the discussion of political participation in India, see Mitra (1991).
9. For a discussion of this point based on an analysis of the local elites in India, see Mitra (1992).

122 When Rebels Become Stakeholders

10. Panchayati Raj, a traditional political institution, rejuvenated and recast as the basic foundation stone of democracy at the local level, first developed in western India and then transported with great success to the communist-ruled state of West Bengal, is a good example. See the chapter on 'Institutional Innovation: The Politicized Panchayats' in Kohli (1987: 108–116) for a discussion of the efficacy of West Bengal's communist regime in making use of the panchayati system in promoting order and welfare.
11. The concept is discussed at length below. The two most useful references to its functioning are Kothari (1964, 1974).
12. The figures are as follows: Left Front voters 68.0 per cent, National Front 61.5 per cent, BJP 61.3 per cent, Congress 59.1 per cent, BSP 55.6 per cent (see Table 5.2a). This shows both the close relationship between partisanship and efficacy, as well as, the widely dispersed nature of the sense of efficacy across the whole ideological spectrum of political parties.

6

Re-inventing the Nation: The Dialectics of Nation and Region in India

Balkanisation—long before Yugoslovia unravelled into violent self-destruction—was the main anxiety of India's leaders and observers, both from home and abroad, during the uncertain decade following Independence, with regard to the chances of survival of the nascent state. Nehru's visionary inaugural words about 'the soul of a nation, long suppressed, finds utterance', ideally, in the body of the modern state—were not enough. There was, as yet, no evidence that the Indian nation commanded the requisite loyalty to subdue the insubordinate provinces. There still isn't enough evidence of that. But, the obsessive pre-occupation with national 'integration' and the fear of 'fissiparous' tendencies is no longer the case. A confident Indian nation, in spite of all the difficulties it still experiences in defining itself, has learnt to live with dissidence—in Kashmir, Assam and other localised sites of 'anti-Indian' risings. The transformation of the early insecurities into the present vitality is a complex story that is beyond the remit of this chapter. Instead, we shall confine ourselves to examining the survey evidence of the ranking of loyalties—to the region and the nation—and draw some explanatory inferences to explain why, in India today, the sum of parts is more than the whole.

While political parties provide the main institutional context within which electoral participation and competitive articulation and aggregation of interests take place, it is the national, regional and local arenas that provide the spatial limits to the operation of institutions. The main reason as to why the spatial basis of politics is relevant to the discussion of social change, is because, conventional theory privileges the general over the specific, region over locality and nation over region. What conventional theory does not clearly indicate is whether these concepts are to be seen in dichotomous terms or as overlapping, inter-penetrating concepts. We argue in this chapter that social change in India has added successive layers to the multi-layered persona of India's political culture, rather than fragmenting it along spatial and primordial divisions. The chapter pursues these issues through the mapping of locality, region and nation upon the political space on the basis of opinions and attitudes of Indians.

Region Against the Nation?

Vitriolic, anti-India, or in a milder form, anti-centre rhetoric as a career move on the part of the local and regional leaders is an element of the everyday reality in Indian politics. The prominent role that many regional parties and leaders play in the formation of coalitions, campaign and post-election jockeying for power in the aftermath of the election, has created an impression of the regionalisation of the national political arena. Many commentators suggest that the national electorate is actually a series of regional arenas, managed by regional and local leaders with their networks; that the calculations of politicians, and by inference, those of the voters are focused on the regional government. Talk of regionalism is not new in Indian politics, but the anxiety which always accompanied such observations in the years after Independence,[1] is a thing of the past. The presence of the region on the national scene is seen by many as something positive, as a part of the process of community formation and empowerment, as 'the emergence of a more competitive and polarised party system and the increasing regionalisation of the party system' (Hasan 1996). Some commentators even see the emergence of the region as a prime consideration in the electoral choice in a positive light. We learn from D.L. Sheth:

> Our representative democracy is indeed moving closer to the people. They now feel more involved and show greater concern for institutions of local and regional governance. They perceive governance from Delhi to be

increasingly remote. Their loyalty and trust are stronger for the local and regional governments than for the centre. More important, the rarefied field of 'national politics' which once pitted the 'nation' against the 'region' has opened up for the regional and 'vernacular' elites.

(D.L. Sheth 1996; *Seminar* 2005)

Nevertheless, doubters persist. In spite of its regular appearance in discussions of the electoral process, the assertion of regionalisation often remains unspecific and empirically unsubstantiated, with dark hints of a monster that has not been entirely put to rest. Regionalisation might infuse new blood into the political system[2] and hasten the decline of national parties (Hasan 1996), but what are its systemic implications? With regionalism rampant, will there be 'vacuum in the party system at the national level' (Yadav 1996a).

Drawing mainly on the opinions and attitudes of the national electorate, we inquire into some of the implications of regionalisation for the resilience of the Indian state. That region is much in evidence is abundantly clear. But its theoretical implication can be seen in two different lights. Is the region merely a convenient spring-board to the national arena, or, is the region an exclusive political space in India's macro-politics? Should nation and region be conceptualised in dichotomous terms, or are they overlapping categories, distinctive and yet mutually enriching and reinforcing?

Some of these issues are salient to the process of electoral choice. Placed in the electoral context, the potential voters have to choose whether to vote at all, and in case one decides to turn out for the poll, whom to vote for. Both decisions are influenced by a multiplicity of factors, including, in ascending order of abstraction—personal links to candidates, family connections, social networks, professional associations, political identification, party membership and ideological leanings.[3] Many of these factors are local in origin; others originate from higher-levels of the system. The salience that voters attach to them and the manner in which politicians manipulate them, are critical inputs into the process of nation-building in a post-colonial context. The candidate and his agents, standing at the interface of the constituency and the state, can strengthen the muscles and sinews of the nation by the manner in which they get the votes, just as they can contribute to its decay by demonising the nation for their own electoral benefit.

A number of empirical instruments can be constructed in order to evaluate the significance of the regionalisation process. A parliamentary election provides an ideal opportunity to apply these measures in order to study the depth of penetration of the national political arena into the regional and the local levels of the system. The perception of the electorate, particularly the way it constructs the salience of the regional arena compared to the national, and their mutual relationship, are the crucial bits of evidence we need for this purpose. But the mere presence of local and regional bigwigs in campaigns, or, national leaders donning colourful local costumes does not necessarily constitute any compelling evidence in favour of the regionalisation conjecture. A certain degree of identification with the locality and region almost always comes across as one of the factors influencing the vote anywhere in the world.[4] Nor does one need to look at the scenario where regional identity acts as an exclusive factor in leading the bulk of voters to the polling booth—as in East Pakistan's ill-fated parliamentary election of 1970—or, to stay away from polls as in Punjab (1992) and Kashmir (1996), in order to establish the importance of regional identity.[5] In such cases the voters have already decided the fate of the nation with their feet.

The strands of regionalism, as a political phenomenon, are many, some of which are difficult to conceptualise in dichotomous terms. Does the electorate recognise region as a phenomenon in its own right? Is it conceptualised in terms of an exclusive identity, pitted against the nation as its polar opposite? Or, is the nation an inclusive category, a Matruska doll that contains layers of region and locality encapsulated within? One approximate measure is to juxtapose the vote share of the regional parties with those defined by the Election Commission as national parties.[6] The empirical issue, then, is to see how the seat and vote shares of the national parties in the Lok Sabha are distributed during the period after Independence.

As the data presented in Figure 6.1 indicate, both in terms of votes and seats, the national parties have collectively stayed at a reasonably high level. The decline of the dominant role of the Indian National Congress, conventionally pegged at 1967, does not appear to have marked a trend in the vote and seat shares of the national parties. At least on the basis of the aggregate data, one can assert

FIGURE 6.1
Votes and Seats Share of National Parties in Lok Sabha (1952–2004)

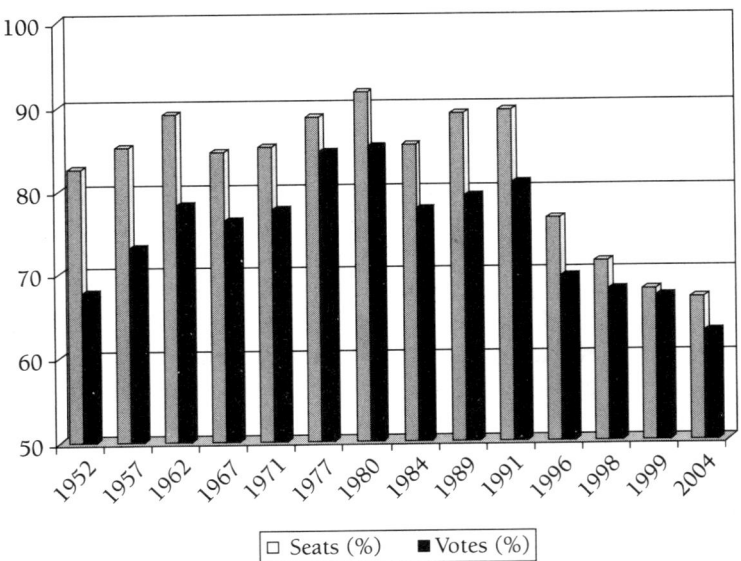

☐ Seats (%)   ■ Votes (%)

Source Data unit, Centre for the Study of Developing Societies, Various years.

that the nation and the Congress party have become independent of one another. Contrary to the assumptions of the one-dominant-party model, national political debates do not any longer have to be mediated by the presence of an overarching Congress party.[7]

Opinions and Attitudes of the Electors: The Micro-political Considerations

Juxtaposing electoral evidence of the decline of the vote and seat shares of the national parties with survey data about the ranking of loyalties to the nation, region and locality reveals interesting, complementary insights. How do individual electors—our ultimate unit of analysis—situate the region and the nation? At the level of the voter, the first question to ask is: How aware is the voter of the region in terms of the information she/he possesses? Next is the question of regional sentiments. Do voters consider their specific regions—loyalty to it and identification with it—as salient values? Finally, do these sentiments extend to parties and institutions? Do voters express greater trust in the regional governments and parties than the national government and parties?

The micro perceptions of region and nation are the crucial building blocs that underpin macro-structures such as political parties and institutions like the Lok Sabha. Without the requisite degree of information and supportive attitudes from individuals, national institutions—like in the majority of post-colonial states—can atrophy and eventually pale into insignificance. Empirical analysis of these issues can be undertaken in terms of the electorate's concern for what the regional government does and information about the regional level of the political system, personal identification with the regional level and trust in the regional government.

Three sets of direct questions (where we have comparative data from 1971, 1996, 1999 and 2004) help us to form the extent of concern for and information about the regional level on the part of the mass public. The first question of the set was: *People are generally concerned about what governments do—some are more concerned about what the government in Delhi does, others are more concerned with what the state government does. How about you? Are you more concerned about what the Central Government in Delhi does or the (name the state government) does?* The responses to this question are presented in Table 6.1.

TABLE 6.1
Concern about Central and State Government (in per cent)

	1971	1996	1999	2004
Neither	24.9	39.7	26.0	9.2
Central government	21.0	11.0	14.8	23.8
Both	14.5	20.9	26.7	22.3
State	18.9	23.0	25.6	23.3
D.K. N.A., Others	20.7	5.4	6.9	21.5

Source NES, CSDS 1971, 1996, 1999, 2004.

Compared to 1967 (Sheth 1975), the trend we get from Table 6.1 suggests an electorate that has learnt to place both the region and the nation in their proper places and that attaches far greater salience to their cooperation than what used to be the case. To measure the extent to which the region and the nation—in the eyes of the Indian men and women—have become co-authors of the joint text of the modern state, we turn to the issue of loyalty to the region. The survey sought to measure this by means of a direct question; We should be loyal to our own region first and then to India. Do you agree to this or disagree? The results are presented in Table 6.2.

TABLE 6.2
Loyalty to Region First and then to India (in per cent)

	1967	1996	1999	2004
Agree	67.1	53.4	50.7	65.4
Disagree	22.3	21.0	21.4	19.8
D.K./No opinion	8.4	25.6	27.9	14.8

Source NES, CSDS 1967, 1996, 1999, 2004.

The high level of loyalty to the region expressed in 1967—this question was not asked in 1971—needs to be seen in the context of the emergence of the regional political forces to prominence in 1967, for the first time since Independence. The Congress party lost control of about half the legislatures in the states. Its strength in the Lok Sabha was slashed down to a bare majority. The resurgent regional forces reflect the high expression of loyalty towards the region on the part of the electorate. Loyalty to the region was still expressed by a majority of the electorate in 1996 and almost equal to the 1967 level in 2004 but a good number of the respondents are not able to put their loyalties towards the region and the nation in the form of a strict dichotomy. Thus, while the region is understood as a distinct category, its preferential position with regard to the nation is, at least for a substantial part of the respondents, not clear.

The same question, when repeated with regard to trust in the capacity of the regional parties (*Compared to national parties regional/ local parties can provide better government in states. Do you agree or disagree to this?*), shows that greater number of respondents prefer regional parties. In fact, by 2004, preference for regional parties has gone up as high as 61.1 per cent (see Table 6.3).

TABLE 6.3
Regional Parties Provide Better Government (in per cent)

	1996	2004
Agree	34.0	61.1
Disagree	20.1	28.1
D.K./No opinion	45.9	30.8

Source NES, CSDS 1996, 2004.

However interesting or suggestive specific survey instruments might be, it is always desirable to seek corroboration of evidence from different sources or other questions in the same survey with some comparable dimension built into it. In order to test the consistency of response, we have cross-tabulated the two measures of trust and loyalty towards region. Not surprisingly, the two individual measures of regional attitude and support to the regional parties are strongly correlated. We report, in the following tables, the results of the cross-tabulation of the two sets of measurements of attitudes towards the region and trust in the efficacy of the regional parties.

The results indicate a strong correlation between attitudes towards the region and trust in the abilities of the regional parties. Once again, it is noticeable that there is a huge consistency between the two questions: those who are not sure that the regional parties could not provide better government also think that the region does not come before the nation (see figures in the top left and bottom right columns of the Table 6.4).

TABLE 6.4
Loyal to Region by 'Regional Parties Provide Better Government' (in per cent)

	1996			2004		
	Regional parties provide better government			Regional parties provide better government		
Region comes before nation	Agree	D.K./No opinion	Disagree	Agree	D.K./No opinion	Disagree
Agree	47.6	34.3	18.1	49.4	22.1	28.5
D.K./No opinion	10.7	86.0	3.3	7.1	87.8	5.1
Disagree	27.8	26.7	45.5	37.1	17.0	45.9

Source NES, CSDS 1996, 2004.

We shall next consider the level of trust in the government at different levels of the system (see Table 6.5).

TABLE 6.5
Trust in Local/State/Central Government (in per cent) 1996

	Great deal	Somewhat	Not at all
Local government	39.0	37.8	23.2
State government	37.2	43.6	19.2
Central government	35.2	42.5	22.3

Source NES, CSDS 1996.

We can combine the results obtained so far in terms of a summary table (see Table 6.6).

TABLE 6.6
Loyalty to Region by Trust in Different Levels of Governments (in per cent) 1996

	Great deal of trust in:		
Regional loyalty	Central government	Regional government	Local government
Loyalty to region before nation	38.3	40.9	42.4
Regional parties provide better government	38.5	45.2	44.8

Source NES, CSDS 1996.
Note Cell entries in the above table are row percentages, that is, of those who consider loyalty to the region more important than loyalty to the nation, 38.5 per cent have a great deal of trust in the Central Government, 41.2 per cent in the regional government, 42.6 per cent in the local government, and so on.

It is important here to recall that the two groups of questions that have been cross-tabulated to produce the composite table, were asked at different points in the questionnaire. The measurement of the sentiments towards the region and attitudes towards the regional parties appeared before the trust in government series. In the latter, the three levels of government in India were measured one after another. As such, each cell entry measures an internally consistent variable that seeks to relate sentiments to measurement of trust in government. In that light, we can suggest that there is a reasonable amount of consistency in the relations of sentiments to trust, that is, a positive sentiment towards the region leads to a high level of trust in the efficacy of the regional government. In both cases, trust in the regional government is higher than the corresponding level for the national government.

What makes this inference problematic for a strong conclusion in favour of a strictly regional mind-set—regional sentiments leading to trust in the regional government—is that, the corresponding figure for the national government is not much different. A large number of those who have positive sentiments towards the regional government also trust the national government as well as the local government, suggesting the possibility that positive sentiments towards the regional level of the political system and to the regional parties do not necessarily preclude trust in the national government.

Regionalisation Conjecture Reformulated

Up to this point, we have operationalised the regionalisation conjecture in the sense that regionalists are people for whom the regional political arena is not only important; it is so in preference to other political levels of the system. That largely answers the first question regarding the popular recognition of the regional level of governance in India. The appreciably high level of people who were unwilling or unable to come down on the side of the regions, or against, suggests that perhaps the nation–region duality might have missed other potential and possible forms of the co-existence of the nation and the region. In order to understand the perplexing anomaly of an astoundingly high 45.9 per cent of non-response in 1996 and 30.8 in 2004 (see Table 6.3), one needs to look more deeply at the data on the social background of the 'regionalists'.

In order to relate social background to attitudes, we have created a new variable, 'regionalists', by combining 'loyalty to region before nation' and 'belief that regional parties provide better government than national parties'. This is a 'strong' specification of the regionalisation conjecture in the sense that only those who have indicated a strong response in favour of regional identity to both the questions are put together in the category of 'regionalists'. The rest are specified as 'others'. Table 6.7 reports the cross-tabulation of regionalists with a number of characteristics describing the people belonging to this category.

TABLE 6.7
Regionalists by Caste (in per cent)

Caste	1996 Regionalists	1996 Others	2004 Regionalists	2004 Others
SC	16.1	19.5	19.1	17.5
ST	8.8	9.7	11.3	7.9
OBC	41.3	35.6	40.5	40.0
Others	33.8	35.1	29.1	34.6

Source NES, CSDS 1996, 2004.

Social Profile of the Regionalists

From the social profile of regionalists, it should be possible to identify those sections of the Indian population that have greater trust in the regional government. The most important social group to be found among those who hold strongly positive attitudes towards the region are the Other Backward Classes.

These are the social groups who did not have the effective access to civil services and professions under the British, nor were they in the forefront of the national anti-colonial movement, which caused the regional and the national party organisations to be dominated by the twice-born castes. Nor could these groups, not being members of either the Scheduled Castes or of the Scheduled Tribes, take advantage of the facilities made available under various reservation laws, at least in the government services and the legislatures. But these social groups did take advantage of the land reforms, particularly the zamindari abolition laws that the Congress governments introduced after Independence. With greater access to land, security of tenure, access to infrastructure and new agrarian technology and—equally important—thanks to family labour, the

OBCs became the main beneficiaries of agricultural modernisation. Their next objective was to capture political power as a part of region-based peasant parties, led by people like Charan Singh in the 1970s and leaders like Lalu Prasad and Mulayam Singh Yadav in contemporary politics. The political experience and linkages gained by them became valuable legacies, which even the return of the Congress party under Indira Gandhi in the parliamentary election of 1971, or the rise of Hindu nationalism in the 1980s, could not destroy. The advent of coalition politics has given this an institutional shape in terms of stable political linkages.

The survey data, which help us visualise the other facets of the social base of regionalists, also show the extent of political change and social mobilisation that have taken place since. The upwardly mobile peasant–OBC–regional forces coalitions of the 1960s have matured into broader political groupings, with other socially and economically marginal forces—bereft of political access that comes from high social status or constitutional guarantee, as in the case of the Scheduled Castes and the Scheduled Tribes—gravitating in the direction of the OBCs and aiming at drawing upon the regional level of the political system as a realistic chance for them to exercise real political power. Some of these conjectures are borne out by Table 6.8.

TABLE 6.8
Regionalists by Religion (in per cent)

Religion	1996 Regionalists	1996 Others	2004 Regionalists	2004 Others
Hindu	81.6	84.8	80.5	79.9
Muslim	12.0	10.2	11.2	11.4
Christian	4.7	2.6	3.1	3.2
Sikh	1.1	1.4	2.4	2.5
Others	0.7	0.9	2.8	3.0

Source NES, CSDS 1996, 2004.

Muslims and Christians used to have a relatively stronger presence among regionalists as compared to non-regionalists (others—in Table 6.8). Upper Hindu castes were mobilised by national political parties already under British rule and occupied positions of leadership in these parties in elections that followed India's Independence. As such, Hindu backward classes and minority communities, once they came on stream, found regional parties more hospitable to their political ambitions. This can be seen to be the case in 1996. However, the emergence of coalition politics acted as an equaliser of chances and the clear relationship between communities and support for regionalists started disappearing in 2004 (see Table 6.8). Table 6.9 shows the higher level of education among regionalists, suggesting that these social groups also possess the educational resources with which to reinforce their intention to use the regional political system for the purposes of political leverage.

TABLE 6.9
Regionalists by Level of Education (in per cent)

Education	1996 Regionalists	1996 Others	2004 Regionalists	2004 Others
Illiterate	28.3	46.5	40.3	32.7
Up to middle	35.7	30.6	24.6	21.9
College, no degree	28.5	17.3	22.3	24.4
College degree and above	7.3	5.3	11.7	20.0

Source NES, CSDS 1996, 2004.

Regionalists are likely to be upwardly mobile educated males, the erstwhile 'bullock capitalists' who first entered politics in a major way in the 1960s. But the trend has levelled off. They have now graduated beyond their exclusive reliance on agriculture to other avenues, increasingly opening up in the countryside, thanks to the plethora of new programmes being introduced by the government as well as by non-governmental agencies. They are into agri-business, working as small-time contractors, acting as brokers for outsiders seeking access to ministers, officials or local markets. As we shall see in the next section, the 1990s, which set the political and the economic processes free from the dominance of the erstwhile political classes—the bureaucracy, the urban power-brokers and, above all, the metropolitan 'High Commands'—has brought great sense of efficacy to the regionalists.

Sense of Efficacy

Several direct questions were asked to measure the sense of political and economic efficacy of the electorate. By cross-tabulating these questions with our two filter questions regarding loyalty to region and trust in regional parties, we are able to check as to what extent the regionalists see themselves as people who matter. Following the conventional measurements of efficacy, questions have been asked about political efficacy and financial success. From Table 6.10, the regionalists in 1996 as well as in 2004, did not have a great sense of efficacy in terms of being able to draw the attention of the government towards popular needs and grievances. But, they were great believers in institutions, and in 2004, they were pulling level with the non-regionalists with regard to institutional legitimacy.

TABLE 6.10
Sense of Political Efficacy of Regionalists (in per cent)

	1996		2004	
	Regionalists	Others	Regionalists	Others
Do you think your vote has an effect on how things are run in this country, or do you think your vote makes no difference? (Vote has effect)	71.1	74.2	65.2	68.5
Suppose there were no parties or assemblies and elections were not held, do you think that the government in this country could be run better? (No. Elections are necessary.)	82.2	86.9	72.7	72.1

Source NES, CSDS 1996, 2004.

Financial Efficacy

The lower sense of efficacy of the regionalists compared to others was in, 1996 reinforced by their general sense of financial well-being (see Table 6.11). But nowhere is this tendency as noticeable as it is in their boldly buoyant view of the shape of things to come. More than half of them expect things to get better. This tendency as the 2004 data show, has levelled off.

TABLE 6.11
Sense of Financial Satisfaction of Regionalists (in per cent)

	1996		2004	
	Regionalists	Others	Regionalists	Others
During the past few years, has your financial situation improved, worsened, or has it stayed the same? (Improved)	31.1	28.5	26.1	28.3
In whatever financial condition you are placed today, on the whole, are you satisfied with your financial situation? (Satisfied)	31.9	27.2	14.1	17.0
Now looking ahead and thinking about the next few years, do you expect that your financial situation will stay about the way it is now, get better or get worse? (Will get better)	60.0	56.1	63.3	67.2

Source NES, CSDS 1996, 2004.

Construction of the Centre from the Periphery

From the distribution of the regionalists over the states that are represented in our sample, people with loyalty and trust towards regions are only slightly more likely to be found in certain parts of India such as Tamil Nadu, Andhra Pradesh and Assam (States with a record of regional movements) than in other states. But they are also found in Karnataka, Gujarat, Haryana and Kerala which have not experienced regional movements of comparative strength. It is best, thus, to characterise regionalism as an attitude, found in a certain section of the Indian population, with specific socio-demographic features. The question we now wish to raise is, whether these people are also distinguished by a specific view of the nature of the state, state–society relations and inter-communal relations in India. The relevant questions from the survey have been cross-tabulated with the regionalists. The results are discussed here.

Communal Accommodation

As the responses presented in the preceding sections indicate, the regionalists have a coherent and distinct view on a range of issues that constitute the core of Indian politics today. At 85.2 per cent approval rate, they are firmly of the opinion that it is the responsibility of the government to protect the minorities (see 1996 data in Table 6.12). The supportive attitude towards minorities is more clearly spelled out in terms of similarly supportive attitudes towards the Muslim community in particular, towards the contentious issue of personal law and a significantly large rate of disapproval of the destruction of the Babri Mosque. The trend continues in 2004. Presumably, the regionalists' state is culturally plural, tolerant, inclusive and committed to distributive justice.

TABLE 6.12
Regionalists and their Attitudes Towards Communal Accommodation (in per cent)

	1996		2004	
	Regionalists	Others	Regionalists	Others
It is the responsibility of the government to protect the interests of minorities (Agree)	85.2	54.7	65.5	61.3
The needs and problems of Muslims have been neglected in India (Agree)	27.8	15.7	33.4	23.6
Every community should be allowed to have its own laws to govern marriage and property rights. (Agree).	54.0	41.3	68.7	47.3

Source NES, CSDS 1996, 2004.

Methods of State Integration

The other issue that polarises India's politics today is the nature of the state itself, particularly with regard to India's neighbours and the use of force to suppress those, contesting the authority of the state rather than negotiate with them. From the responses to the question on Kashmir (*People's opinions are divided on the issue of Kashmir problem—some people say that the government should suppress the agitation by any means while others say that this problem should be resolved by negotiations. What would you say: should the agitation be suppressed or resolved by negotiation?*), the regionalists are keener on negotiation, both within as well as outside India (see Table 6.13). On the issue of Kashmir, the regionalists are less likely to be indecisive than the non-regionalists. Fewer of them plead ignorance of Kashmir: 9.6 per cent of the regionalists have not heard of Kashmir as compared to 36.1 per cent among the non-regionalists (in 1996); as per the survey data of 1996, 33.5 per cent of the non-regionalists do not know the best line to take on Kashmir as compared to 27.7 per cent for the regionalists. The regionalists are also somewhat more likely to invoke force against militancy but the most important difference is the attitude towards resolution of the conflict through negotiation. About half of the regionalists are for negotiations compared to a little over a quarter of the non-regionalists who share this opinion in 1996. However, the proportions of 'not heard of' or 'cannot say' drastically declined in 2004, and the gap between the regionalists and the non-regionalists almost disappeared.

TABLE 6.13
Regionalists' Attitudes Towards Kashmir Issue (in per cent)

	1996		2004	
	Regionalists	Others	Regionalists	Others
Resolved through negotiation	49.0	28.0	58.5	59.5
Should be suppressed	12.5	10.8	10.0	8.3
Other	1.4	1.4	1.2	1.5
Respondent cannot say	27.5	33.7	20.1	21.7
Not heard of Kashmir	9.6	26.1	10.2	8.9

Source NES, CSDS 1996, 2004.

One point that comes across clearly from the analysis of attitudes towards Kashmir is that the average regionalist is unlikely to be the 'my region, right or wrong' variety. As we have seen, their attitudes towards centre–region issues are not specific only to *their region* but to the general way in which they would like regional issues to be solved.

Partisan Preference

In terms of partisan preferences, the regionalists have a general tendency to prefer regional parties and a corresponding tendency not to vote for the national parties. Well-known regional parties like the TDP, the AGP, or the DMK are beneficiaries of this tendency, whereas the national parties like the Congress and the BJP are worse off in consequence (see Table 6.14).

TABLE 6.14
Regionalists and Partisan Preference (in per cent)

	1996		2004	
Parties	Regionalists	Others	Regionalists	Others
INC	24.9	27.9	25.5	24.6
BJP	16.5	22.2	20.6	20.7
Janata Dal/JD(U)	6.8	7.0	1.8	1.9
CPI	2.1	1.2	0.7	1.1
CPI(M)	5.2	4.6	2.6	4.2
TMC	3.7	1.4	–	–
DMK	4.4	1.8	1.0	1.6
TDP(Naidu)	3.6	1.3	2.1	2.3
AGP	2.1	0.6	0.5	0.4
AIADMK	1.2	0.3	1.9	2.1
BSP	3.2	3.4	5.8	3.4
SP(Mulayam)	2.8	3.3	4.7	3.4
BJD	–	–	1.0	1.3
Shiv Sena	2.3	1.9	0.9	2.3
RJD(Lalu)	–	–	1.2	1.4
LNJP(Paswan)	–	–	0.8	0.7

Source NES, CSDS 1996, 2004.

This tendency of the regionalists to favour the regional parties gets further intensified when we concentrate on specific regions with a history of regional movements. The emergence of the regional parties like the Asom Gana Parishad, Telegu Desam Party or Akali Dal as ruling parties illustrates this process. Recent Akali politics is an important example of the containment of regionalism. The point is borne out by the following statement of Parkash Singh Badal, made on the 75th birth anniversary of the Akali Dal.

> [The] Shiromoni Akali Dal is a symbol of the aspirations and hopes of Punjab. The Dal has always struggled for human rights, Punjab, Punjabi and the rights of Sikhs. For this the Akali Dal has made innumerable sacrifices. He went on to add, 'we are committed to peace and shall not allow it to be disturbed at any cost. We have full faith in constitutional methods. We shall curb corruption and shall strive to give a clean government ... when today we are celebrating our 75th anniversary we reaffirm our commitment to our goals.' He then confirmed the resolve of the Akali Dal to 'rejoin the national mainstream'; 'now regional parties and national parties who believe in internal autonomy for States are coming together. Akali Dal is very keen to co-operate with them'.(Chum 1996)

Re-inventing Nation from Regions

The data from the Lok Sabha electoral results and the survey findings strongly indicate the presence of a keen awareness of the region as an important level of the Indian political system. That the region is present in a distinctive way does not, of course, suggest that it is exclusive, or that the regionalists necessarily pit the region and the nation as polar opposites, separated by a chasm of distrust and conflict of loyalties. The survey data support the existence of the region and the nation as separate and distinct entities on the basis of popular perceptions. However, the relationship of the two emerges as much more complex than is commonly supposed. The bark of the regional chauvinist is louder than his bite; the political scientist measuring the depth of national integration can accept the separatist rhetoric of the regional leader, at its face value as an indicator of the imminent dissolution of national unity, only at his peril.

The regionalists who were identified in the course of the analysis presented here, emerge as a significant section of the Indian electorate which has had the benefit of greater education, is upwardly mobile and is confident in its ability to negotiate its way through the economy and the policy process. It has a tendency to back the best agent available to promote the regional interest in a given arena. Thus, when a credible regional party is available, the 'regionalists' prefers it to its nationalist competitors. But, they are unwilling to do so mechanically or uncritically. The annihilation of Jayalalitha's AIADMK bears this out. On the other hand, self-confessed regional parties are able to come to terms with the national parties in a manner that promotes common interest. The vote-trading of the two major alliances, namely, the UPA and the NDA bear testimony to this.

The existence of the regionalists in the mass electorate provides the popular base for the formation of the regional parties. From the point of view of the social forces concentrated in a specific part of the country, control of the regional government appears both as a desirable and achievable goal and an effective method for achieving the objectives important to regional movements, such as the use of the mother tongue as official language, cultural hegemony, control over the practice of faith in everyday life, religious property, law and order, agricultural and developmental subsidies and various forms of state-administered welfare.

Having established themselves in their regions, the regionalists have, in this new phase of Indian politics that we have now entered, set their sights at constructing the kind of nation that would be appropriate to the new scheme of things. Increasingly, rather than remaining content with their own region, they are stretching out their hand, and—using their alliances with similar forces from outside—beginning to define the nature of the national community in their own way. Recent experience has demonstrated in different parts of the country, that the pursuit of these goals can not only co-exist with similar aspirations elsewhere, regional movements can, in fact, reinforce one another by pooling their political resources. Hence the unprecedented scenes of the regional leaders from one part of India campaigning for regional parties in other parts of the country in local and regional elections in addition to elections to the Lok Sabha.

The inter-weaving character of the nation and regions can be seen from the complex relationship of the 'regionalists' and the stakeholders (see Table 6.15).

TABLE 6.15
Self-rule and Shared-rule: Regionalists Cross-tabulated by
Stakeholders (1996 and 2004)

	1996				2004			
	Stake-holders	Others	Rebels	Total	Stake-holders	Others	Rebels	Total
Regionalist	26.8	23.2	31.9	25.4	28.6	31.8	34.6	**30.3**
Others	73.2	76.8	68.1	74.6	71.6	68.2	65.4	**69.7**
Total	**45.1**	**48.1**	**6.8**	**100.0**	**53.4**	**40.5**	**6.1**	**100.0**

Source NES, CSDS 1996, 2004.

Conclusion

Those with long memories of Congress rule during the period of its hegemony would recall that the High Command had its own way of ensuring coordination between the nation and the provinces. It used to send 'observers' from the centre to attempt re-conciliation among warring factions in the states and these observers were invariably people from other regions. Also, local and regional Congressmen—a Govind Ballav Pant here, an Atulya Ghose there—were even allowed to take on local colours and rhetoric at variance with the central line. The big difference between the contemporary multi-party democracy and the days of one-party-dominance is that, whereas earlier these expressions of local and regional interests were tolerated rather than encouraged, legitimacy of the regional idiom and the construction of different variants of the nation out of these multi-colour regional beads is now the norm. During the period of Congress hegemony, the outside 'observer' came very much as a central representative—a stern bearer of the message of party unity with little room to manoeuvre of his own—rather than as a fellow regional leader with similar problems. That is no longer the case, because, leaders like Lalu Prasad or Jayalalitha, visiting other regions during national campaigns, can be seen both an insider and outsider to the regional way of looking at things. The Congress system encapsulated the expressions of the local and regional interests and symbols at lower levels of the system; the new element in Indian politics makes these processes of consultation a systematic way of bringing out bits of India's outlying areas and people, and weaves them into different ways of defining what the nation is about and who has the legitimate right to speak in its name.

The politics of coalitions that has replaced the Congress hegemony, has greatly facilitated the process of the integration of the local and regional for the purpose of launching a new debate on the nature of the nation and for identifying the variable boundaries of the nation and region. In consequence, looking for regional allies has now become an imperative for all the national parties. This explains the remarkable stability of both India's ruling and opposition coalitions.

Having come to their own, the regional parties are increasingly self-confident in terms of working out deals with one another as well as with the national parties. The Congress's return to power in 2004 was in fact the result of its successful alliances with regional parties like the RJD, the TRS, the JMM, and so on, a strategy to which it was opposed earlier. The Congress is still somewhat suspect, but that may change once the after-glow of the Congress hegemony has completely burnt out, leaving the Congress to behave much as any other political party. One sure sign of this is that, the terms of political discourse are no longer mediated by the salient values that once defined the core of India's high politics. The regionalists—who, as a group, draws in people from India's periphery in terms of religion, elite caste-status, or geographic distance from the Centre—are able to generate a different construction of the nation-state that is in sync with our times in its ability to reconcile the demands for regional autonomy and self-determination with the need for national unity. When speaking in the national mode, the regionalists do not count out the need to be well informed and decisive in defence of the security and integrity of the nation. But in terms of actual policies of the state, the regionalists are much more willing, and in view of their social base, able, to listen to the minorities, to regions with historical grievances, to sections of the society that entered the post-Independence politics with unsolved, pre-Independence (in some cases, pre-modern) grievances. It is thanks to these regionalists that the emerging multi-party democracy of India is not merely an anomic battle for power and short-term gain, but a manifestation of the releasing of pent-up creativity and visions that provide a fertile and cohesive backdrop to the realignment of social forces. Far from being its antithesis, region has actually emerged as the nursery of the nation.

The analyses of opinions and attitudes, that connect national and regional sentiments, help establish an important point of reference in the unfolding of the Indian nation. As things stand, we are able to see how the different forms of the construction and representation of national identity—in the east and the west, the south and the north, not ignoring the Hindu–Hindi heartland—have become legitimate parts of the national political discourse. Thanks to these insights, national identity in India emerges as a Matruska doll, such that, once we strip off the upper layers, one begins to discern a series of identities, carefully constructed by the political actors in a manner that optimises their chances of achieving a life of affluence and dignity, in a secure environment.

Notes

1. Harrison (1960) was one of the first to articulate this fear of disintegration.
2. See the report on the new faces in the 11th Lok Sabha. See (*India Today* 1996).
3. For a discussion of the modelling of these factors that contribute to both electoral participation and partisanship, see Riker and Ordeshook (1973).
4. A scrutiny of the presidential campaign in the United States—as the national leaders press the flesh and seek to humour local worthies—would prove the point.
5. The Pakistani national elections of 1970 which the Awami League won massively in East Pakistan were fought on the basis of the salient issue of regional autonomy. The success of the Awami League precipitated a serious political crisis, eventually leading to the Liberation War of 1970–71 and the secession of East Pakistan. The Hurriyat in Jammu and Kashmir has been campaigning for a poll boycott in order to bring pressure on the Government of India to concede the autonomy of Kashmir.
6. Which party is a national party is not always a straightforward question. Is it enough for a party to present itself as one? We have opted for the standard

definition of the Election Commission which defines a party as a national party if it is present in at least three states.
7. In the one-party-dominance system, national political debates took place mostly between factions of the Congress party and privately, between them and members of the opposition. Now, such debates take place publicly, between the national parties, the regional parties, and the local.

7
Poverty, Welfare and Social Opportunity in India

Ownership is the essence of economic citizenship. Beyond actual possession, a sense of personal welfare and ownership, or at least the hope of achieving them, constitute a necessary and important complement to being stakeholders in a society. While efficacy and legitimacy are necessary attributes of political agency, from the political actors' point of view, to be counted among those who see themselves as part of India which is on the economic march, adds a vital component to political democracy. We address the issues of economy and politics and popular evaluation of the issues of social justice and opportunity, on the basis of the perception of India's new economic policy.

Economic Change and Political Discontent

The triangular relationship of economy, society and politics remains essentially contested in a post-colonial state where political mobilisation brings new aspirations and social forces into the political arena. The hierarchical social structure and subsistence economy that underpin it are both challenged by new groups of haves and have-nots who replace traditional social relations based on reciprocal economic and social associations. Social and economic domination—which, in the past might have been seen as natural, organic and necessary—now appear contested, political and therefore, susceptible to change. The political consequences that emerge from this conflict of interests are variable. In a society where the political process provides the room to manoeuvre, as argued in the introduction (Figure 1.1), elite agency can enhance legitimacy and governance through a combination of the maintenance of law and order and strategic reform, aimed at enhancing welfare and identity.[1] If the elites in charge—through a combination of force, fraud and constitutional manipulation—deny the opportunity for articulation and aggregation of the demands of deprived groups, the result may be a temporary lull in the extent of manifest social conflict. But history warns of the long-term implications of the policy of benign neglect or outright repression in terms of angry explosions, with disastrous consequences for the political order.

Even after six decades of Independence, mass poverty, continues to remain a salient fact of India's politics and a painful stricture on her democratic credentials.[2] Right from the outset, a range of policies, aimed at the eradication of mass poverty, was designed by the government and left to be implemented by a sprawling Central, state and local bureaucracy. Under the leadership of Jawaharlal Nehru and an egalitarian consensus that prevailed within the Congress 'High Command', from the very beginning, the state committed itself to the norms of social democracy. Nehru's bold and visionary 'Freedom at Midnight' speech, at the Constituent Assembly, New Delhi on 14th August, 1947, spelt out both the ultimate objectives of Independence and the political means of attaining them. 'The achievements we celebrate today', Nehru said, 'is but a step, an opening of opportunity, to the great triumphs and the achievements that await us.' The task included 'the ending of poverty and ignorance and disease and inequality of opportunity.' (Drèze and Sen 1995:1)

The political and administrative resources at the disposal of the government headed by Nehru were, however, the result of a compromise between many sets of contradictory values and interests.[3] The departure of the colonial rulers and the creation of the Republic formally barred princes and zamindars—arch enemies of the Congress-sponsored vision of Independence, democracy and modernity—from a formal presence within the executive. However, many of them were brought back to power through the logic of the electoral process, which inevitably seeks out the wielders of social and economic power as peddlers of influence and hence potential recruits to the circle of the political elites. Thus, unlike revolutionary countries like China, or war-ravaged societies like South Korea, independence and the transfer of power created no major dent in the structure of social power in India. Nor did it affect the form of its administration. The police and bureaucracy maintained structural continuity with the past. So strong was the sense of corporate identity and administrative autonomy of these vital organs of the state, that this continuity remained unaffected by the departure of large contingents of British civilians and police officers. Their places were rapidly filled in by Indians, deeply steeped in the culture of the Raj.

Eventually, the burden of administrative implementation of Nehru's vision fell on those who neither necessarily shared the values nor their political implications. Finally, the political context of economic decision-making was to be composed of the complex structure of a mixed economy. The state and private capital were to enter into a partnership, with the state providing the long-term vision and investment in areas of the economy that were vital for the whole, but were unlikely to yield immediate profits and the private sector providing the link between investment and the efficient production and distribution of goods and resources.

Thus, the constitutional structure bore the marks of the compromise in terms of sharp measures of control, holding enormous potential for bureaucratic power over the economy and society and a series of exceptions. That provided a useful entry point for interest groups—operating through politicians—which could influence regulations and lower public accountabilities, slowing down the economy as a whole. The fundamental rights to property and occupation were thus hemmed in by a number of restrictions in favour of the equalisation of chances and economic reform. The Congress governments at the centre and in the states, immediately after the first General Election in 1952, set about giving legislative shape to these norms. Rather than letting the free play of the forces of the market (for it was argued that a fully developed market with consumers in a position to harness the potentials of the market to the greatest welfare of the society did not yet exist), the government took over the onerous task of bringing about an equitable distribution of material resources in the country.

As we have already seen in the introduction to the book, India's subsistence economy at the time of Independence and her resolve to eradicate mass poverty and mal-distribution of resources, while operating from within the structure of parliamentary democracy, was greeted with incredulity by the specialists of economic development. Among the major countries of the world, India was the only one to follow this path. Not surprisingly, over the years, in a cruel twist of irony, the poverty of India's economy has been matched by the plenty of scholarship on it. The relative transparency of India, availability of good and reliable data, legions of home-grown, skilled economists, post-war interest in democratic poverty alleviation through foreign aid, and, most of all, the tradition of building global models of political economy where India is present as the quintessential embodiment of underdevelopment, account for such ubiquitous presence of India in the development literature. Both at home and abroad, India has often been made the exemplar of everything that was not right with economic policy and its implementation.

The debate on growth versus redistribution got a new impetus following the attempt by the government of Narasimha Rao in 1992 to liberalise the economy by gradually dismantling the restrictions on the free play of market forces—a regime that had acquired the title of a 'licence–permit–raj'. Other supplementary measures like the facilitation of foreign investment in India through joint-ventures and, reciprocally, facilitation of Indian investments abroad, were introduced. These measures have, since then, deeply affected the nature of India's economy and its performance as well as the financial outlook of ordinary men and women. Instead of delving into the actual statistics of growth, redistribution and poverty, the chapter concentrates on the perception of poverty and prosperity by individuals. A battery of three questions has been asked to measure this sense of relative improvement of the life chances of the individual and his progeny. The issue of distributive justice is studied with the help of specific questions about economic and social reform. In view of the importance of policies of structural adjustment, we would focus our attention on its perception by the Indian electorate with the help of questions related to integration with the international market economy and privatisation of public sector enterprises.

'Objective' and 'Subjective' Measurement of Deprivation

We have followed two complementary methods of measuring welfare. The first, 'objective' method entails the aggregation of data of things that an individual owns, developing a poverty index that divides people into four categories ranging from very poor and poor to the middle and upper classes. The 1996 and 2004 surveys formulated these indicators in terms of occupation, ownership of assets, type of house and an assessment of monthly income of the household as a proxy for the economic standard of living of the interviewee. A class variable was constructed by combining the responses to these questions. The class variable, thus produced, was cross-tabulated with other background variables in order to establish the social profile of the poor and the well-to-do. The 'subjective' measurement involves responses to three questions regarding the perception of the economic past, present and future by the individual.

On the whole, the relationship between ownership and social status in Indian society appears to remain stable, though, one notices a slight increase of the very poor and a tiny diminution of the upper class over the two surveys (see Table 7.1). In the 1996 data, the Scheduled Castes and the Scheduled Tribes are more highly represented at the lower end of the class scale. Respectively 30.1 per cent and 14.7 per cent of the very poor are Scheduled Castes or Scheduled Tribes; whereas the comparable proportions in the population as a whole for the SC and ST are 18.8 per cent and 9.5 per cent. The pattern is generally repeated in 2004 as well. The upper castes are present at the higher levels of the class variable: respectively 46.4 per cent and 69.4 per cent of the middle and upper categories of the class variable belong to the elite castes, whose proportion in the population as a whole is 33.9 per cent.

TABLE 7.1
Cross-tabulation of Class with Caste (in per cent)

	1996					2004				
Class	SC	ST	OBC	Upper castes	Total	SC	ST	OBC	Upper castes	Total
Very poor	30.1	14.7	39.9	15.3	**30.6**	28.0	13.9	40.5	17.6	**32.0**
Poor	19.5	11.1	42.4	27.0	**31.0**	17.8	9.0	43.5	29.7	**33.2**
Middle	11.6	5.1	23.4	46.4	**25.2**	9.9	5.2	40.8	44.1	**23.8**
Upper	5.0	2.1	23.4	69.4	**13.2**	5.0	3.5	31.5	60.0	**11.0**
Total	**18.8**	**9.5**	**37.7**	**33.9**	**100.0**	**17.8**	**9.1**	**40.6**	**32.6**	**100.0**

Source NES, CSDS 1996, 2006.

Among the poor and the very poor, the proportion of elite castes is respectively 27 per cent and 15.3 per cent—a far cry from their proportion in the population as a whole.

A similar pattern is sustained by the cross-tabulation of class and education (see Table 7.2), which shows a clear correlation of the economic class with education. The poor and the very poor are much more likely to be illiterate than the middle or the upper classes. At the upper level of the economic scale, the middle and upper classes are much more likely to be educated as compared to the poor or the very poor. The comparable figures are even more pronounced in this direction for college education or above, namely, 13 per cent and 10.2 per cent for the upper and middle classes, as compared to 2.4 per cent and 0.1 per cent for the poor and the very poor respectively (according to the data of 1996).

So far, we have dealt with indicators that are objective, in the sense that they are invariant with persons and apply uniformly to all people within specific social and economic categories. Class in that sense is a social phenomenon and the indicators that measure it are not socially 'constructed'. At a different level, however, the individual's sense of his or her own welfare is essentially *personal*. People have a tendency to evaluate their personal situation in terms of their own life experience and their personal expectations out of life.

As such, past affluence or deprivation, one's own situation in comparison to the reference group, future expectations, or for that

TABLE 7.2
Cross-tabulation of Class with Education (in per cent)

	1996					2004				
	Illiterate	Up to primary	Middle school	Higher secondary	College and above	Illiterate	Up to primary	Middle school	Higher secondary	College and above
Very poor	63.2	20.8	8.2	7.7	0.1	56.4	26.1	9.0	7.3	1.1
Poor	44.4	21.1	15.3	16.8	2.4	34.5	26.7	14.4	20.5	3.9
Middle	27.0	17.2	15.2	30.5	10.2	18.8	19.9	14.6	32.8	13.9
Upper	32.2	15.7	14.3	24.7	13.0	12.4	11.7	9.7	33.8	32.3
Total	**41.9**	**18.9**	**13.1**	**20.2**	**5.9**	**35.3**	**23.2**	**12.2**	**20.7**	**8.5**

Source NES, CSDS 1996, 2006.

matter, the life chances that one expects one's children to have, are important determinants of the subjective evaluation of one's state of welfare. These are, what one may call, the actor's categories of welfare as compared to the objective measures which, in this sense, are observer's categories.

The findings reported in Table 7.3 show three interesting trends. The first and the most striking aspect of these findings is that they do not sustain the image of a strongly polarised society where the conventional cleavages of class, status, or generation would represent diametrically different levels of personal experience with regard to the satisfaction with development. The levels of satisfaction, reported by different sub-groups, are invariably within a few percentage points of the sample average for the population as a whole. In this sense, these findings lend certain credibility to the image of incremental growth and redistribution presented by Lewis (1995). This is true particularly with regard to the robust optimism about the future one envisages for oneself and for one's children, which remains consistently above the levels of satisfaction with the past and the present. They suggest a revisionist view that questions the earlier image of immiserisation and class conflict. India's achievements in this area, point towards a democratic 'bonus', thanks to the knowledge and expertise that have been 'quietly' accumulating in India's policy community now for over two decades. India's top policy-makers, the implementers of public policy in the national and regional bureaucracies and the generations of middle managers whom they have trained, have taken charge of policy and have created a culture where things happen, perhaps slowly, but registering nevertheless incremental and linear growth.[4]

The second important aspect of these findings is that, the difference in the levels of satisfaction of the different sub-groups presents a striking linearity along the conventional lines of social conflict. In spite of the generally optimistic picture created by the data, Table 7.3 indicates effects of gender, age and class on the opinions that the respondents have about the financial situation and its implications for their welfare. Men tend to be more optimistic than women, reflecting the relative powerlessness of women making

Poverty, Welfare and Social Opportunity in India **155**

TABLE 7.3
Perception of Financial Satisfaction by Socio-demographic Groups (in per cent)

	1996			2004		
Groups	Financial situation has improved	Satisfied with present financial situation	Financial situation will get better	Financial situation has improved	Satisfied with present financial situation	Financial situation will get better
All Groups	**29.2**	**28.4**	**47.9**	**26.5**	**16.0**	**49.2**
Gender						
Men	31.6	31.0	50.5	28.7	17.0	51.8
Women	26.7	25.7	45.3	24.3	15.1	47.0
Locality						
Rural	26.6	25.8	45.1	25.8	15.7	48.2
Urban	37.3	36.6	56.9	29.8	17.7	54.7
Age group						
< = 25 years	32.9	29.9	52.5	30.2	17.0	55.3
26–35 years	31.2	28.0	50.1	28.9	16.6	51.8
36–45 years	27.4	27.5	45.7	24.8	15.4	49.2
46–55 years	25.9	29.1	46.9	24.1	14.9	45.9
56 years or more	24.3	27.4	40.1	22.5	16.1	41.2
Education						
Illiterate	22.3	22.0	39.5	19.6	11.8	39.7
Up to middle	27.8	27.1	47.5	26.0	16.1	51.5
College, no degree	39.9	38.7	60.0	34.0	20.8	58.5
College+	49.0	47.4	69.4	41.0	22.9	61.1
Religion						
Hindu	29.1	28.6	47.9	27.4	16.7	50.2
Muslim	26.6	25.9	45.2	21.1	12.6	45.8
Christian	34.6	31.2	59.1	24.0	9.6	51.0
Sikh	48.4	34.1	52.4	32.9	24.8	49.9
Caste						
Scheduled Caste	24.5	28.6	47.9	22.3	12.8	45.6
Scheduled Tribe	25.3	25.9	45.2	24.9	11.2	49.9
OBC	25.7	31.2	59.1	25.8	15.3	49.1
Upper caste	36.4	34.1	52.4	30.7	20.2	52.2

(*Table 7.3 continued*)

(Table 7.3 continued)

	1996			2004		
Groups	Financial situation has improved	Satisfied with present financial situation	Financial situation will get better	Financial situation has improved	Satisfied with present financial situation	Financial situation will get better
Class						
Very poor	18.1	17.7	37.5	17.5	10.6	41.9
Poor	27.5	25.8	46.7	24.6	14.0	49.0
Middle	34.6	43.0	54.3	34.9	21.0	56.3
Upper class	51.2	50.2	68.7	42.9	29.2	61.1

Source NES, CSDS 1996, 2006.

them more cautious and non-committal. Similarly, urban India is clearly more optimistic than rural India. The upwardly mobile tend to migrate to urban areas, which reflects their more robust attitude. It may also be the case that the new economic *mantra* of liberalisation, initiative and the visible material consequences of integration with the world economy through the ownership of household appliances are more pronounced in urban India than in the rural areas.

The attitudes of the young as opposed to the elderly are generally more optimistic. This may reflect the effect of education which closely parallels the same trend. But either way, it shows that, *ceteris paribus*, the sheer generational change would increase the chance of the greater spread of the atmosphere of buoyant optimism and positive attitudes towards liberalisation.

With regard to the attitudes of religious groups, the findings reported here should be treated with caution and seen only as a first approximation of a complex reality. Thus, the Muslim attitude towards the three different measures of one's personal experience with the economy—generally lower than the national average— confirms the fact that there are perhaps some underlying factors responsible for the condition of that community. But more research is necessary to conclude if the fact that they tend to be less optimistic about their financial situation is reflective of their community, class, level of education, or the historic residue of the Partition which separated the educated and upper class Muslims from their hapless brethren. The same argument holds for the Sikh community, which is placed above the national average on all counts. Once again, it is perhaps reflective of their class and education, rather than of the idiosyncratic factor of religious affiliation.

The caste variable operates on predictable lines, with the upper castes reporting higher scores on all four indicators compared to the lower castes. However, it is interesting to note here, that the absolute differences between the scores reported by the two extremes of the caste-status are not very sharp, as compared to the effects of education, or more significantly, class. Education and class are not, like caste, primordial factors of life. One invests time and effort to gain them and, in the process, becomes conscious of differential rewards in life. Caste identification without caste consciousness can actually dull the edges of anger and resentment at the injustices of life. Higher status in terms of education and higher class status are the main factors of political consciousness and hence create a greater sense of relative deprivation. The latter two are the most discriminating in terms of their impact on the subjective perception of welfare, with the college educated or the upper class being in some cases twice more well-off compared to the illiterate or the very poor. And finally, one would observe a general decline between 1996 and 2004 which, to some extent, goes against the media hype of India Shining, and explains the defeat of the NDA in 2004.

Devising a Combined Measure of Deprivation

On the basis of the generally positive and linear relations of the perception of welfare along the lines of conventional social cleavages, we have devised a general index of achievement–deprivation. A new variable, 'deprivation', with four levels, was created by combining the two. The social profile of the new measure of deprivation is presented in Table 7.4.

The new 'deprivation' index divides the sample into four categories. In the first are the most deprived who perform the worst both in terms of class (where they appear among the very poor) and

TABLE 7.4
Social Profiles of the Most and Least Deprived (in per cent)

Groups	1996 Most deprived	1996 Moderately deprived	1996 Moderate achievers	1996 High achievers	2004 Most deprived	2004 Moderately deprived	2004 Moderate achievers	2004 High achievers
All Groups	**11.4**	**23.6**	**42.4**	**14.8**	**14.1**	**27.4**	**40.7**	**10.0**
Gender								
Men	9.8	24.4	43.7	16.6	12.8	27.4	41.7	11.0
Women	13.1	22.7	41.1	13.0	15.9	27.3	39.5	8.7
Locality								
Rural	13.4	23.4	45.5	10.5	15.7	26.3	42.5	8.3
Urban	5.1	24.2	32.8	28.4	8.2	31.4	34.2	16.2
Education								
Illiterate	17.9	22.2	47.0	5.7	22.2	26.0	40.3	3.8
Primary	10.6	24.3	46.6	11.0	15.4	25.8	45.3	7.1
Middle school	7.4	27.1	41.0	17.0	10.0	28.4	43.3	10.2
Higher secondary	4.2	24.2	35.7	27.4	6.3	29.8	39.6	17.1
College and above	2.0	21.6	23.0	43.9	2.4	31.7	29.7	26.0

Age group							
Up to 45 years	11.0	23.0	43.2	15.7	13.4	26.4	42.2	10.5
46 or more	12.6	25.2	40.5	12.3	15.9	29.8	36.9	8.5
Religion							
Hindu	11.5	23.7	42.3	14.9	14.2	26.7	41.8	10.3
Muslim	13.0	24.4	42.6	12.3	15.0	31.3	37.3	7.2
Christian	6.1	15.1	54.5	13.8	15.9	25.5	40.6	7.6
Sikh	2.4	31.0	20.6	35.7	6.4	34.2	28.4	19.6
Caste							
Scheduled Caste	16.6	23.5	46.9	5.7	20.3	23.9	42.8	4.2
Scheduled Tribe	12.5	17.1	56.3	5.9	16.6	22.6	49.5	4.7
OBC	12.9	23.3	45.6	11.8	14.8	27.8	41.5	9.1
Upper caste	6.3	25.8	32.3	26.0	9.3	30.0	36.1	15.6

Source NES, CSDS 1996, 2006.

the general subjective satisfaction variable where they are among the lowest achievers. This group of 11.4 per cent (according to the data of 1996) thus represents the bottom of the pyramid in terms of the material and the psychological achievers of India. Symmetrically opposite to them are the top 14.8 per cent, the 'high achievers' who perform the best on both the general indicators. Interspersed between the two categories are the 'moderately deprived' group of 23.6 per cent who perform relatively well on the class variable but not in terms of psychological satisfaction with their achievement and the 42.4 per cent of the 'moderate achievers' who perform well on the psychological dimension of achievement but not on the material side.

The findings in Table 7.4 help define the profile of achievement and deprivation in India. The most deprived are more likely to be women rather than men, and the achievers, both moderate and high, more likely to be men than women. Similarly, people living in rural areas are more likely to be among the low achievers of India.

The performance of urban dwellers is actually quite striking among high achievers. A quarter of urban dwellers count themselves among the highest achievers compared to just over a tenth of rural dwellers, a phenomenon that indicates the double effect of the larger concentration of opportunities in urban India on the one hand, and the effect of self-selection, for it is the more highly motivated and resourceful who migrate to towns and once there, these tendencies are further reinforced through the peer group pressure of other aspiring high achievers.

The effect of education on achievement is the most important among the socio-demographic features reported in Table 7.4. The illiterate, as compared to those with higher secondary or above level of education, are quite unlikely to be the high achievers of India, for only 5.7 per cent of the illiterate, in the 1996 data, make it to this select group, compared to the 43.9 per cent of those with college education or above. At the other end of the scale, only 2 per cent of the college educated and 4.2 per cent of those with education up to the higher secondary level are among the most deprived, compared to about 17.9 per cent among the illiterate. The same trend is observed in 2004 as well.

As before, the performances of religious groups should be treated with caution, lest we confuse religious affiliation as the cause of under-achievement. The Muslims appear to be among the lower achievers compared to other religions. The Christians perform better than the Hindus, whose achievements are higher than that of the Muslims. But the best performers are the Sikhs, with a more than twice the likelihood of being among the highest achievers of India compared to the sample average. But religion at the first approximation represents only a grouping of individuals; much more detailed statistical analysis is required to establish the role of religion in the causal path towards high achievement. There are complex historical factors at work here, indicating the long-term effect of migration of the Muslim middle class to Pakistan after Partition and the role of the missionaries and colonial rule on the material and psychological situation of India's Christians. That the Sikhs of India are generally high achievers is usually acknowledged; how much of this can be attributed to the propensity of the Sikh community to reinforce these high-achieving tendencies and how much can be attributed to the fortuitous combination of factors essential to high growth and sociological factors inimical to large concentrations of wealth (Punjab's ryotwari land relations, compared to the zamindari systems of land tenure in Bihar and Orissa under colonial rule, for example) appear as pointers towards further investigation.

Finally, the relationship between caste and achievement is on predictable lines. The Scheduled Castes and Tribes are more likely to be among the most deprived of India as compared to the upper castes and the upper castes are more likely to be among the highest achievers as compared to members of the Scheduled Castes and Tribes.

Normative Basis of Social Justice

How one construes the path from low achievement to high achievement depends on a number of factors. At one extreme is the belief in the fatality of one's individual situation. For some, the main responsibility for misery or the good fortune of a high standard of living lies mainly with one's *karma*. At the other extreme are those who believe in *purusakara*, the symmetric opposite of passive fatality. For them, a combination of individual initiative and the optimal use of all one's resources is what makes the difference. Most people evince a combination of attitudes, with elements of belief in individual initiative judiciously added to a passive resignation to fate. The role of the state and the effect of government policies, however, increasingly appear as important factors responsible for what happens to the material and moral life of individuals. The government can make a difference by bringing about policies of major structural change such as redistribution of property, changing laws of landownership, or for that matter, it can roll back the unfettered control that the bureaucracy had gained on the free flow of goods and services. Similarly, even without necessarily changing the structure of property relations, the government can bring about measures of egalitarianism by giving hand-outs to the less advantaged. A democratic society assumes that such legislative and administrative measures are undertaken as a result of popular pressure or in anticipation of popular approval. Our objective in this section is to see to what extent the people are aware of some of the crucial measures taken by the Government of India from the outset, and, to the extent that people are aware of them, how their opinions are distributed across these key issues.

In order to examine the attitudes of the different sections of the population towards the policies of economic and social reform, the following question was asked with specific reference to land ceiling: *Some people say that the government should pass legislation so that people are not allowed to own and posses a large amount of land and property. Others say that people should be allowed to own as much land and property as they can make/acquire. What would you say*?

The findings reported in Table 7.5 show, first of all, how strong the belief is in limiting ownership at all levels of society. Roughly 70 per cent of the Indian society believes that there should be some form of limit on ownership of land and property in India. Failure to have an opinion on this issue is also an interesting finding. Predictably, the illiterate are more likely not to have an answer compared to the educated: about one-fourth of the illiterate do not know

TABLE 7.5
'Ownership should be Limited' by Social Background
(in per cent)

Groups	1996 Limit ownership	1996 No ceiling on property	1996 Don't know	2004 Limit ownership	2004 No ceiling on property	2004 Don't know
All Groups	**68.9**	**17.8**	**13.3**	**67.8**	**17.3**	**14.9**
Gender						
Men	72.6	18.5	9.0	72.1	17.6	10.3
Women	65.2	17.0	17.8	62.9	16.8	20.3
Locality						
Rural	68.8	17.3	13.9	67.0	16.3	16.6
Urban	69.5	19.2	11.4	70.6	20.6	8.8
Age group						
<= 25 years	68.7	18.2	13.1	67.3	19.0	13.7
26–35 years	69.6	18.2	12.3	69.9	17.2	12.9
36–45 years	70.3	16.9	12.8	67.5	17.0	15.4
46–55 years	67.7	17.2	15.1	67.4	17.1	15.5
56 years or more	67.3	17.8	14.8	65.2	15.4	19.5
Education						
Illiterate	64.1	13.6	22.3	60.7	13.5	25.9
Up to primary	71.9	17.4	10.7	68.7	17.3	14.0
Middle school	73.3	20.4	6.3	71.8	19.4	8.8
Higher secondary	73.4	21.8	4.7	74.2	20.3	5.4
College+	68.4	28.3	3.2	73.7	22.6	3.7

(Table 7.5 continued)

(Table 7.5 continued)

	1996			2004		
Groups	Limit ownership	No ceiling on property	Don't know	Limit ownership	No ceiling on property	Don't know
Religion						
Hindu	68.5	17.4	14.1	67.9	17.1	15.0
Muslim	72.9	16.1	10.9	68.4	16.7	14.9
Christian	65.7	30.1	4.2	70.3	18.0	11.7
Sikh	61.9	25.4	12.7	62.1	25.5	12.4
Caste						
Scheduled Caste	71.6	14.0	14.4	68.8	13.8	17.3
Scheduled Tribe	71.9	11.8	16.4	65.3	15.7	19.0
OBC	68.4	18.1	13.5	69.0	16.4	14.6
Upper caste	67.1	21.3	11.6	66.5	20.6	12.9
Class						
Very poor	71.1	13.8	15.0	66.5	12.2	21.3
Poor	71.4	15.4	13.2	67.8	16.7	15.5
Middle	67.8	19.6	12.6	69.5	20.8	9.7
Upper class	63.9	28.5	7.5	68.9	25.8	5.3
Most deprived	69.8	9.9	20.3	60.6	12.8	26.6
Moderately deprived	67.3	17.9	14.7	67.0	18.3	14.6
Moderate achievers	71.2	17.4	11.4	70.1	16.9	13.0
High achievers	67.4	24.4	8.2	71.8	22.2	6.1

Source NES, CSDS 1996, 2004.

if the government should limit the extent of land and property by legislation, compared to less than 4 per cent of those with college education or above who do not pronounce an opinion on this. Equally interesting is the variation around the position opposed to legislating upper limits to land and property: the Christians, the Sikhs, the upper castes, the upper classes and the high achievers are more likely to want to have no such upper limits than the Indian population as a whole.

The normative justification for ceiling on property as reported in Table 7.5 (the similarity in the pattern of relationships between 1996 and 2004 is striking!), goes in the 'right' direction. Taking the preference for 'no ceiling on property' as an indicator, we see that about 14 per cent of the very poor pronounce themselves for this option, whereas the proportion of the upper class taking this position (at 28.5 per cent in 1996 and 25.8 per cent in 2004) is twice as large. The remarkable point that emerges from this Table is the high consensus in India for some sort of social control over property. Not only is the level of support for limiting ownership is high at all levels of achievement; the difference between the most deprived and the high achievers is only about 2 per cent.

Democracy and the Politics of Liberalisation

The overwhelming support for limits to land and property within the populace describes the core of post-Independence political culture of India. It grew as a consequence of the socialistic ideals that underpinned the struggle for Independence. Subsequently, it was further reinforced with the structure of planning that the Congress party, under the leadership of Nehru, adopted as the basis of the model of mixed economy. However, the control of the economy steadily passed into the hands of those who did not have any immediate stakes in it. The lack of competition from within or from outside had produced no incentives to *innovate*, but merely to *replicate*. When the government of Narasimha Rao took advantage of the desperate financial crisis of 1991 in order to open

India's economy to the operations of the market process, the country started making basic changes in the structure of the economy without much debate within the public sphere. Liberalisation had not figured prominently in the election campaign; and in the best of times, the immediate austerity and the sharp turns of the economy, at least in the short-term, hurt many powerful interests. The policies of liberalisation are rarely the best methods to win elections. The government, nevertheless, kept the momentum for further liberalisation on a steady course, and, urged on by the World Bank and a section of the Indian elite, soon reached a point of no return so far as the two key components of the policy of liberalisation—namely, giving the multi nationals access to the Indian market and the privatisation of the public sector undertakings—are concerned. Popular responses to the two questions are analysed below.

The structure of planned development and the mixed economy assumed tariff barriers and other mechanisms through which India was intended to achieve import substitution. Naturally, there was little room for foreign multi national companies in this scheme of things. Now that the main policy has changed, the survey posed the following question in order to test the extent of public knowledge and sympathy or antipathy towards this policy: *Foreign companies should not be allowed free trade in India. Do you agree or disagree with this?* (see Table 7.6).

Liberalisation was possibly an elite-initiated policy with little popular support or knowledge at the time of its original inception and it certainly remained so even after a full term of the Rao government, which made it the cornerstone of its politics. In the 1996 data, only about a fifth of the population approved of the policy of integration with the international market economy, particularly with regard to the open access to multi nationals, and 37.1 per cent were opposed to this policy. Roughly two-fifth of the population was not aware of this policy initiative, or considered it so far removed from every-day life that it had no opinion on the issue. But Table 7.6 makes it clear that strong support for this form of liberalisation did exist within some vocal and articulate sections of the population, namely, the higher secondary and college educated, urban, upper-class people and the high achievers.

TABLE 7.6
No Free Trade for Foreign Companies by Social Background (in per cent)

	1996			2004		
Groups	Disagree	Don't know/ no opinion	Agree	Disagree	Don't know/ no opinion	Agree
All Groups	**21.8**	**41.1**	**37.1**	**30.1**	**31.1**	**38.8**
Gender						
Men	26.3	28.8	45.0	33.5	22.7	43.8
Women	17.3	53.8	29.0	26.2	40.9	33.0
Locality						
Rural	21.7	45.3	33.0	28.9	34.7	36.4
Urban	22.1	28.1	49.8	34.6	17.9	47.5
Age group						
< = 25 years	24.2	37.3	38.5	33.0	26.7	40.3
26–35 years	21.9	38.3	39.7	30.7	28.7	40.6
36–45 years	21.7	42.2	36.1	30.1	32.0	38.0
46–55 years	20.0	45.3	34.7	27.5	33.0	39.5
56 years or more	19.5	47.8	32.8	27.5	39.0	33.5
Education						
Illiterate	16.2	60.9	22.9	22.6	51.0	26.4
Up to primary	20.0	40.3	39.7	29.2	30.8	40.0
Middle school	25.5	30.4	44.1	34.1	22.4	43.6
Higher secondary	29.7	18.1	52.1	37.5	13.4	49.1
College+	33.0	5.0	62.0	39.8	5.8	54.4
Religion						
Hindu	22.1	40.9	37.0	29.5	31.6	38.9
Muslim	21.8	40.6	37.6	32.2	29.6	38.3
Christian	20.2	40.1	39.7	37.7	25.3	37.0
Sikh	17.5	54.0	28.6	34.8	26.4	38.8
Caste						
Scheduled Caste	19.9	44.7	35.4	27.5	38.3	34.2
Scheduled Tribe	17.1	57.3	25.6	26.7	38.1	35.2
OBC	21.8	43.1	35.1	30.1	30.8	39.2
Upper caste	24.3	32.1	43.6	32.5	25.8	41.7
Economic Class						
Very poor	16.6	53.9	29.5	24.8	43.6	31.6
Poor	21.1	42.1	36.9	30.1	32.1	37.8
Middle	25.6	33.1	41.4	33.5	21.8	44.7
Upper class	29.1	20.7	50.2	36.6	15.2	48.2
Most deprived	15.8	55.7	28.6	23.7	49.9	26.4
Moderately deprived	21.2	41.2	37.6	29.7	31.8	38.5
Moderate achievers	21.6	42.3	36.1	30.4	28.9	40.7
High achievers	28.9	22.3	48.8	37.7	14.8	47.6

Source NES, CSDS 1996, 2006.

The issue of integration with the world market certainly divided the electorate into those keen on the protection of India's own business and industry, people essentially with a *swadeshi* view of the policy towards liberalisation and those supporting the opening up of the domestic market to global competition. Taking education as a characteristic, we can see that, in the 1996 data, non-response falls from a high of almost 61 per cent among the illiterate, to five per cent among the degree educated and above. But as we go up the educational ladder, both the levels of support and opposition go up, respectively, from about 16 per cent to 33 per cent for support, and from about 23 per cent to 62 per cent for opposition. This appears to be the trend when we take age (the younger are less likely to be without opinion), or class, or deprivation as the criterion. In each case, the better provided for are both more opinionated (that is, less likely to say 'don't know') as well as fragmented. A similar trend is seen in 2004.

The second question (*Government companies should be given to private hands. Do you agree or disagree with this?*) was asked to test popular opinion on the other important aspect of liberalisation, namely, privatisation. Table 7.7 reports on this.

The picture we get here is a replica of the previous image: In the data of 1996, over two-fifths of the population without any specific knowledge of the policy (to the extent they do not have an opinion on the issue); meagre overall support (23 per cent) and rather substantial opposition (over 34 per cent). Like before, people without an opinion on the issue are more likely to be women, rural, illiterate, old, the Scheduled Caste and the Scheduled Tribes, very poor and those who have not had much direct participation in the fruits of economic development. Support, on the other hand, comes from the symmetrically opposite groups: men, urban, higher secondary and college educated, middle and upper castes but quite strongly from the high achievers and the upper class. But the pattern of opposition also grows, indicating a polarisation of opinion towards liberalisation within the population as a whole. It is interesting to note that between 1996 and 2004 the perception of 'don't knows' has declined and majority of them seem to have aligned with those opposed to privatisation.

TABLE 7.7
Privatise Government Companies by Social Background (in per cent)

	1996			2004		
Groups	Disagree	Don't know/ no opinion	Agree	Disagree	Don't know/ no opinion	Agree
All Groups	**34.5**	**42.2**	**23.3**	**46.2**	**30.2**	**23.6**
Gender						
Men	41.4	29.9	28.7	51.2	21.9	26.9
Women	27.4	54.8	17.8	40.4	39.8	19.8
Locality						
Rural	33.6	45.9	20.5	44.3	34.0	21.7
Urban	37.5	30.5	32.1	53.0	16.5	30.5
Age group						
< = 25 years	36.7	38.8	24.5	48.8	26.6	24.5
26–35 years	35.8	40.6	23.6	47.3	27.6	25.1
36–45 years	35.8	40.8	23.4	45.5	31.0	23.5
46–55 years	33.0	45.2	21.8	45.9	32.0	22.2
56 years or more	28.0	50.1	21.9	41.4	37.8	20.8
Education						
Illiterate	25.3	61.2	13.6	33.4	49.8	16.8
Up to primary	33.9	41.3	24.8	48.5	29.3	22.2
Middle school	43.4	31.7	24.8	51.7	22.6	25.7
Higher secondary	45.5	20.0	34.5	57.9	12.6	29.4
College+	44.6	9.1	46.3	56.5	5.7	37.8
Religion						
Hindu	34.4	41.9	23.6	45.8	30.7	23.5
Muslim	34.4	43.2	22.5	47.4	28.7	23.8
Christian	40.4	40.1	19.6	52.3	24.3	23.4
Sikh	21.4	52.4	26.2	44.5	26.7	28.8
Caste						
Scheduled Caste	37.0	43.5	19.4	44.7	35.5	19.8
Scheduled Tribe	30.4	53.5	16.0	41.8	38.4	19.8
OBC	31.3	45.5	23.2	45.5	30.3	24.2
Upper caste	37.9	34.4	27.7	49.0	25.1	25.9
Economic Class						
Very poor	28.7	55.3	16.0	39.6	42.2	18.2
Poor	35.3	42.2	22.5	45.9	31.4	22.6
Middle	39.9	34.1	26.0	51.1	21.4	27.6
Upper class	38.2	24.5	37.2	54.3	14.7	31.0
Most deprived	26.3	58.3	15.4	37.1	48.4	14.5
Moderately deprived	35.1	41.3	23.6	46.6	30.8	22.5
Moderate achievers	35.4	43.0	21.6	47.2	28.1	24.7
High achievers	39.6	25.8	34.6	52.5	15.4	32.1

Source NES, CSDS 1996, 2004.

Conclusion: Does Democracy Promote Social Opportunity and Economic Security?

India's liberalisation policy is probably an extreme example of surreptitious attempts to bring about structural change in a democracy where political participation and transparency are strongly in place, thanks to a vigilant press, zealous judiciary and contentious parliament. The circumstances under which this initiative was taken are well known and have already been mentioned in the text. The fact remains, however, that even after 15 years of application and propagation, as we have seen above, liberalisation is not an overwhelmingly popular policy. What implications does this have for the functioning of democracy in India, particularly with regard to the initiation and implementation of economic policy?

The question acquires a specific meaning when we put the issue in comparative perspective. A case in point is China where specific economic policies, considered rational and necessary by the leadership, have been implemented with exceptional brutality in the past. Commenting on the terrible costs of Maoist policies, meant for revolutionary economic growth, Waldron writes,

> ...in China between 1959 and 1961, cannibalism was perhaps more widely practiced than at any other time or place in human history. It was the consequence of probably the greatest famine of all time, which was directly caused by Communist policy and cost somewhere between 30 and 60 million dead. (Waldron 1997)

It is a smug and therefore dangerous idea to suggest that such things could not take place in India which has a culture and tradition that is more respectful of life. One needs only recall the terrible costs of the 'man-made' 1943 Bengal famine where, by one calculation, between two to three million people died out of starvation (Sen 1981).The question that arises here is, to what extent is there a potential for the elite 'hijacking' of the economic policy from popular control, and, to the extent that we have some evidence to prove this assumption to be true(which is plainly the case with regard to liberalisation), why does Indian democracy indulge her political elites under careful observation? In order to explore this issue further, several questions with some bearing on economic policy and leadership were cross-tabulated with the main deprivation–achievement variable (see Table 7.8).

TABLE 7.8
Deprivation and Attitudes Towards Social Policy (in per cent) 1996

	Most deprived	Moderately deprived	Moderate achievers	High achievers
The poor and deprived enjoy better status than before	30.5	39.5	54.2	62.8
India needs determined leadership	62.5	69.0	74.2	82.2
Government policies are not responsible for poverty of the people	20.6	22.3	29.1	31.4
Government generally takes care of the common people	28.3	32.4	44.2	44.3
Representatives take care of what people like you think	12.3	17.8	25.8	29.5
Poor and needy benefited from government development schemes[5]	16.2	22.7	31	40.1
Not personally benefited from any government scheme	14.2	15.8	17.6	14.6

Source NES, CSDS 1996, 2004.

The survey shows that the relatively more deprived among the people are aware of the fact that development has not benefited all sections of the society equally. Nor are they all cared for in the same manner; the government stands guilty of this asymmetry as much as the political representatives. But, even among the most deprived, over 60 per cent believe in strong leadership and would presumably concede the government the authority to take initiative in matters of high policy of the state. The percentage goes up among the high achievers.

172   When Rebels Become Stakeholders

The high achievers present the paternalist image that one often ascribes to India's elite. They are, as we find in Table 7.8, overwhelmingly in favour of strong leadership (82 per cent as compared to 63 per cent for the most deprived). They are more likely to absolve the government of its responsibility for poverty and are more likely to believe than the most deprived (about 44 per cent as compared to 28 per cent) that the government generally takes care of the interest of common people. They are more than twice likely to repose their faith in elected representatives as compared to the most deprived (30 per cent as against 13 per cent). They also have relatively greater faith in the redistributive capacity of the Indian political system. Of the high achievers, around 63 per cent believe that the poor and needy enjoy better status now than before, compared to 30 per cent for the most deprived. The corresponding figure, when it comes to the belief that the benefits of development have gone to the poor and needy as well as the well-to-do, is at about 40 per cent, more than twice as high for the most deprived, only 16 per cent of whom share that opinion. The only area where the high achievers are behind the most deprived, is in the confirmation that they have actually availed of some government welfare schemes, such as housing, employment, old age pension, loans, or subsidies. When one looks at the moderate achievers of India, who at 42.4 per cent (Table 7.4) are the largest group, their attitudes run parallel in every respect to the high achievers, except this one.

What one learns from secondary sources, however, shows a trend towards incremental progress on both counts. The economy has gained momentum. The extent of mass poverty has been reduced in comparison to the situation at Independence. This raises two questions in terms of our study. How did a poor country, which takes democracy and reform seriously, break out of the low level equilibrium trap? Even more importantly, why does the discourse of poverty and justice in India remain overwhelmingly democratic?

Some of the findings, reported in this chapter, give credibility to the claim that some of the progress made by Indian economy has indeed trickled down, to the point where, even the bottom of the social pyramid has some participation in the economy to report. Comparable findings have also been reported by Lewis

(1995), who finds support in the new writing on India's economy. Citing the work of Ranade (1991), Lewis shows how 'leakage' of developmental resources, through corruption and inefficient utilisation, has not been as extensive or damaging as previously believed.[6] The Integrated Rural Development Programme (IRDP) is credited with having reached the poor, including the very poor, and increasing their productivity. The policy implication, in this respect, is to identify the most opportune point in the social matrix where a developmental intervention would be most effective.

Those familiar with the American prognosis of the Indian situation in the 1960s, will find a contrast here. There is a remarkable turnaround in Lewis' own line of thinking itself. In his *India: A Quiet Crisis*, Lewis (1962) had foreseen an impending crisis, born out of the Indian inability to sustain policy formulation and implementation. Fears of the impending political and economic crisis were also voiced by the other main political commentator of the period, Harrison (1960). Three decades later, with the halcyon days of Jawaharlal Nehru and the hegemonic role of the Congress party only a fading memory, Lewis has set the record straight in *India's Political Economy. Governance and Reform* (1995). The findings belie some of the prognoses of *Redistribution with Growth* (Chenery et al. 1974)—a classic landmark from the 1970s—ironically through the application of some of the policies, such as irreversible transfer of resources and reformist political coalitions, which were not thought of—in the 1960s scholarship—as likely to take place in India.

So, what actually happened in India and to what extent do our findings help us understand this? One of our main contentions is to draw attention to the disjunction between political prominence and articulate policy-makers on the one hand, and entrepreneurship and real economic power on the other hand. Though they were not in the limelight during the years of socialist planning, entrepreneurs at every level of the economic system have quietly persisted in their quest for opportunities. With allies in unlikely places, these agents of the new economic policy of the 1990s have pressed ahead over the past decades. This interface of the town and the village—where the new political elites operate—lies beyond the scope of any conventional analysis of the Indian economy, which concentrates on either the 'commanding height' of the economy, located in metropolitan capitals, or in the hopeless misery of the most deprived villages. But this is where an opinion survey can be most helpful. The 'room to manoeuvre in the middle', that democratic politics has brought to this politics of the meso level, has also given a new lease of life to the village economy, besides generating a sustained basis for agrarian productivity, at least in those parts of India where the new agricultural technology has been matched with adequate infrastructure.

The new policies of liberalisation and the older structure of redistribution have combined to blunt the edges of radical politics and have brought an added measure of legitimacy to the political system. The interaction of protest movements and new economic processes has opened up greater room to manoeuvre for marginal social groups. This, in turn, has produced new challenges, sometimes stretching the resilience of the system to the limits. The further implications of this issue are the main themes of the next chapter.

Notes

1. There is, as a matter of fact, room to manoeuvre in every society; for it is difficult to imagine a situation where the writ of one person might run so effectively that no consultation or participation is needed. As Scott (1985) shows, in most situations, the formally powerless has a range of techniques through which to bring pressure on the decision-makers. But the real scope of participation might vary radically from one political system to another, depending on the constitutional structure that underpins it, the values and norms of the society, the nature of group consciousness and organisation of the groups in society.
2. The challenging combination of poverty and democracy was the main thrust of Moore's (1966) pessimistic reading of the Indian situation. In comparison, a more optimistic case for the effectiveness of democratic intervention for the removal of mass poverty has been made by Drèze and Sen (1995) and Lewis (1995).
3. Austin (1966) gives an excellent introduction to the process of constitution making as a result of compromise, the elusive search of consensus, and the necessary accommodation of contradiction.
4. See the interviews with the state-level administrators in Subrata Mitra (2005).

5. The full question asked was: Some people say that whatever progress was made over the last few years, through development schemes and programmes of the government, has benefited only the well-to-do. Others say, no, the poor and needy have also benefited from them. What would you say? Have the benefits of development gone only to the well-to-do, or have the poor and needy also benefited?
6. Citing the work of Ranade (1991), Lewis (1995: 361n) provides an account of incremental progress. On the basis of a study of the rate of growth of real consumption expenditure of the bottom four deciles of India's rural population, Ranade shows that their average consumption has increased from 0.46 per cent annually during 1970–77 to 1.85 per cent annually from 1977–83.

8

Building Social Capital from Above and Below: Locality, Region and Trust in India

The sense of being someone who matters, and of having rules that correspond to what one considers right and proper, are essential to one's self-definition as a citizen and stakeholder in politics. Similarly, as we have argued in the previous chapter, the experience of personal welfare and upward mobility are necessary attributes of being stakeholder in the national economy. In this chapter, we move on to citizenship—the third and vital component of the stakeholders' approach to democracy. Citizenship encompasses the range of sentiments and attributes that go under the name of social capital. These refer to trust, shared norms and membership in community networks which are not confined to any primordial group.

The chapter delves into this theme with a focus on institutional mechanisms at the lower and higher levels of the political system that catalyse, promote and supplement these attributes of social capital in India. We examine in this chapter, how, institutional innovations like Panchayati Raj and the regional states (that are culturally more cohesive compared to the former provinces), have contributed to the building of political communities out of a diverse population. Under the relentless networking by the majority-seeking politicians, democratic politics has emerged as the lowest common denominator of all possible identities and a common currency of transactions, be it for enhancing one's share of allocable resources or the assertion of contested, collective values. Where the processes of support from below—in the form of successful local democracy—and assistance from above, work hand in hand, the result has been the enhancement of trust, democracy and governance. Where panchayats have failed to make their mark and regional governments have remained faction-ridden, corrupt and paralysed, the opposite has been the case. A sample of Indian states, selected in a manner that speaks for India's diversity, demonstrates these assertions.

The analysis undertaken in this section seeks to juxtapose the survey data with aggregate statistical data at the regional level. Six regions have been chosen for the preliminary analysis of regional diversity. The selection of these states, as representatives of India's diversity, is based on the assumption that diversity is a function of poverty, geographic location, ideological leaning of the party or coalition in power at the time of analysis, social basis of the ruling elite, institutionalisation of the class–party linkage, popular perception of law and order, so on and so forth[1] (Mitra 2005). The six regions, namely, Bihar, Gujarat, Maharashtra, Punjab, Tamil Nadu and West Bengal, were chosen to reflect the extremes of these variables. These selected states, which represent the 'four corners' of India, regions at the highest, lowest and middle levels of affluence, regions which have satisfactorily solved the problem of regional identity and those still struggling with it, and finally, regions representing political ideologies of the Left, Right and Centre, were chosen for the study of variation in trust in the local, regional, and national governments. Out of these six, three— Maharashtra, West Bengal and Bihar—were chosen for more detailed and in-depth analysis of the process of local democracy.

Community and Conflict in India

After six decades of Independence, for many Indians and observers of India, 'community' remains an elusive goal. Each communal riot comes across as a violent invocation of the memory of Partition, as it seeks to partition the local political and social spaces on the lines of religion, caste or tribe. The difficult transition from kin-society to a community that cuts across kinship is not a new phenomenon. Despite the frequent reference to Bharat Mata ('Mother India') and other cultural symbols of Indian nationhood during the struggle for Independence, the potential threat of fragmentation along the lines of religion was an ever-present theme. Just as 'divide and rule' became the dictum of British rule during the last decades prior to Independence, and as the British took every possible advantage of the cultural, linguistic and religious divisions of India, the Congress party, under the leadership of Gandhi and Nehru, found its effective counter-strategy in its resolve to 'unite and oppose', which effectively put the issue of community-building on the backburner. But, if unity brought strength to the top leadership, some of the costs of keeping the community off the agenda had to be borne by the cultural, religious and social minorities at the lower levels, because, the political need for unity made it imperative to play down differences. Where such differences were the results of resentment against past oppression or exploitation, or against social marginalisation, the support of the aggrieved party could be at best lukewarm, or absent altogether. The Poona Pact of 1935, which denied proportional representation to Harijans is a good example.

As we learn from the tragic history of India's partition, even a deliberately contrived 'thin' definition of the Indian nation was not effective in retaining the loyalty of the majority of India's Muslims, who preferred the more categorical and exclusive definition of an Islamic nation-state and followed Jinnah and the Muslim League to Pakistan. The retention of the loyalties of the other non-Hindus—the Christians, the Sikhs, the Buddhists, the Jains, the Parsis—was relatively less problematic and could be accommodated within a fuzzy definition of a twin identity—India, and Bharat.[2] At Independence, therefore, the nebulous 'nation' of Nehru, which, after centuries of oppression and denial had found 'utterance', actually started its career as an ambiguous construct, with community and conflict written on its two faces. This tenuous unity—kept under wraps as the 'Congress system' institutionalised this duality in many formal and informal ways—has gradually come unstuck, as the inexorable logic of political transaction has relentlessly driven home the reciprocal realities of communal cohesion and inter-community conflict.

With regard to this problem, the role of the local government and politics, in the making of political communities and public spheres, remains an unresolved issue. The proponents of modernity have sometimes seen the local and the provincial as sectarian and backward, and have reposed their faith in the urban intelligentsia as the flag bearer of the secular and progressive modernity.[3] We contest the pessimistic view of the potential of the local arena for acting as a motor for the creation of political community, and argue that the dual focus on locality and region makes it possible to analyse the building of civil society from an unusual angle.

Panchayati Raj and the Building of Civil Society from Below

Both the Panchayati Raj and the linguistic states are post-Independence innovations that assume a special significance in the building of civil society in India. Formal democracy and universal adult franchise, right from the outset, brought the legal right to participate to all existing social groups, sectional interests and spatial levels. This guaranteed their juridical existence; in addition, the functioning of competitive elections ensured a certain degree of strategic room to manoeuvre as well. Out of the moral and political considerations, many from within India's struggle for Independence sought to avert a repetition of the tragic consequences of European state building for the local and the socially marginal, in the course of economic transformation.[4] Others were equally keen to follow what they considered the natural course of history, on the path towards the great transformation from tradition to modernity. Not surprisingly, there was considerable difference of opinion on the role of the local and marginal social groups, suggesting deeper differences at the highest level about the form of the future state and nation in India. Just as Gandhi held on to the role of the village republic as the necessary building bloc of the nation, the state and society in India, Nehru as already mentioned above, famously held the opposite view.

Not surprisingly, Panchayati Raj drew a lot of criticism from those committed to structural change as a precondition of democracy and development in India. One of the most ruthless criticisms came from Barrington Moore. Writing in the 1960s, shortly after the implementation of the recommendations of the Balawant Rai Mehta Commitee's recommendations for the introduction of a three-tier local self-government at the village, bloc and district levels, Moore wrote:

> ...if democracy means the opportunity to play a meaningful part as a rational human being in determining one's fate in life, *democracy does not yet exist in the Indian countryside* [emphasis added]. The Indian peasant has not yet acquired the material and intellectual prerequisites for democratic society. The Panchayat 'revival'... is mainly romantic rhetoric. (Moore 1966: 408)

This duality—the conflict between two opposite ways of characterising the nature of the state and nation in India, variously referred to as the modern and the traditional, the scientific–rational as opposed to the endogenous–vernacular, the macro view of Delhi as opposed to the micro perspectives from India's regions, districts and villages—has characterised the value conflict that underpinned the political discourse in India from Independence onwards, surfacing in India's high politics at regular intervals.

Panchayati Raj was installed because it offered several attractive features to the post-Independence policy community, namely:

1. non-violent and incremental structural change;
2. communal mobilisation of resources in a decentralised context;
3. a micro basis for the local initiative, crucial for the structure of mixed economy and;
4. a potential source of unlimited patronage to serve the needs of the Congress 'system'.

Democratic decentralisation in India has been the result of an incremental evolution, rather than a revolutionary creation. A perusal of the history of the relation between the Central Government of India and the administration at the local level over the past centuries shows how the two have kept in step with one another. Looking back at the past five decades, one can see that, with regard to the local government and its relation to the local political system and beyond, India's politicians have gone through radical changes of policy from time to time. The local government, which had already acquired a rudimentary presence under the British rule in the 1880s, made a formal appearance after Independence in terms of the legislative enactment by the provincial governments. This was formally enshrined in the Constitution (Art. 40). Following the report of the Balawant Rai Mehta Committee (1957), and its incorporation into the recommendations of the Planning Commission, a three-tier structure was expected to become the institutional basis for local self-governance for the whole of India.[5] Maharashtra took a lead with the V. P. Naik Committee report, which recommended the devolution of the power of taxation and disbursement of development funds to the Zila Parishad, the majority of whose members were to be elected directly. However, a period of decline set in soon, which lasted from Nehru's death up to the revival of the idea of panchayats as the basic units of the political system by Rajiv Gandhi in 1985. Khanna (1994) lists a number of factors as responsible for this decline, among them, the food grains crisis of the early 1960s, followed by the introduction of the cluster of policies known as the Green Revolution, which transferred the initiative for production and distribution of vital agrarian resources to the state government departments.

Programmes for poverty alleviation such as agrarian reform, special programmes for small and marginal farmers, or drought prone areas, or specific programmes such as 'Food for Work' were often conceived, financed and administered by Central agencies. Besides, under the dominant Central Government of Indira Gandhi, many state governments turned on the local democracy with the same authoritarian measures as the Centre, namely, postponement of elections and the supersession of the local political institutions by the administration which cut off the periodic infusion of new blood into these institutions. The Janata Party, upon taking office in 1977, set up the Asoka Mehta Committee in order to revive local autonomy and participation. However, in spite of its recommendations, which are of great theoretical implication for the understanding of local politics in India, very little changed in terms of ground reality (Government of India 1978). Internal conflict greatly paralysed the central initiative during the brief Janata Party rule of 1977–80. Except in West Bengal, where the Left Front government seized the initiative (Bhattacharya 1998: Chapter 4), the central administration and co-ordination of all the developmental activities in the districts, under the auspices of the District Rural Development Agency, (DRDA) became the rule. The next radical change in policy came from Rajiv Gandhi, who initiated the move to institutionalise Panchayati Raj in terms of a distinct tier of the federal system with constitutionally guaranteed power.[6] Though the initiative failed to get through the parliament, leading to an amendment of the Constitution, the idea was not entirely lost. It resurfaced in 1992 in the form of the 73rd Amendment of the Constitution which gives constitutional recognition to Panchayati Raj as a tier of the federation. Elections to panchayats have been made mandatory, to be supervised by an independent State Election Commission. Similarly, the Panchayati Raj bodies are to be endowed with independent taxation power and Central funds whose disbursement is to be supervised by a State Finance Commission.[7] The panchayats today, potentially, have far more power than before and in some parts of India, they have become viable political units in their own right, playing a crucial, catalytic role in bringing about largely peaceful and incremental political change.[8] Why and how it came about, what makes it effective, and how it varies from one region to another are issues which will be taken up in this chapter.

As a form of governance, Panchayati Raj has two main elements: (a) local autonomy, that is, the extent of real power in the hands of local representatives, and (b) local democracy, that is, the sharing of this power by local people through participation in free and fair elections. The 73rd amendment of the constitution (1992) gives an institutional shape to both conditions.

Region: A Crucial Link between Nation and Locality

Though they vary in the extent of autonomy they are willing to concede to the 'room to manoeuvre' at the disposal of the state to meet challenges from social groups (to one another or to the state itself), mainstream theories of the state in India have recognised the ability of the state to accommodate regional, local and sectional interests while acting as the crucial building bloc of legitimacy in India. The basic commitment on the part of the state to negotiate solutions to conflicts over distribution of resources and allocation of values is the essence of statehood in India. The most substantial statement of this commitment on the part of the state, and within reasonable measures, its ability to deliver, comes from Rudolph and Rudolph.

> Like Hindu conceptions of the divine, the state in India is polymorphous, a creature of manifold forms and orientations. One is the third actor whose scale and power contribute to the marginality of class politics. Another is a liberal or citizens' state, a juridical body whose legislative reach is limited by a written constitution, judicial review and fundamental rights. Still another is a capitalist state that guards the boundaries of the mixed economy by protecting the rights and promoting the interests of property in agriculture, commerce and industry. Finally, a socialist state is concerned to use public power to eradicate poverty and privilege and tame private power. Which combination prevails in a particular historical setting is a matter for inquiry. (Rudolph and Rudolph 1987: 400–401)

The mainstream view, which has drawn some criticism from the Left (Byres 1988), has been further refined in subsequent research. On the basis of the analysis of a broad spectrum of India's regions, Kohli (1987) has shown that the state is at its most effective when it is reinforced by a regime at the regional level, also committed to the same objectives as the national state, and has the political support of a well organised political party with its own links to the peasantry. The negotiating stance of the state could be a crucial variable on its own. When the state sends mixed signals—such as its readiness to negotiate on transactional issues like redistribution but resistance to such transcendental considerations as the territorial integrity of the state, or secular basis of the nation—its legitimacy is considerably enhanced.[9]

Set free from the formal control of the National Planning Commission and the informal control by the Congress party, India's regions have increasingly appeared as the foci of political initiatives in the direction of economic development and community formation. Commenting on this new face of regional governments, James Manor shows how, in Andhra Pradesh, the government of Chandrababu Naidu has come up with a programme of political accountability, intended to promote good governance.[10]

On the basis of the mainstream position on the state in India, empirical research, in search of explanations for the variations in the effectiveness of the state in time and space, has branched off into the nature of political institutions, political parties and movements, interventions in the economy in terms of public policy and other specific points. The role of the local political arena in the spread and deepening of democracy in India—the puzzle specific to this chapter—provides an important insight into the functioning of all these sub-systems because local institutions, political processes and their leadership are the ultimate interface between the state and the people.

The contrast with the stable western democracies could not be more striking, for in India, democratisation has taken place in a society where, unlike in the stable democracies—as we learn from the history of nation and state formation (Tilly 1985, Gilmour 1992; Rudolph and Rudolph 1987)—the obstacles to this form of governance were violently cleansed prior to the introduction of liberal democratic institutions. India at Independence faced a different and, from the point of view of the modern state, a difficult scenario. Juxtaposed to the macro-political structure, based on the assumption of a rational–legal authority, were half a million rural political systems, sustained by an opposite set of values. Nehru would have seen in them bastions of caste dominance, religious bigotry, feudal social and economic relations and gender oppression. The democratic constitution and universal adult franchise ensured that the project of modernisation and nation and state formation would not be in a position to jettison the weight of traditional society. Marginalised by the process of economic change and urbanisation, the vulnerable social groups, drawing on the full range of democratic participation and radical protest, using their international visibility thanks to the electronic media, would be in a position to hit back, unlike their hapless counterparts in Europe during the period of enclosures,

Industrial Revolution and crushing of religious and ethnic minorities. Looking six decades back, comparing India's multi-party democracy and incremental economic growth with the dire predictions, one is entitled to ask: how could these 'undemocratic roots', ensconced within the traditional world of local politics, sustain a democratic system, based on radically different values?

We contend that local democracy is at its most effective when local institutions enjoy the trust and confidence of local elites and are politically accountable to the local electorate. Frequent and competitive political participation of the local electorate is crucial to the viability and efficacy of local governance and the legitimacy of the state. The rich associational life, interpersonal trust and networks depicted by Putnam (1993) as necessary to local democracy are, in fact, the consequence of the existence of political competition and not its cause. A brief resume of the impact of panchayat and community-building in West Bengal illustrates this point.

Trust in Levels of Government: Local, Regional and National

We do not have any independent survey evidence to determine the extent to which Moore's rather dismissive comments about the viability of local governments as units of development were true for his time. However, assuming that they offer a reasonable bench mark, survey data from 1996 give a picture of the considerable gains that local political arenas have made in the intervening three decades. Results of a question, *How much trust/confidence do you have in the Central Government—a great deal, somewhat or no trust at all?* and repeated for the 'state government' and 'local government/ panchayat/municipality', are reported in Table 8.1.

Considering India as a whole, the level of trust in local government is actually higher than either regional or Central Government. At the lower end are Punjab and Bihar, where trust in all three levels of government tends to be low. At the upper end are West Bengal and Maharashtra, where trust in government is higher.

Since trust in government is affected by the visibility and effectiveness of the governmental structure, we need to examine the

TABLE 8.1
Regional Variation in Trust in Central, State and Local Government (1996)

High trust in different levels of government	Central	State	Local
All India (N=9589)	**35.3**	**37.5**	**39.9**
Bihar (880)	29.9	30.0	29.9
Gujarat (484)	22.7	22.1	39.7
Maharashtra (860)	30.8	34.0	40.7
Punjab (194)	14.9	16.0	13.9
Tamil Nadu (699)	28.6	36.5	40.3
West Bengal (769)	35.9	40.8	50.6

Source NES, CSDS 1996.

brief history of implementation of Panchayati Raj in India in order to explain the variation in the levels of legitimacy accorded to the local government. Until the passing of the 73rd Amendment of the Constitution, which radically altered the picture and brought about a certain measure of uniformity in the institutional structure of Panchayati Raj all over the country, the states of India had very different practices. They could be divided roughly into three different types: states like Maharashtra where Panchayati Raj became a reality before other regions of India; West Bengal which entered the race for successful Panchayati Raj later, but a combination of circumstances made panchayats the focus of state activity, leading to spectacular success; and those like Bihar, where a mobilised, politicised rural population, divided on the lines of class and caste conflict, has found in panchayats their main arena of the battle for supremacy, reducing the institution to low levels of efficacy and trust. In order to examine the variation in terms of regions and within each region, across social classes, we need first to look at the history of implementation of Panchayati Raj in these regions.

Implementation is seen as the classic Achilles' heel of developing countries, thanks to the bureaucracy and its hangers-on, who—in view of the inadequate development of intermediary groups—often find themselves as the main link between society and the political system, and manage to skim off vital resources, besides diluting the norms of rational management and contributing to the misperception of development resources as consumption goods by their recipients.[11] Successful implementation of Panchayati Raj requires a balance between retaining the support of the local rich and professional classes, while increasing its legitimacy through the participation of the local poor. The division of the trajectory of implementation into three different types is based on their temporality, the type of political linkages and their perception by rural elites in the states.

Mobilisation from Above: Maharashtra

Maharashtra belongs to the group of states where Panchayati Raj was introduced in the first wave (Khanna 1994; Sirsikar 1995). The panchayats became the bastion of local elites, then dominated by the landowning, relatively high status regional castes. Subsequently, as political mobilisation brought in the lower social classes into the local political arena, the richer, erstwhile social elites fled the panchayat arena to higher-level political arenas, to more lucrative markets abroad, or to take refuge in such non-egalitarian arenas as co-operatives, where membership is not by democratic franchise but by the un-democratic ownership of the means of production. In Maharashtra, the panchayat is an administrative outlet of the largesse of the welfare state, the more important political decisions and their implementation being more under the control of the regional government and co-operatives, and coalitions of agri-business, NGOs and caste associations. Panchayat elections have become less regular than during the heyday of their early prominence. Even 'the important subjects pertaining to "co-operation and industries" which were initially entrusted to the zila parishads have been [subsequently] withdrawn' (Khanna 1994: 213).

Mobilisation from Below: West Bengal

West Bengal represents the category of regions where Gram panchayats became the chosen political and legal instrument for the implementation of state policy with regard to land reform, distribution of surplus land, registration of land records, rights of share croppers, tenancy rights and distribution of state subsidies, welfare and loans. Politics from above (in this case, the CPM led state government) favoured these changes; politics from below (the political machinery of the CPM and allies) was in a position to take advantage of these new political resources and harness them for its own political purposes, leading to the creation of red panchayats. Panchayats in this case emerged as the focus of both implementation and legitimisation. Though the normative and legislative basis of Panchayati Raj were already present at an all-India scale already by the 1970s, a fortuitous set of circumstances led to the Panchayati Raj being adopted as the main focus of the state government. The explanation in this case goes beyond the politics of the state to the partisan preferences of the CPM, for reasons that we shall see now. Towards the late 1970s, the CPM was locked in a battle on two fronts in the Bengal countryside. On the one hand, the Party felt that without the countervailing institutional power of the state, the Left Front would not be able to break the dominance of the *jotdar*s (local rich peasants), nor implement its agrarian programme because of the apathy of the lower bureaucracy towards land reform and redistribution and, in some cases, its active collusion with the *jotdar*s, who largely constituted the support base of the Congress. On the other hand, taking recourse to peasant activism held the potential of getting out of hand and developing into insurrectionary violence, both politically damaging to the electoral prospects of the CPM and a likely harbinger of direct Central rule on the grounds of the deterioration of law and order. Out of this double bind was born a consensus that saw the panchayat as the optimal strategy to promote the political goals of the party and empowerment of the poor in the most effective way.

Stalemated Conflict: Fragmentation and Anomic Violence in Bihar

This is a situation where the mobilised poor, taking advantage of their numbers, have often succeeded in capturing panchayats. But the local social and economic elite, who see power ebbing away from their control, have not found any alternative arena.

As a result, panchayats and local politics have become the scene of sporadic violence and caste conflict. Reports on Panchayati Raj in Bihar suggest that the institution has made its appearance as early as 1949, though the 'upper two tiers, the Panchayat samiti and zila parishad, functioned only in some parts of the state continuously from 1964 onwards, and all over the state from 1979 onwards till their supersession in 1986' (Khanna 1994: 84). Khanna rates the contribution of Panchayati Raj in Bihar to the 'politico-administrative system, democratisation and development' as limited. Two government-appointed committees, the Bage Subcommittee of 1973 on Gram Panchayats, and the Tyagi Subcommittee of 1973 on Panchayat Samitis and Zila Parishads recognised the malaise and made specific recommendations. Little action was taken towards the implementation of these recommendations. Khanna, drawing on the observations of a number of 'social scientists', sums up the state of affairs in local politics and local institutions in Bihar.

> Traditional local leadership has been dominating the Panchayat Raj, by and large. However, recently this domination is beginning to weaken at several places. Factionalism, casteism and use of violent means continue to afflict working of a large number of Panchayati Raj institutions. Decentralisation of administrative power and financial resources of Panchayat Raj institutions is very inadequate so far, thereby restricting their role. Neither the Panchayati Raj leadership nor its bureaucracy has appropriately a clear understanding of the concept and practice of democratic decentralisation. They have therefore shown 'little commitment to development and democratic processes'.
> (Khanna 1994: 87–88)

Political and Social Dynamics of Panchayat Elites in West Bengal

By all accounts—in terms of the regularity of elections, auditing of accounts, the volume of political transactions, local legislations, matched by the perception of the Bengal interviewees of the efficacy of their local government and their trust in it—West Bengal is undoubtedly one of the most successful cases of the implementation of the Panchayati Raj in India today. However, the violent controversy surrounding land acquisition in Singur and Nandigram for the creation of SEZs (Special Economic Zones), which has taken some of the shine off the West Bengal case, also indicates the limits of the Bengal 'model' of community building through panchayats. One of the main achievements of the Left Front government has been to have persuaded the *jotdars* (owner cultivators) that their best chance of achieving moderate affluence and security was by conceding legitimacy to the panchayats as the intermediary between them and the agricultural workers, their class enemies. Once in place and effective links between the rural society and the state were established, panchayati democracy became an optimal instrument of 'parliamentary communism'.[12] The instruments, through which this has been achieved include the recording of the sharecroppers, distributing land deeds to poor peasants and causing a more accessible and transparent bureaucratic process. Thanks to these initiatives, the panchayat assumed a significant role. From arranging credits to the supply of seeds and fertilisers, from rationalisation of the available employment opportunities in the village to the determination of a uniform wage rate, everything is channelled through the panchayat. Bhattacharyya writes,

> As a political institution the panchayat became the most immediate structure of democratic representation; the villagers turned into its functionaries and the courtyards of their houses were now used as venues for its meetings. Suddenly the esoteric rule of the state got partly de-mystified and the villagers themselves became witness to, if not actual participants in, the planning and prioritisation of administrative works. In addition to this, and this is important, the Panchayat eventually gave the village a common identity by formally unifying the entire village into a single unit and liquidating the divisions based on caste based localities [...] As an arbitrator between individuals and families in disputes, the panchayat and the entire population of the village involved and delivered a process of adjudication which is quicker, cheaper and more transparent. (Bhattacharyya 1996: 22–23)[13]

The functioning of West Bengal's panchayats takes place in the context of a panchayat-friendly legal environment. The Left Front government has ruthlessly implemented the ceiling laws regarding ownership of agricultural land. It has secured legal right of share for about its 2,00,000 sharecroppers and has stopped for good their coercive eviction from land by the landlords. Finally, it has instituted a three-tier panchayat system (at the village, block, and district levels) on competitive party lines and has held four successive elections to these bodies since 1978, the last (1993) of which had sent more than 91,000 elected representatives (a third of them women).

The rural elites are the crucial links between the local government and the local people. Further questions, such as the actual role of the rural elite, particularly those directly involved with the panchayats, their social origins, the dynamics of the social process in which they are ensconced, require us to look beyond the survey data and into an in-depth case study of West Bengal's panchayats. From anecdotal evidence, it becomes clear that the symbiotic relation of the Communist Party and the Panchayati Raj, which has served both rather well, also sets limits to the success of the experiment.

The West Bengal CPM has developed an effective policy with regard to the functioning of the panchayat institutions. The CPM has developed a specialised party organ—the PPN, *Panchayat Parichalona Nirdeshika* ('Directives on running the panchayats'), in the form of a newsletter issued directly by the West Bengal State Committee of the CPM and sent to every panchayat and municipality through the district committee, in order to coordinate its ideological and political work with that of the panchayat institutions. The Panchayati Raj institution is part of the public manifesto of the CPM and the party is keen on defending its record on this score. In an interview, a party spokesman explained the founding of the party's panchayat newsletter as part of its efforts to '*strengthen democratic method* [s] in running the panchayats, and to encourage *more active popular participation in panchayats*' (Bhattacharya 1997: 41 [original emphasis]). The less visible private face of the party is keener on the political and ideological dividends that this bourgeois democratic initiative might bring.[14] This constant struggle between the public and the private—in an environment that has increasingly become more conscious of the democratic rights and the need for transparency—has become the hallmark of CPM politics in contemporary West Bengal.

Trust in Local Government by Region and Social Class

The focus on West Bengal in the context of comparative regional analysis raises further issues: Is West Bengal unique? What implications, if any, can be drawn for India as a whole from the case study of Bengal? Now that the 73rd amendment provides a national legislative context, what scope is there to achieve a transfer of knowledge from one region to another, so far as the know-how of local governance is concerned?

We shall go back once again to the survey finding on trust in government. Trust is a product of personal experience; affected in turn, by the life situation of the actor as well as the effectiveness of the institutions and processes that constitute his political world. The variation in trust, thus, offers some insight into the performance of local governments and their implications for people in different regions and in different social situations. Table 8.2 reports the distribution of people, showing a great deal of trust in the local governments. By comparing across columns and rows, one can make a comparison across regions and social classes.

Looking at the distribution across the urban and rural population in the three states, one can see the spectacularly low level of trust in local institutions among Bihar's urban residents. Exactly opposite is the case with the urban population in West Bengal, a possible consequence of the good performance of the Bengal panchayats and good communication of this performance by the state government. On the different perceptions across gender and religion, Bihar, once again, lives up to the image one has and the reports one gets of violence against women and minorities. Once again, West Bengal represents the symmetric opposite, with women and Muslims being either close to the same level as men (and Hindus) or better. The same scenario continues with caste-status in Bihar where members of Scheduled Castes and Tribes are below the upper castes, unlike Bengal, where the Scheduled Tribes are actually far ahead of the rest of the population. On education, Bihar presents an almost linear relationship with the level of education and trust in the local government, the level going down

TABLE 8.2
Trust in Local Government across Regions and Socio-economic Strata

	Bihar	Maharashtra	West Bengal	All India
All Groups	29.9(263)	40.7(347)	50.6(389)	39.3(3744)
Locality				
Rural	31.2	45.3	50.0	42.5
Urban	18.2	30.0	59.3	29.3
Gender				
Men	35.5	39.7	52.7	42.9
Women	24.0	41.6	48.2	35.6
Religion				
Hindu + Jain	30.0	42.6	50.6	39.1
Muslim	29.2	33.0	51.5	43.8
Christian	–	–	–	34.8
Sikh	–	–	–	29.1
Other	–	34.3	–	32.1
Caste				
Scheduled Castes	27.0	41.7	52.5	39.2
Scheduled Tribes	6.55	50.0	57.1	38.9
OBCs	33.6	44.6	48.4	40.9
Upper castes	31.7	31.5	50.0	37.3
Education				
Illiterates	23.5	42.2	56.5	35.8
Up to primary	37.6	43.6	47.6	43.1
Middle school	38.6	38.3	39.4	40.6
Higher secondary	43.9	38.8	51.5	42.4
College +	36.1	34.7	58.6	38.9
Age group				
Up to 25 years	34.5	37.3	42.9	38.2
26–35 years	30.2	43.1	50.0	40.4
36–45 years	23.9	40.9	56.1	39.2
46–55 years	30.7	38.5	56.1	37.6
56 years or more	28.1	43.2	52.1	40.6

Source NES, CSDS 1996.

somewhat for those at the highest level of education (the small number of cases of $n = 13$ reduces the statistical significance of this observation somewhat), but not dipping to the level of illiterates, and staying way above the average. Bengal presents an interesting curvilinear relation, levels being high at the highest and lowest levels of education (possibly active adherents of the Left Front, where party ideology compensates for the low trust, 'normal' in the illiterate caused by personal inefficacy, and lower trust in the most highly educated from an elitist disenchantment with mass democracy). The true surprise of Bihar is the relatively high trust in local government among the youngest—at 34.5 per cent, not far from the comparable level in the national sample and way above other age groups in Bihar. Bengal, on the other hand, expects the youth possibly to serve their time before they can stand up and be counted, and be in a position to have a relationship based on trust with the local government. The CPM banks heavily on the trusted and loyal middle aged cadre in key positions and inducts the locally influential as candidates for the local elections, who are allowed to compete under its symbol even if they do not belong to the party. Neither of the two tactics favours the rapid induction of the youth into playing an influential role in the panchayat structure, unlike in regions which are relatively less institutionalised and where the younger and the more educated have fewer organisational hurdles to cross. The Maharashtra data confirms the image one gets from the literature of moderately performing panchayat institutions which have lost some of their earlier prominence and trust from the upper and more educated strata, but continue to be strong, welfare administering institutions, inspiring more trust in women than men (unlike the national average and unlike our two other regions), but not from Muslims, who are significantly below the Hindus when it comes to trusting the local government.

Conclusion

We have argued in this chapter that the judicious use of the local—the lowest spatial unit in its literal sense, but more broadly, of the subaltern and minority social groups and their ideas—has infused new political resources into the political system of India, has enhanced legitimacy of the state, and has given resilience to the political community in India. This has come about through a number of national legal and political initiatives, and, has been more successful in those parts of India where a competitive party system, in combination with the regional policy, has created a successful integration of the local with the national. By extension of the same argument, the experimentation in local democracy has been the least successful in those regions where no autonomous empowerment of the subaltern social groups has taken place, and no persistent attempt has been made by the regional governments to integrate the local in their legal and public policy framework. The survey data related to popular attitudes towards the role of the regional and local governments, as compared to the Central, reveal the general picture. The analysis of the case study and interview data from the secondary sources help examine the theoretical implications of the survey findings.

India's achievement in the field of lifting people out of social marginality provides a striking contrast to the record of the majority of post-colonial states. A governmental system, based on multi-party democracy and free, fair and regular General Elections, has gradually emerged from the hegemonic rule of the Congress party and the Congress system of the first decades after Independence. A federal state, that has been able to retain the bulk of the territory with which it started its life as a Republic in 1950 through periodic redrawing of internal boundaries and radical constitutional innovations to give juridical shape to sub-national identities, has helped contain separatist tendencies. Finally, and perhaps not with the same degree of success, it is becoming a multi national society where the constitutionally stipulated ideal of communal accommodation is in the process of being continuously negotiated within the boundaries of the political process.

Our findings help put the pessimistic prognoses of 'deinstitutionalisation' in the 1980s in perspective. Leading this collective despair of India's chances of surviving as a multi-party democracy, Manor had spoken of anomie, Morris–Jones of a state of civil war, Kohli of the crisis of governability. Paul Brass, describing the extant Indian politics as an alternation between centrally coordinated patronage and the dramatic rhetoric of crisis management, typical of Indira Gandhi, had given voice to these misgivings: 'The system, therefore, shifts back and forth between jobbery and demagoguery and fails to confront effectively major issues concerning the economic future of India and the spread of lawlessness and violence in the countryside' (Brass 1997: 335).

Looking back, many, though not all the authors of 'deinstitutionalisation', have emerged as the key players in building community and democracy in India's localities and regions. These local and regional leaders, often functioning on their own without the benefit of central directions, have drawn on whatever resources they could, and, working within the local culture, context, and economy, they have produced an integration of the national–secular and the vernacular–traditional themes. These processes, taking place at the fringes of the national mainstream, both challenged and enriched it and in the process, in evident testimony to the robustness of India's federal process.[15] (Khare 1997), have been transformed to the extent where they could enter into negotiations with the national and international political agents. Some of these resources constituted a national pool of leadership which, in spite of its dismal failure in the first Janata experiment at the national level in the 1970s, succeeded in reinforcing multi-party democracy in the states and finally, at the centre.

The chapter, drawing on evidence from survey, and from archival, documentary and interview sources as well as from anecdotal narratives, shows that democratic participation has become the 'normal' form of politics for a very wide range of people. However, there are tremendous variations across the regions in the depth and breadth of involvement with the local government. The main thrust of our findings is to show that since political power in the Indian political system emerges from coalition formation at the lower levels, everyone engaged in the game has a vested interest in keeping the 'democratic' game going, though, once again, the stakes are not the same for everyone. Democratic participation can very well co-exist with legal and political irregularities, unfair and unequal distribution, corruption and venality. True, General Elections often succeed in throwing the rascals out, but it also inducts some rascals in, and the political process turns some into rascals once they are within the government. In the final analysis, the resilience of Indian democracy is the outcome of the 'Million Mutinies' against historical and current injustice and the successful political management of the 'crisis of governance' that the radical articulation of injustice often leads to. This is how the three levels of Indian democracy are intertwined, with the Election Commission and the Supreme

Court providing relatively fixed points of reference at the macro level, the numerous local arenas introducing new social elites into the political process, and the regional leadership striking a dynamic balance between the desirable and the possible.

Instead of thinking of India's regions in idiosyncratic terms, this chapter has concentrated on understanding their experience with regard to local governance as the consequence of a cluster of factors, most of which are general to all regions, and, in some sense, collectively describe the nature of the state and the political process in India. While it takes a capable and imaginative leadership at the regional level to put many of the legislative, political and material resources to work in order to produce the required results in the local governance, those resources are generally available. West Bengal in this sense is not unique and the other states of India could profitably transfer some of the knowledge gained from the West Bengal 'experiment' with great profit. Important among this moveable feast of good practices are cooperatives, proper use of local bureaucracy, effective implementation of land reform and minimum wage legislation. The CPM's presence happens to provide sufficient political condition at the local level to bring all these resources to their optimal use; but it is not a necessary condition. The crucial test cases are regions with non-CPM governments. Karnataka could be one such state.

The local institutions (and the *neta*s that populate them, many of whom are in fact the second generation beneficiaries already of local self-government of the 1960s) connect the modern state and the traditional society. By creating new opportunities for popular participation, providing information and creating interest, setting up horizontal and vertical networks, the local institutions open up greater 'room to manoeuvre in the middle'.[16] In consequence, in those parts of India where local government and local democracy have been successful, the state seems to 'work' better. That this result has been achieved by the governments of both the Left and the Right in the Indian states goes on to show to what extent statecraft can be independent of rival ideologies of state.[17]

The emphasis on the local, also suggested by the new communitarianism of Putnam (1993) and others, has an important implication for post-colonial societies. It suggests that one should accord legitimacy and the status of full actors to pre-modern social structures and groups as these countries start their long march towards state and nationhood. This sits uncomfortably with the more conventional theories of social and political change, born out of the historical and political context of European nation-states. The incorporation of variables such as social networks, interpersonal trust, or shared norms into conventional theories of social and economic change creates a dilemma for the development planners and the builders of states and nations. Can the State reconcile the twin tasks of accumulation, extraction, transformation and rationalisation on the one hand. and the legitimisation of these measures within the framework of representative democracy on the other?

Caught in this double bind of contemporary norms of political correctness, which require Central Governments to be responsive to the interests of marginal social groups and deprived regions, and the norms of rational management, whose criteria of efficiency often dictate otherwise, politicians—in Yeltsin's Russia, Mandela's South Africa, or Lalu Prasad's Bihar—prefer to fudge the issues and muddle through, with the usual combination of rhetoric and inaction. Broadly speaking, India has been generally successful in negotiating its way through a combination of leaders with vision and administrative talent, and the historical good fortune of institutional capital at the time of Independence. As the analysis undertaken here shows, in spite of stubborn problems of regional separation and residual discontent in some sections of the population, the state and the nation are firmly set on a steady course. Presenting these occasionally contradictory challenges within the broader context of Indian politics would be the main theme of the next chapter.

Notes

1. See Mitra (2005) for details with regard to the selection of the sample.
2. Note the ambiguity built into the Indian Constitution: 'India, that is Bharat, shall be a Union of states' (Art. 1). The grouping together of different religions in Art. 25, and opening up the Hindu religious institutions to all sections of

the Hindus can also be seen in this light, as part of the attempt to create an inclusive nation in India.
3. 'I do not understand why a village should necessarily embody truth and non-violence. A village, normally speaking, is backward intellectually and culturally and no progress can be made from a backward environment. Narrow-minded people are much more likely to be untruthful and violent.' (Nehru 1960: 508). Equally dismissive of the current reality and future potential of the village as a political unit for the building of the new India was Ambedkar:

> That they (the villages) have survived through all vicissitudes may be a fact. But mere survival has no value. The question is on what plane they have survived. Surely, on a low, selfish level. I hold that these village republics have been the ruination of India. I am therefore surprised that those who condemn provincialism and communialism should come forward as champions of the village. What is the village but a stink of localism, a den of ignorance, narrow-mindedness and communalism? I am glad that the Draft Constitution has discarded the village and adopted the individual as its unit, (*Debates of the Constituent Assembly*, Vol VII (1): 39.)

4. The marginal social groups of the contemporary stable democracies had neither the legal status nor the political power to resist a fate they did not approve of. The social history of the eighteenth century Europe is replete with accounts of their suffering and resistance. This was no accident of history. The causal relation between this massive destruction of the life styles and habitats of these people and the building of new state and economic forms is now reasonably well settled.
5. See Khanna (1994) for a detailed account of the growth of local self-government in Indian states.
6. The initiative lost bipartisan support in the Parliament when it appeared that Rajiv Gandhi might have been motivated by the prospects of having a more pliable instrument of government in a nationally constituted prefecture of local governments as compared to the more assertive regional Chief Ministers.
7. For details of the 73rd amendment, see Khanna (1994: 34–35).
8. Bhattacharyya (1993) suggests that as much as 50 per cent of public funds in West Bengal pass through the hands of the Gram Panchayats.
9. For further discussion of these arguments, see Mitra (1990).
10. Commenting on Naidu's programme, Manor said:

> His main emphasis is on information technology, which he thinks can provide not just new jobs and wealth but also what he calls SMART governance. The capital letters stand for Simple, Moral, Accountable, Responsive and Transparent government. He couples this with

200 When Rebels Become Stakeholders

promises of greater popular participation and visionary leadership. What Mr Naidu has done is to provide a more disciplined, effective administration. He has begun building information infrastructure that disperses and collects ideas through electronic kiosks across the state, which has a population of 72 million. Citizens will soon be able to register their views in 'social audit' on the performance of government programs (Manor 1998).

11. The phenomenon has been described as 'bureaucratic rent' by Krueger (1974), '*pyraveekar*' by Reddy and Hargopal (1985).
12. See Kohli (1983) for a detailed discussion of this point.
13. Both the non-partisan character of Bengal's panchayats and the extent of their efficacy in creating a village community might have been somewhat overstated. See Bhattacharya's account or a critical analysis of the role of the CPM in the running of Bengal's panchayats.
14. Bhattacharya (1997: 42) quotes from an inner party document (Hoogly District Committee) to suggest as much:

> That the activities of the panchayat will be performed by elected members of panchayats alone is the outlook which is opposed to the long term political objective of the Party. In order to transform panchayats into the weapons for struggle, what is necessary is strong party control over panchayat units, collective decision and leadership and regular check up of Panchayat activities in party committee meetings.

15. See Harish Khare's article in the special issue of *the Hindu* (Khare 1997) to mark the 50th anniversary of India's Independence. Several articles in this collection point in the direction of this main theme.
16. For further discussion of this point, see Mitra (1991).
17. Rudolph and Rudolph (1987: 19–59) have a comparable formulation in their convergence hypothesis, especially the chapter entitled 'Centrist Politics, Class Politics and the Indian State'.

9

India at Sixty: Social Change and the Resilience of Democracy

How quaint and bold and yet, how visionary Nehru's inaugural address—'Tryst with Destiny'—now seems, when we compare the state of affairs in his precarious, nascent Republic with that in the buoyant economy and robust institutions of India at 60. By all accounts, democracy has become the normal method of functioning of Indian politics, much more so if one is to go by the manner in which issues like nuclear energy and security, that are the preserve of secret diplomacy in many stable, western democracies, have been debated in the public domain.[1] The pace of economic change has been sustained less successfully than in countries like Taiwan or South Korea, but those countries were not full-fledged democracies during the period of rapid social expansion, whereas India has remained democratic almost continuously, all the while ensuring incremental and continuous growth of enfranchisement, entitlement and empowerment.

In this chapter, we recapitulate some of our main findings in the light of this puzzling co-existence of democracy and development. This brings us back to the central issue of Indian politics. How comfortably do *jati*, *varna* and *dharma*, the core concepts of Indian tradition, fit within the corpus of a modern, liberal, secular nation-state, as envisioned by the Constitution? How does one reconcile the empirical evidence of the robust vitality of Indian democracy and the periodic occurrence of intense inter-community violence? And finally, if the neo-institutional model of dynamic and democratic social change has delivered the positive results that we have considered in this book, then where is the evidence of its continued applicability?

The Correlates of Democratisation

The empirical evidence that underpins the main arguments in this book has been primarily gathered from two major opinion and attitude surveys of India's adult population. Of course, one needs to be careful about the claims one makes with regard to the intellectual links with the social world one speaks about, because survey research, even by the permissive standards of the social sciences, cannot claim to be a 'scientific' discipline, much less can it provide a comprehensive *explanation* of the social phenomena. Social and attitudinal measurement in the context of a complex, multi-cultural society like India, is a relatively new phenomenon. Even in its role as a technique of precise description of a complex social situation, the survey researcher often finds himself playing second fiddle to the shrewd observer, working alone, equipped with nothing more ostentatious than the day's newspaper and a few well-placed phone calls. Even under the most rigorously controlled conditions, a survey is, at best, only a still picture of a dynamic reality, so much so that even the use of survey data for the simplest description of reality would require a complex montage, inviting charges of trickery from the uninitiated.

With this elaborate caveat, we would still hold, that the use of survey data is the only reliable method of investigating the linkage of democracy and social change. Where attitudes, beliefs and opinions play a crucial role, it is the only method that one might pursue for a satisfactory empirical verification of hypotheses, derived from an analytical model of democratic social change. The empirical conjectures—derived from the model specified in chapter one (Figure 1.1)—that describe the course that a pyramidal society, bound together in reciprocal and hierarchical social relations, takes in its transition towards a competitive political universe, based on universal adult franchise—have been tested with reference to a number of specific variables. The analysis has involved the discussion of continuity and change over successive generations, elections and the party system, the nation and the region, economic and social policies in India, always focusing on the perception of the institutions and processes by the electorate of India, and particularly, by the rebels and the stakeholders. The overall finding is one of a steady and incremental growth of democracy.

The results of our investigation can be summarised in the form of the correlation of all the empirical phenomena relevant to our model (see Table A3.6 in the Appendix 3 for a correlation matrix). In the main, three observations should be noted from this matrix. The first refers to the overall positive correlation of political legitimacy—constituted mainly with process variables, such as the accountability of the government and how people view the efficacy of political parties and elections in communicating the popular will to the commanding heights of the government—with all the other indicators of the interaction of the state and society in India. Thus, those with a greater exposure to campaigns and political meetings hold the legitimacy of the political system to be high. Similarly, those who perceive the financial situation to be generally positive, the present by itself and in comparison with the past, together with the perspective of future outcomes for themselves and their children, have a positive evaluation of the legitimacy of the system. Institutional trust, a structural variable that measures trust in the local, regional, national governments and the other major arms of lawful and legitimate governance in India, namely the judiciary and the Election Commission, also correlate positively with the process-based measure of legitimacy. Those better informed about politics, scoring positively in our stringent measure, based on the ability to recall the names of the Chief Minister, the Prime Minister and the Member of Parliament from the constituency of the interviewee, correlate positively with legitimacy. The correlations with the policy variables are, however, weaker, with liberalisation at 0.03 performing better than the performance of the government in areas pertaining to social harmony—such as the conflicts based on caste, class, land ownership, or atrocities with reference to Dalits and minority religious communities. The correlation for the latter is weaker, though still positive, at 0.02. Interestingly, there is no significant correlation between the perception of the legitimacy of the government on the one hand and the state of law and order in the country. The second major observation to be made here is on the set of positive correlations with other components of the institutional aspects of the state and society in India that reinforce the picture of overall legitimacy. Thus political efficacy (a measure based on the individual's assessment of the value of his vote and the accountability of those elected to the bodies wielding power and influence), which correlates positively with legitimacy, also have a positive correlation with exposure to campaigns and political meetings. Those who are closer to the political process but are themselves not necessarily holders of office, have a positive correlation with institutional trust and political information. Political efficacy correlates positively with financial efficacy, institutional trust and political information. Financial efficacy correlates positively with political information and institutional trust with the state of law and order.

While the positive correlations reported so far indicate an overall positive assessment of the political system and the democratic political process, the evaluation of specific policies is, however, uneven and in some crucial areas, negative. The third major observation points to the negative assessment of the policies of liberalisation by those who consider themselves to be politically efficacious, who have financially benefited from the political process and who have more political information. Liberalisation does not correlate significantly with either political exposure, or with institutional trust. Similarly, law and order are seen negatively by those who have more political information and political exposure. These are the same groups whose perceptions tend to correlate negatively with social harmony as well.

Of course there are still grey areas in the quickening and deepening of democracy in terms of trust in the institutions, but not among those actually in charge of them. However, India's political system has shown the institutional capacity to tackle these problems and the people have rewarded precisely those institutions—the Election Commission and the Supreme Court in particular—in terms of high trust in them. The rejuvenation of India's political institutions comes as a timely correction to the picture of political decay and deinstitutionalisation, to which many specialists had drawn our attention, particularly in the wake of violent ethnic conflict in Punjab, separatist movements in Assam and Kashmir and the demolition of the Babri Mosque.

Those with long memories of Indian politics, particularly of the politics of poverty alleviation of the 1960s, might wish to note a radical change in the tenor of politics when compared to what one finds in the survey and in the general political rhetoric. The regional and local leaders today do not aim at state hand-outs; they want to wield power in their own right. The Janata victory of 1977 was the big dividing line. Indira Gandhi's authoritarian interlude of 1975–77 taught people that politics was everything, and power was its focus. The timid experiments of the 1960s gave way to the bold ventures of the 1970s in terms of the politics of coalitions. The intensive experimentation with coalitions and alliances and the culture of negotiation and accommodation that it has given rise to, are the legacies on which India's multi-party democracy is based today.

Mainly, three consequences have followed. In the first place, knowledge of and direct access to power, on the part of the previous subaltern classes, is no longer an aspiration but a reality. Today's regional figures like Bihar's Lalu Prasad, Dalit leaders like Mayawati from Uttar Pradesh or Chandrababu Naidu from Andhra Pradesh, are full-fledged leaders in their own rights, aspiring to national prominence on the strength of their regional power. In the second place, there is a general understanding of these changes on the part of politically conscious groups in all levels of society. There is, surprisingly, no Indian equivalent to the great 'white flight' in the United States, of the spectre of the affluent middle classes bolting representative politics altogether and escaping to the leafy suburbs or to gated communities. Our data show that the upper castes have accepted the legitimacy of the new parameters of politics in India; hence the support for reservation for the SC/ST, backwards, women, across all social classes. Those socially and economically better off, as we learn from the regional comparisons[2] and from our findings from this survey, make it abundantly clear how the upper crust of society has learnt to make do with the new rulers.

The form in which the upper-caste *angst* and frustration at the democratic rise of the masses express themselves is the third important aspect of contemporary Indian politics that emerges from the study. Shut out from social privileges, automatically generating access to power, the upper echelons of the Indian society have adopted a two-pronged strategy, consisting of support for the parties of the right, a category where we can place the tendencies for social conservatism, religious and cultural nationalism and the increasing adoption of the market as an alternative to politics as a career. The integration with the world market comes as yet another way in which they can escape popular democracy's inexorable march, nibbling away at social privilege. Not surprisingly, the upwardly mobile sections of the Indian society are enthusiastic supporters of globalisation and staunch defenders of meritocracy and yet, remaining all the while firm believers in the Indian model of accommodation and social justice.

These three main aspects of contemporary Indian politics manifest themselves in many forms and combinations. Under their impact, the regions have become social laboratories for cumulating skills of administration, transfer of the knowledge of governance from one region to another, of the transformation of the local to the regional elite, and of the regional elite to the participants in the high politics of Delhi. That is the other side of the picture of the invasion by the vernacular elites of the hallowed halls of power in Patna and Lucknow. This questioning of the norms and institutions is also a manifestation of the quickening and deepening of Indian politics. That alone can keep democracy going, rather like Gandhi's intervention in the 1920s, which, ridiculed by the elites of his time, dramatically changed the nature of Indian politics and put the freedom movement on a firm footing among workers and peasants.

The findings from the survey data are supported by larger developments that one can pursue at the level of aggregate data and institutional changes in Indian politics. Thus, hung parliaments and coalition governments create a spectre of governmental instability in India; a perusal of regional politics, firmly ensconced stable party systems and party-cleavage linkage at once question this image. The combination of federal and constitutional norms has put to rest the fears of Balkanisation. Today, one finds robust confidence about the stability and resilience of the states, and as such, an acceptance of the inclusive character of the national and regional identities.[3] Hence the nation and regions appear as 'layers' of identity. The picture of social harmony is moderated with the implicit presence of class conflict, so, the support for liberalisation is moderated with a reminder of the interests of the less advantaged. There is great support for the institutions but less for the actors. However strange this might sound at a time when the rhetoric of intolerance has entered politics in a big way, democracy in India is no longer seen as an imported and exotic concept, nor as the creation of an enlightened, determined minority. It is a style of governance that has neatly fitted the lifestyle of a majority of Indians, even if the fit is partly by default. The 1996 Parliamentary elections, in many ways, mark the beginning of a new phase in Indian politics. This beginning, however, also portends changes that may prove to be counter-productive for Indian democracy.

The 'Grey Area' of Multi-party Democracy in India

So far, we have concentrated on the hypotheses that explore the basis of the functioning of multi-party democracy in India and found reasonable evidence for its acceptance by the main actors in Indian politics. Is this, however, an act of faith, an unconditional commitment, or, a limited commitment, conditional on performance? The question arises from the fact that Indira Gandhi, the unrepentant author of the 1975 Emergency, was actually brought back with popular acclaim in 1980 when the Janata Party, who were the heroes of the anti-Emergency movement, failed to deliver stable and efficient governance. In this section we shall explore the reasons for the residual doubts about the stability of multi-party democracy in India. Once again, India is not alone. In historical and comparative perspective, the collapse of an established party system is known to occur when it fails to accommodate the interests of an emerging social group, or, fails to aggregate the interests of groups who are articulate and assertive about their demands.[4] How does India fare on this score?

High Trust in Institutions but Distrust of Actors

The presumed collapse of India's institutions has been the staple of academic (Kohli 1990, Sen Gupta 1996) and journalistic discourses on Indian politics (Akbar 1988) since the early 1980s. The deinstitutionalisation prognosis was greatly reinforced by the destruction of the Babri Mosque in 1992 and gets prominent mention at every outbreak of communal violence. As such, it is important to examine the level of trust and confidence that the people of India have in her major institutions and in the people responsible for running them. When asked: *How much trust/confidence do you have in different institutions of India*—the results are highly positive for the institutions but more negative for those who are responsible for running those institutions (see Table 9.1).

TABLE 9.1
Evaluation of Different Institutions and Actors

	Great deal	Somewhat	Not at all
Election commission	45.9	31.1	23.0
Judiciary	41.6	34.2	24.2
Local government	39.0	37.8	23.2
State government	37.2	43.6	19.2
Central Government	35.2	42.5	22.3
Elected representatives	19.9	40.4	39.7
Political parties	17.4	43.6	39.0
Government officials	17.2	40.4	42.3
Police	13.0	29.9	57.1

Source NES, CSDS 1996.

In order of positive evaluation, the Election Commission, which, under the high profile leadership of T.N. Seshan, made elections much more orderly than before, gets the best score of 45.9 per cent of 'great deal of confidence' and 31.1 per cent of 'somewhat confidence'. The judiciary, again the beneficiary of the high profile public interest litigation and prosecutions leading to the exposure of financial misdemeanour of politicians at the highest level, comes next in the order of positive evaluation. Local government, which, since the democratic decentralisation under the initiative of the Balwant Rai Mehta Committee of 1957 has steadily spread all over India, gets a positive evaluation from three-quarters of the population. Next in order comes the state and Central governments of India. There is a precipitous fall however when it comes to the elected representatives and the political parties, for both of which the negative evaluation exceeds the positive score. Government officials do no better and the police do the worst.

Trust in the local government, next to the Election Commission and the Judiciary, followed by the state and then by the Central Government, tells us two things. First, that the performance of the lower level governments appears to be better judged than that of the Central Government and second, people seem to be more concerned about the lower units of governance than the higher ones. It may be matched with the identification the Chief Minister vis-à-vis the Prime Minister and also with interests in the state or national governments. While the issue of nation–region will be discussed later, it may be noted that 23.0 per cent of the people admit to have more concern with the state government as against only 11.0 per cent in the Central Government while 20.9 per cent in both and 39.0 per cent in none.

To sum up the discussion, we may conclude, that the growth of a competitive party system and the existence of inter-party consensus on key issues affecting civil liberties are crucial facilitating conditions for the civil society. The party system, in turn, is effective and seen as legitimate only insofar as it succeeds in getting itself accepted by the social groups as an effective means for the articulation and aggregation of demands, failing which, a politically mobilised people has every incentive to turn to other agencies like the army, the clergy, radical groups of the Left or the Right, and, last but not the least, to mob violence, none of which has a proven record of an abiding commitment to the civil society.

From the data and the results of the present survey, multi-party democracy appears to have struck roots in India. This is seen, particularly, from the linkage of partisanship and social cleavages, a broad-based sense of political efficacy and legitimacy and cross-cutting value conflicts and partisanship. And yet, some doubts about the stability of multi-party democracy linger on, reinforced by such events as the national Emergency of 1975–77, the destruction of the Babri Mosque in 1992, continuing communal conflict and tension, and the sub-national movement in Kashmir. The danger to multi-party democracy from these issues is muted because, as we have seen in the data, opinions within India's political parties as well as social groups on these crucial issues are divided, with a substantial percentage of supporters within each major political party and across major social groups in general, coming up with responses that provide a commitment to the civil society in India.

The local and regional disturbances are not unusual in many post-colonial and post-revolutionary countries. The issue is, why do they not become cumulative or terminal in India? As we have already seen from the survey data, there is a significant number of individuals who feel themselves to be efficacious but do not accord a great measure of legitimacy to the institutions of the state, nor to the political parties as the most effective instrument for the implementation of the popular will. This provides some insights into these grey areas of Indian democracy. As long as the system responds, either through policy change or by the change in the rules of the game, the process of democratic politics bounces back. Research on the potential for a responsive political system to gain strength from protest movements and the ability of the Indian political process to accommodate 'rational protest' as a complement to institutional participation, provides an additional explanation to the resilience of multi-party democracy and civil society in India.[5] (Kaase 1972, Marsh 1977, Mitra 1992).

Democratic Politics and the Ambiguities of Identity

The fact that under the compelling rationality of political choice, the Indian voter and those desperately soliciting his support, have put all available resources into instrumental use is a theme that has been implicitly present all throughout this book. Democracy flourishes only when the political market is seen as an integral part of public life. In that sense, the fact that the electoral process draws on all possible sources of social influence is by no means unique to India. Where the issue becomes complex and controversial is the limit that one can legitimately place on the reach of politics, either because it is against the law or because the indiscriminate use of certain political resources have dire implications for the very stability of the nation and state in India. It is in this context that the political use of caste, religion and region gain considerable salience.

The role of primordial identities in societies caught in the process of transition from the agricultural to the industrial has received considerable scholarly attention.[6] Today, the linear view of modernisation, which once defined the leading view among specialists, is questioned by radical divergences from the predicted path. Looking back, the Indian Constitution, one of the first acts of self-definition among newly decolonised societies, appears to have been prescient, for in its first article itself, it gave voice to India's double identity: 'India, that is Bharat, shall be Union of States.'[7] 'India' represented the legal structure based on the individual, fundamental rights and participation and the 'scientific spirit' of which Nehru was the main inspiration, while Bharat was evocative of links with India's pre-colonial past. The competitive political process that the constitution had foreseen has brought this duality into its most explicit statement, simultaneously drawing upon the primordial identities in order to mobilise members of those traditional groups for the purposes of political support, but also making it possible for groups of very different social origins to work together as members of larger political coalitions or as parties to the formal institutions of the state and thus, to inculcate the values of equal citizenship. Thus, caste, religion and region are much talked about but the concepts, as used in politics, are far from what they might indicate in their social context.

When Jawaharlal Nehru inaugurated the new Republic of India with the famous speech on Freedom at Midnight, he gave voice to a section of the Indian elite that wished to see India transformed into a modern, secular state. Their aspirations were enshrined in the constitutional norms of equal citizenship, fundamental rights to equality and liberty—irrespective of caste, creed, religion or place of birth—and the judicial and bureaucratic apparatus of a modern state with which to implement these lofty ideals. Four decades after Independence, some of these hopes lie shattered in the ruins of the Babri Mosque of Ayodhya and in the killing fields of Bihar and other places, routinely afflicted with caste wars. The emergence of the politics of identity, where groups based on caste, religion, tribe and region, appear as the main actors, once again raises an issue that gave rise to the original Orientalist discourse: are the institutions of liberal democracy appropriate to India? Nehru, intensely aware of the dangers of communal violence, was familiar with the problem. Reproachful as they were, the modernist leadership of the Congress had watched with helpless fascination as the Muslim League, wielding religion as a vehicle of mass mobilisation, had fought for and won the right to have a separate homeland for the Muslims. The stigma of the failure to resist the demand for the partition of India on the basis of religion and the communal carnage that marked the birth of the new Republic, had convinced Nehru that the evils of caste and religion had to be firmly kept out of the public arena. In Nehru's view—shared by the ruling elite, drawn from a largely urban, professional and western educated background—the scientific spirit, technology, planning, social legislation and a rational bureaucracy were the answer.

Why does caste, after six decades of social legislation, modern education, and liberal democratic politics, continue to be a significant factor in India's public life? The question, posed to the Oriental circles at the turn of the century, would have raised few eyebrows, because Indian society was meant to be like that and, the thin modern coating added to it by the British rule notwithstanding, could not behave in any other way. Today, an active electorate of 500 million people questions some of the premises of the Orientalist approach which considered the Indian society incapable of self-definition or self-regulation. Nevertheless, as the spectre of 'caste war' and communal violence live up to a scenario all too familiar to the Orientalists, there is the occasional throwback to the heady days of Orientalism among 'essentialists', who present caste as the immutable essence of Indian society. Opposed to this is the instrumentalist approach which presents caste as merely a politically convenient self-classification for the purpose of material benefits.

All through this book, tangential references have been made to the issue of the resilience of caste with reference to essence and agency, two views of caste that compete, and occasionally conflate, in the context of India's vibrant political process.

In view of the aspirations of India's modernising elite, the ability of castes to survive large-scale social and economic change and to mutate into modern forms like caste associations continues to be a puzzle. That caste 'survives' is clear from several diachronic studies based on fieldwork, the campaign rhetoric of practically all political parties including those explicitly committed to 'secularism', electoral alliances and evidence from the various surveys. What remains unclear is exactly which attributes of caste survive and why. Its protagonists constantly slip in and out of the two faces of caste—the traditional endogamous status groups, organised around specific occupations—and caste associations where people come together, using social ties for the purpose of promoting collective interest. Thanks to its liminality, caste appears as the quintessential Janus of Indian politics, with a *jati* face, turned towards the *varna* scheme and through it, to Indian tradition and identity, capable of moving people in ways and areas beyond the reach of modern institutions; and, an associational face, which links it with the institutional fabric of the modern state. The political actor deftly manipulates both faces in order to generate power through this complex repertoire.

Interpreting caste, therefore, leads to the larger issue of how to relate the ontology of *jati* and *varna* (of which caste and the caste system are but inadequate representations) to the moral basis of society and state in India. Here, the battle lines are clearly drawn. Essentialists and Orientalists have a similar understanding of Indian tradition. Both views hold that castes, ensconced in the *varna* scheme, are the bedrock of Indian tradition. The secular modernists of India, on the other hand, view caste as synonymous with underdevelopment, hierarchy and prejudice. They wish to jettison it altogether. Essentialists, whose instinctive and political sympathies are for preserving the pure spirit of Indian civilisation in amber, ridicule such attempts as derivative and ultimately self-defeating. However, the fact that in reality caste survives and mutates, serves only to throw empirical doubts about both the rival schools.

India's political discourse with regard to caste today, is full of references to the various conceptual *avatars* of the concept itself. Thus, Dumont's theory of caste—with references to *homo hierarchicus* (1966) and purity and pollution, complete with a theory of the natural subordination of the inferior to the superior—is interspersed with other ramifications of caste—those of caste as a grid of identities, constituted by the local *jati*, the regional *varna* schemes and the all-India Hindu *varna* system; caste as *Jajmani*, exchange of economic needs and status, reinforced by power; caste as the essence of a traditional society. The traditional caste system is the institutionalisation of this essence as well as a mode of resistance to all of the above. That the traditional view of caste survives—in spite of the efforts of the modern state and democracy, posited as challenges to the ideology of the caste system and its institutions and the various legislative efforts after Independence, such as the Untouchability Offences Act 1955, various forms of reservations, electoral and political mobilisation and the long-term effects of urbanisation—continues to puzzle. The empirical evidence discussed in this book, seen in the larger political context, provides some insights into the resilience of caste and its mutations. While these issues would surely form the subject of more detailed and theoretical explorations in future research, some indications of the kind of questions that can be raised, can be given through the suggestion of two analytical categories.

Primordial Identities and Competitive Politics

The introduction of limited franchise under British rule had already created a stir among the Indian electorate. The ensuing competition and the differential mobilisation by the untouchables had led to a strong reaction among the Congress leadership which saw the communal electorate as an attempt by the British to divide and rule. One of the legacies of the Poona Pact (1936), which symbolised a historic rapprochement between the leaders of the untouchables and the Congress leadership, was to set aside a quota for the representatives of the untouchables. The second legacy was the knowledge that the local hierarchy could be renegotiated at the level of high politics, through competitive electoral mobilisation. The lesson was not lost on the electorate, particularly among the less privileged sections, when, after Independence, universal adult suffrage was introduced in one full swoop. There was an initial interlude, during which the locally dominant castes transformed the *Jajmani* relations into a veritable vote bank through, what the Rudolphs have called, 'vertical mobilisation'. However, intra-elite conflict and land reforms, which helped further loosen the dependent relations between the locally dominant caste and those who worked for it, quickly led to a situation of factional conflict and short-term political alliances, called differential mobilisation. By the 1960s, electoral mobilisation had led to a new phenomenon called horizontal mobilisation, whereby, people situated at comparable levels within the local caste hierarchy came together in caste associations. One consequence of horizontal mobilisation was the formation of new parties like the Republican Party, the BSP, primarily supported by former untouchables or the various *kisan* (farmer's) parties and movements like the Lok Dal which drew their support mainly from the backward classes and aggressively promoted sectional interests through the electoral arena.

One of the main consequences of six decades of competitive electoral politics on the local caste hierarchy has been to render all inherited relations of power necessarily contestable. The congruence of status, power and wealth—tenuous even at a period when little recourse for status negotiation was available outside the local arena—has been further contested. As Washbrook reminds us, '....the merest sight or smell of privilege in any area of society instantly provokes antipathetic response among those who see or smell it. No privilege is inherently legitimate and no authority exists uncontested' (Washbrook 1989/90: 227).

For the ease of presentation, we can conceptualise the role of caste as a factor in political behaviour in terms of an analytical scheme (see Table 9.2). Membership of a caste, ensconced within the local caste hierarchy, can be perceived by some of its members as an obligation to support their social superiors. As the logic of political participation has spread through the Indian electorate and the percentage of people taking part in elections has grown, 'vote banks' which functioned on the basis of vertical obligation have become progressively rare. As things stand now, it is common to find factions—short-term political alliances—where one can find voters following their own interest and utilising all political resources at their command, including the membership of a caste.

TABLE 9.2
Caste and Political Competition

	Caste domination	Political competition
Value	Hierarchy	Egalitarianism
Instrument	Primordial (essence)	Rational (agency)
Norm	Obligation	Interest
Modality	Jajmani	Political organisation
Structure	Vote bank	Multi-caste association
Form of Mobilisation	Vertical	Differential/Horizontal

The scenario of contestation that Washbrook describes from the case of Tamil Nadu is repeated daily in all parts of India.[8] Underneath the violence and atrocities perpetrated in its name, caste is actively present as a factor in electoral mobilisation. Does caste consciousness perpetuate inherited caste related inequalities? What might sound counter-intuitive is, in fact, one of the enigmas of caste, for caste consciousness, in fact, destroys precisely those attributes of the caste system—such as traditional social obligations, hierarchy, and dominance—which, the essentialist view used to present as necessarily fixed in time and space. The point will be discussed at greater length in the following section.

Caste, Community and Modern Politics

Formation of communities is the predictable outcome of the new atmosphere of competitive, modern politics, where the logic of numbers and the scarce resources are increasingly becoming clear to the social groups trying to acquire new privileges or to hold on to what once appeared securely theirs but is now coveted by other groups. The politics of community formation can be presented in terms of an analytical schema (see Table 9.3). Unlike the 'modern' or 'traditional' organisations, a community is a necessarily liminal structure, with a vernacular face, turned towards the local society to which it appeals in terms recognisable to the local arena and a universal associational face, turned towards the modern state and the market. The caste association is the most frequent (but not the only) type of community one is likely to come across in contemporary Indian politics.

TABLE 9.3
The Politics of Community Formation

Social base	Identity	Territorial boundary	Political strategy
Localised caste (*jati*)	thick	insular	close
Community (*sampradaya*)	thin	broad	open

Seen as communities, castes are uniquely Indian in form but universal in content. Under the impact of six decades of electoral competition, social legislation, new economic opportunities and new political linkages have developed. Caste, as its correlations with the political attitudes and the social visions discussed in this book show, is far from the rigid, timeless essence of an unchanging India. The use of caste as a form of identification is primarily strategic.[9] The introduction of competitive politics and democratic institutions has quickened the pace of change in the social and political organisation of castes, increasingly perceived as communities in which people come together to promote collective interest. Castes are now perceived not as rigid but flexible by their members, who treat them more as vehicles of self-promotion rather than a structure of domination by the powerful and of self-censorship by the powerless. 'Scholars', as Inden argues, kept India 'eternally ancient' by attributing to her various 'essences, most notably that of caste' (Inden 1990). A new perspective, which can depict India's institutions and political discourse as instruments through which her people seek to influence the course of their history, therefore, should start with a re-evaluation of caste.

The use of caste for electoral purposes is an example of using a primordial identity. There are similar uses of other primordial identities such as region, language, religion and tribe. This is done quite deliberately as a collective political strategy. The emphasis here is on the fact of collective deliberation and optimisation of all political resources. Therefore, to depict the electoral process as a mechanical manifestation of caste arithmetic, based on the fact that the primordial identities are salient in the campaign, would be an inadequate representation of reality. The second important point to infer, from the manner in which the primordial identities are used for political purposes, is the concept of de-linking one from the other when it suits the actor. We find an excellent example of how religion—once its salience was regionally established—receded into the background and the localised *jati* resurfaced as the main anchor of political mobilisation, in a case study from an Assembly Election in Uttar Pradesh. Reporting a 'conversation that took place between an old woman (possibly an *ahir* by caste) and a BJP canvasser', Singh (1996) shows how the political actor is able to put religion 'in its place' once the religion-based political movement has made its point, so that, the everyday politics of caste and community interest can take over.

Canvasser: Oh! mother, are you Hindu?
Woman: Yes.
Canvasser: Do you believe in Rama?
Woman: Yes. He is our god.
Canvasser: Do not you want a grand Sri Ram temple built in Ayodhya?
Woman: Sure. It must be built. I too have contributed for this purpose during 'shila pujan'.
Canvasser: Then you should vote for the BJP because it is the only party which will get Sri Ram temple built at Ayodhya.
Woman: Yes-yes. I shall vote for it. (A small pause.) But will you tell me the caste of the candidate who is fighting on the BJP ticket?
Canvasser: Yes. He is a *rajput*.
Woman: No, my son. I cannot do that. When everybody is voting for his caste, how can I go against that? I will also vote for my caste men.[10]

The above exchange brings out the strategic character of the electoral discourse, in which people from all levels of society take part and where, depending upon the occasion, all political resources are put into effective use. When traditional networks and primordial identities are drawn upon, the intention is clearly political and not exclusively social. But this complex repertoire is drawn on the 'modern' identities of class as well. If the electoral process continues to sharpen the 'binary opposites of caste and class', the exigencies of practical politics continue to fuse them in the organisational mode of the political caste, which is neither purely interest nor identity but intersects both, in a manner that the actors concerned consider optimal (Sheth 1996). In the process, the politics of primordial identities has called into question their traditional roles as the building blocks of society. Commenting on caste in particular, Sheth says, 'The singular impact of the competitive democratic politics on the caste system thus was that it delegitimised the old hierarchical relations among caste, facilitating new, horizontal power relations among them' (Sheth 1996). The process has come full circle with the voter choosing the type of primordial identity he or she would allow a given party to use effectively at a given point of time. The use of religion in particular, in a multi-religious society, where the largest religion itself is deeply fragmented on caste, sect, regional and linguistic lines, clearly has self-imposed limitations.

Finally, while the democratic character of the Indian political system has probably acquired the requisite resilience to withstand challenges from the non-democratic ideologies of the Left and the Right and has actually transformed these anti-system movements into legitimate partners in government, the future of political parties as the preferred mode of democratic government is not so secure. There is the impatience of the newly enfranchised electors who do not think highly of elected party politicians, visible evidence of corruption in high quarters within the political parties and the Gandhian nostalgia for a non-party, decentralised, direct democracy, based on village panchayats. Some of these ideas that were written into the Constitution have gradually found their way into law, political institutions and practice. These potential conflicts, between the principles of partyless direct democracy and party-based parliamentary democracy, did not matter very much during the early years after Independence, when the first 'Independence' generation, presided over by Jawaharlal Nehru, was in charge. India could have her consensus-based, accommodating Congress system which linked it to the tradition of the united struggle against the British, the Gandhian legacy of non-partisan character of the village community and the Nehruvian commitment to the party-based parliamentary democracy. As if in recognition of the British and the implicit faith in the British constitutional practice, the Indian constitution provided for no guaranteed role nor dedicated state finance for political parties.[11] As we have seen from the record of India's short-lived Emergency in the centre and countless replications of it at the regional level, Nehru's successors have taken greater liberties with the internal restraints on authoritarianism that have been built into the informal, customary basis of the British parliamentary practice.

It follows from the arguments of the previous section that India's multi-party democracy will continue to have a grey area surrounding it, not so much around its democratic institutions and practices as around the stability of the party system on which it is based. If the present regime, based on multi-party democracy, fails to deliver the goods, it is certainly possible for an authoritarian populist to seize the opportunity and raise the banner of non-party democracy as the most effective instrument of the popular will and cultural nationalism as the legitimising device of its power. In order to improve the odds against such a possibility, it will probably not be a bad thing for India to take a leaf out of the German rules book and add a suitable amendment to the Indian Representation of People Act, reinforcing the necessity of the political parties.

Crowding the Middle: The Central Tendency of Indian Politics

To the distant observer, the violent rhetoric of Indian politics might come across as a sure sign of an imminent implosion. There is animated talk of majority rights and minority obligations, of revolutionary seizure of all assets and their just redistribution and, equally of the market principle substituting all else, of jettisoning the slow moving democracy in favour of more effective leadership.

But somehow, in the end, reason appears to prevail, heated discourse gives in to moderation, adversaries become partners—all of which leave the world more confused than ever about the mystical working an increasingly, Indian mind. How does one account for this?

One possible answer to this question lies in the underlying distribution of public opinion on the composite measure of the contents of the nation—soft, accommodationist, multi-cultural or hard, exclusivist, mono-cultural. Our data show a convergence to the mode for practically all sub-populations (see Table 9.4).[12]

The most outstanding aspect of Indian politics that comes out from Table 9.4 is the general tendency to be close to the sample mean of 7.29. On a scale based of 10 items with a maximum value of max = 20, where lower figures indicate proximity to the accommodationist and the inclusivist view of the nation in India, the sub-groups indicate rather small variations. The data, from this point of view, appear to support what the Rudolph and Rudolph (1987) have called the tendency towards 'centrist politicy' in India.

TABLE 9.4
Mean and Standard Deviation on the Accommodation Scale 1996

Sample		Mean	Std. Dev.
Total		**7.29**	**3.00**
Education	Up to primary	6.95	3.01
	Middle school	6.70	3.32
	Illiterate	7.28	2.52
	Higher secondary	7.37	3.34
	College and above	8.78	3.60
Class	Very poor	6.87	2.68
	Poor	7.11	2.80
	Middle class	7.57	3.21
	Upper class	7.75	3.23
Locality	Rural	7.21	2.85
	Urban	7.53	3.40
Caste	SC	6.99	2.69
	OBC	7.00	2.82
	ST	7.10	2.59
	Other	7.83	3.40
Gender	Female	7.16	2.84

(*Table 9.4 continued*)

(*Table 9.4 continued*)

Sample		Mean	Std. Dev.
	Male	7.41	3.15
Religion	Muslim	4.81	2.57
	Christian	6.08	2.61
	Others	6.16	2.47
	Sikh	7.54	2.83
	Hindu and Jain	7.64	2.90
Elite status	Non-elite	7.27	2.95
	Elite	7.36	3.29
Party voted for	Left Front	6.62	2.75
	National Front	6.93	2.75
	BSP	6.96	2.75
	Congress	7.00	2.94
	BJP	8.41	3.06
Regionalist	Regionalist	6.37	2.99
	Non-regionalist	7.60	2.94

Source NES, CSDS 1996.

Parties representing the scheduled castes (example, the factionalized Republic Party of India), the scheduled tribes (a large variety of local parties) and the Muslims (various Muslim leagues and several Uttar Pradesh parties of short duration) have proved notably unsuccessful in mobilizing and holding the support of the minority status groups they hoped to lead and represent. (Rudolph and Rudolph 1987: 424).

But the Muslim attitude towards the state and nation in India, particularly in view of their position on the overall inclusion–exclusion scale, calls for a more detailed analysis. Their sub-sample average of 4.81, with a standard deviation lower than the Hindus, indicates both a major difference with the view of the nation and significant homogeneity within the community on this issue. The Muslim view of the nation is one of the leading political questions of India, deliberately made into a non-issue during the long years of Congress rule. The partition provided only a semi-solution to the question in the sense that those Muslims who stayed behind did not, thereby, automatically disown the two-nation theory. The fuzzy position on the issue of the role of religion within the structure of the state, suspended between that of the wall of separation and equidistance, opening up the possibility of opportunistic manipulation, did not give many choices to the religious communities either. The dangerous potential of a sullen 'majority' community and distrustful 'minorities' has powerfully manifested itself in the context of the tragic incident of the Babri Mosque. Its distant echo can still be perceived in our data, where the supporters of the BJP, along with those with college education and above, constitute the groups most inclined to an exclusivist definition of the nation in India.

As India copes with yet another round of electoral consultation in search for effective and representative government and the media get saturated with campaign rhetoric from politicians whose venality and corruptibility are often beyond any doubt, one may be forgiven the moments of weakness when one questions the fit between Indian society and the political institutions of the postcolonial state and look somewhat wistfully at the exacting standards by which the western democracies, the original source of many of these institutions, judge their leaders. This book should help the hard pressed democrat in those moments of doubt from becoming cynical. For the evidence analysed here gives some insights into where and how the Indian democracy is at its most effective. It also gives some food for thought about how the state, in search of a nation, is the beneficiary of the efforts from below to discover a common basis of civility, of tolerance and accommodation, of quiet pride in the nation and a reinforcement of its inclusive character. The Indian democracy, in that sense, has definitely 'thickened' the nation, necessarily thinned by the needs for centrally prescribed communal amnesia as the price of unity against the masters of divide and rule and the long years of the one-dominant-party system when the same spurious basis of communal unity remained frozen, the fear of another partition and guaranteed vote banks being the political fuel that nurtured it. Six decades of vigorous political transaction has made the people of India discover the political basis of accommodation. So, they converge to the mean on the 10 point scale of exclusion and accommodation. Political competition has thus produced the basis of the dynamic consensus, which underpins social change in India.

The attitudinal data on legitimacy and nation formation, presented in this book, should provide further insights into the process that provides a bridge between the post-colonial state and the people. The mission, as Partha Chatterjee observes, might be impossible, for 'Nationalism sets out to assert its freedom from European domination. But in the very conception of its project, it remains a prisoner of the prevalent European intellectual fashion' (Chatterjee 1986: 10). Some supportive evidence for the process Chatterjee envisages can be found in the institution of representative democracy which provides multiple points of entry for the people. The Indian state, through the deepening and broadening of federalism, extension of representation in effective ways to groups historically excluded from participation, through the judicious use of affirmative action, and through strategic tolerance and covert encouragement to rational protest movements, has opened up myriad ways in which to be active in promoting one's own welfare. The Indian experiment has established an important point of reference for state formation and nation-building for the post-colonial states.[13]

Conclusion: The Centrality of Stakeholders to India's Countervailing Forces

What is the guarantee that the Indian democracy has the requisite dynamism to continue its linear growth? As one can see from the analysis undertaken in this study, stakeholders are likely to be present in all the crucial nodes of the Indian system. The implications of the Indian case for a general theory of democracy and social change would be considered in the next chapter. The general consideration of our empirical findings in this chapter has shown the institutions and processes of the Indian democracy at work, though they are not always visible because of the political froth—of secularism engaged in noisy battle against Hindutva, or liberalisation as compared to socialism—that comes in the way of their visibility. Our analysis has pointed out that the real choice is not between being for or against the market, but of deciding what the socially acceptable and politically feasible basis of integration with the world market is. Similarly, the issue with regard to cultural nationalism is not whether religious and cultural values have a role in politics, but in what form the traditional values of India should explicitly and publicly constitute the basis of the nation and state in India. The preoccupation with secularism (and now liberalisation) has tended to take attention away from the fundamental issues of poverty and illiteracy, just as one can also forget that the price of populism—the product of democracy in the context of weak and unstable political parties—is power without accountability. Our findings, particularly with regard to political trust, emphasise the salience of the judiciary and a politically accountable professional bureaucracy, the tired but vigilant workhorses of the state, and the press—India's great asset—to come to the aid of democratic social change.

Notes

1. The crisis generated by the demand of the Leftist parties for a debate in the parliament on the 123 Agreement with the United States provides an important window to observe the working of India's parliamentary democracy and public debate on issues of high politics.
2. Gujarat social elite in the study village, at the time of the study still dominated by the landholding *patels*, had learnt the democratic game enough to extend running water and electricity to the tribal parts of the village, the expenditure being borne by the panchayat. 'Even if we do not give it to them, they will take it from us any way. This way we shall have the pleasure of giving, and keep the village unity intact', was the answer of an elderly *patel*, member of the panchayat, when asked why the panchayat spent the money for the electrification of the tribal parts of the village and to extend the pipelines to their houses, whereas the original water and electric facilities for the upper-caste parts of the village were borne by their residents themselves. The Orissa upper-caste elites were a study in contrast. There was little communication or commonality between them and their scheduled caste and tribal fellow villagers. The results of this comparative study were published in Mitra (1992).
3. Contrast, for example, the tones of Harrison (1960) and Mitra and Lewis (1996).
4. In the National Election Studies, conducted in 1996 and 2004, the main question asked to measure this phenomenon in the survey was: *Would you say that the persons we elect by voting generally care about what people like you think, or that they don't care?* An alarmingly high percentage (63.1) says that the elected representatives do not care. The larger implications of this would be discussed in the next section at length.

5. See Marsh (1977), Kaase (1972) and Mitra (1992) for applications of these theoretical conjectures.
6. In the euphoria over the post-war decade of development, when decolonisation was sweeping the face of the globe, a natural and necessary dissolution of the primordial identities into the modern forms of citizenship was considered the norm. It was also the main moving spirit behind the mainstream development literature which suggested a linear and incremental course of modernisation of the traditional societies as the likely shape of things to come. History has proved to be rather different from such predictions. One of the early warnings of a different possibility, informed by a different theoretical construction of the nature of interaction between tradition and modernity was provided by Rudolph and Rudolph (1967).
7. Art 1, the Constitution of India. Curiously, the Hindi version of the Constitution reverses the order where 'Bharat' precedes 'India'.
8. For theoretical and empirical discussions of resistance from within the Indian social system and the various forms it takes, see Robinson (1988). Also, on the theme of resistance from below by marginal social groups, see Scott (1985). For an insight into the long process of caste consciousness as a form of resistance to the caste system, partly instigated by the missionaries and the new value system introduced into the Indian society by the British rule, see Hardgrave (1968), Washbrook (1989/1990), Haynes and Prakash (1991) provide several historical and contemporary examples of resistance against social dominance.
9. Electoral campaigns are replete with anecdotes of the strategic use of caste identities and solidarities. Vijay Bahadur Singh explains the role of caste as follows. 'In order to consolidate his position further Balaram [the candidate] attempted to create a fear psychosis among Muslims and to warn the backward castes against the malign attitude of the forward castes, particularly the *rajputs*.' Singh cites the comments of a speaker at a meeting organised by Mulayam Singh Yadav, describing how rajputs use them for political purposes:

> They are clever in exploitation, cruel in oppression and, above all, they unleash atrocities on the poor, especially the dalits. They use us as a driver uses a stone or a brick as a stopper to his vehicle on the road. After we have been used, we are kicked in the same fashion as the driver kicks the stopper which he must have very earnestly searched for all around the place (Singh 1996)

10. V.B. Singh reports: 'This conversation I overheard on the outskirts of a village in the constituency, 16 November 1993', ibid., p. 127.
11. There is a Representation of People Act, but no equivalent of the German *Parteienrecht*. The Indian Election Commission has recently moved in this direction by directly requiring parties to be accountable for the campaign expenses and more importantly, to hold internal elections.

12. It should be added here that four out of the 10 items that have been given into the construction of the scale of inclusion–exclusion (see Appendix 2) relate to issues of great significance for the Muslims. As such, the overall position on the scale might be weighed in favour of the confessional component of nation-building in India, not taking into account the other areas of social, economic, and political integration. Conversely, the finding also points us in the direction of the unsolved role of religion in Indian politics, for long (thanks to the equivocation of the politics of accommodation) a non-issue in Indian politics.
13. The findings reported here provide supportive evidence for the assertions with regard to the role of the state in India made by Rudolph and Rudolph (1987: 400–401).

10
Beyond India: Democracy and Social Change in Comparative Perspective

Does democracy promote orderly social change? Reciprocally, does social change reinforce the moral and material basis of democracy? To the dismay of confirmed democrats and populists of all hues, the evidence is, at best, mixed. The tragic ends of Zulfikar Ali Bhutto, and his nemesis, Sheikh Mujibur Rahman, both of whom had sought to latch their political wagons to radical rhetoric, illustrate how serious the consequences of a growing hiatus between popular expectations and state capacity can be. Examples such as these do not inspire confidence in the happy marriage of democratic institutions and popular mobilisation in the context of the poor, post-colonial societies. The Chinese, wiser in these matters than their South Asian counterparts, have stood by the political wisdom of curtailing democracy to suit the needs of rapid economic growth. The crushing of the democracy movement at Tiananmen and the uprising in Tibet, and the accommodation of both by the western liberal democratic states are pointers to the limitations of the universal claims made in the name of democracy. Even the recent political events from western Europe do not provide much reason to cheer for the easy road to social democracy. England's 'Winter of Discontent' in the mid-1970s, under the Labour government which paralysed the country and the ultimate revival of economic momentum under the stern leadership of Margaret Thatcher, illustrate the difficulty of negotiating large-scale structural changes in stable, industrial democracies. Nor does the United Kingdom stand alone.

The trouble that the German grand coalition has faced with reforms in the labour market regulation since its inception in 2005, and the uphill battle that has been predicted for President Sarkozy of France following his electoral victory, provide comparable evidence of similar difficulties with regard to the making of democratic social change.

Instead of pointing towards India's idiosyncrasy, the core model that we have employed in our analysis (Figure 1.1) has drawn attention to the political calculations of decision-makers at the elite level and the stakeholders at the level of the mass public that account for the course of political change. When the political process succeeds in transforming subjects into citizens who participate in politics, feel that they matter and hold the system to be legitimate, the result is a functioning democracy. When the course of social change transforms the indifferent into the involved, and rebels into stakeholders, and individual strategies lock in with one another to produce social outcomes, the case for a stable basis to democratic social change is made. This concluding chapter reviews the theory that underpins our empirical findings, considers the Indian data in the light of South Asian attitudes and beliefs with regard to democracy, and moves towards a reconciliation of the procedural and substantive views of democracy in general.

India's 'Exceptional' Democratisation in South Asian Comparison

Does India stand alone? How does the strategy of 'turning rebels into stakeholders', as India's chosen path from colonial rule to multi-party democracy, compare to the states of South Asia? The similarity of shared rule under the British, language, religion and culture and the dissimilarity of post-Independence political development provides a unique opportunity to compare the contribution of elite strategy to the democratic transition. Thanks to the availability of the comparative data on democracy in India's neighbouring states (CSDS 2008). We are in a position to compare some essential features of India's democracy with that of her South Asian neighbours.

The analysis undertaken in this book has chosen the legitimacy of democracy as a form of government and the sense of personal efficacy as the foundational concepts of India's democratic process. The findings on both indicators are presented in Table 10.1. Asked, *which of the following three statements do you agree with most? 1. Democracy is preferable to any other kind of government; 2. In certain situations, a dictatorial government can be preferable to a democratic one; 3. It doesn't matter to people like me whether we have democratic or non-democratic governance*, one finds very strong support for democracy everywhere with the exception of Pakistan. The Pakistani experience with regard to the efficacy of one's vote is also lower than other South Asian states. Where does that leave the 'exceptional' democratisation of India?

TABLE 10.1
Preference for Democracy as Compared to Authoritarianism

	Bangladesh	India	Nepal	Pakistan	Sri Lanka
Democracy is preferable	69	70	62	37	71
Sometimes dictatorship is better	6	9	10	14	11
Doesn't matter to me	25	21	28	49	18
[My] vote makes a difference	66	67	75	50	65

Source *The State of Democracy in South Asia*, CSDS, 2008.

'South Asian democracy is more than an Indian story' (CSDS 2008: 6). 'If India shows greater depth in its support for democracy and pro-diversity policies, Bangladesh reflects much deeper political identification and levels of political participation, Pakistan has a higher sense of national pride and Nepal proves the vitality of people's aspirations and ability to struggle for a republican and democratic order. And Sri Lanka trapped in a seemingly intractable civil war, has a civil society wedded to peace' (CSDS 2008).

Post-modernity in the Non-Western World: Democracy's 'Trojan Horse'?

By promoting all actors to agency, the post-modern approach to politics has opened up a new agenda of political research on changing societies. The individual actor no longer needs to be equipped with the 'right' attitudes to be able to participate in politics properly; nor does the system, by an extension of this argument, need to achieve the preconditions set up by Lipset and other modernist scholars, to be able to qualify as modern and democratic. But, if this new approach opens up the Pandora's Box of political creativity and agency, then it also brings a further problem in its train. If post-modern political actors like Mayavati and Lalu Prasad make their way into the privileged world of upper-caste politics, is this, in the end, a victory for the old order that has neutralised opposition through accommodation, or is this the birth of a new world, inspired by new categories that are somehow more authentic and representative of India than the post-Independence brand of Nehruvian modernity? At issue here are the core questions of knowledge and power, and re-use of the pre-modern categories for the sake of a more authentic modernity. If Indian politics is to be understood in terms of *Indian* political categories, then what are they? More fundamentally, does politics make the terms of discourse, or do terms of discourse define the difference between politics and anti-politics?

The debate extends beyond the frontiers of Indian politics. As we see in the occupied territories of Iraq and Afghanistan, the resolve by the 'alliance of the willing' to declare democracy the only game in town has driven non-liberal politics underground. With the unresolved issues of religion, language, identity and class as political anchors, groups of political actors have found a novel argument in the revival of archaic social practices, terrorism and the 're-use' of cultural and religious symbols for political purposes. The consequent rift between a society and its intellectuals, and the failure of the state to mediate between the two has led to a condition of enduring political crisis. The theoretical implications of this crisis should be familiar to those who look askance at the rising ethnic conflicts and the plethora of the new vocabulary of political discourse in India and many sites of political conflict in the non-western world.[1]

The difficulty of explaining substantive political problems is further compounded by a terminological confusion. Running in parallel to established concepts, such as democracy, participation and development, are such unofficial concepts of indeterminate legality as *gherao, dharna,* boycott, *rasta roko, jail bharo*.[2] Larger structural changes within Indian society have produced these new concepts of resistance to the authority of the state and the encroachment by the market on the life styles and traditional means of livelihood of the victims of rapid change. In their counter-strategy to neutralise these terms of struggle, both the state and the market have devised new concepts such as *loan melas* and *garibi hatao*, further enriching the vocabulary of Indian politics.[3] This extraordinary range and richness of the conceptual and empirical material do not, however, appear to have affected the conceptual framework with which one seeks to understand it.

One explanation for this relative lack of synchronisation can be found in the 'derivative' nature of Indian political science and its relatively narrow institutional focus.[4] Those, with longer memories, will remember a failure on a similar scale on the part of the social sciences during the freedom struggle when millions were moved by *swaraj* and *swadeshi*, while the political scientist was restricted to the narrow empirical range of British constitutionalism applied to India, or, to the ethereal spheres of philosophical speculation. Indian reactions against this conceptual inadequacy have been articulated in terms of the call for a rejection of the universal categories and a return to the authentic endogenous categories, a solution which is not without problems of its own.[5] The importance of the underlying problem can be seen from the debate that has surfaced intermittently in national as well as international forums, articulated, mostly but not exclusively, by students of sociology (Bailey 1957) and political science (Mehta 1987, Sathyamurthy 1971, 1986), and in the more specific context of the historiography of the colonial rule in British India (Guha 1983, Hardiman 1987).

Two epistemological puzzles that arise out of this crisis are of interest to us. First, how meaningful are the terms of academic discourse such as *democracy* and *secularism*, in societies that have not gone through the historical process that led to these terms in the liberal democratic states of the western world? Second, to what extent is it possible to map the terms of the academic discourse that have arisen from the political practices such as *gherao, dharna,* boycott, *chamcha, julum shahi*, without a significant loss of meaning, into the categories of political analysis? Effective empirical data analysis is not possible without an understanding of the meaning and significance of the key categories of the political discourse. We approach this larger debate through an analysis of the Western scholarship on Indian politics in order to set the stage for the survey data to follow. While it specifically focuses on the literature which has its origin in the intellectual community of the West, the larger implications that the book seeks to draw are also applicable to Indian academics who have based their work on the methods and the substantive conclusions of Western scholars. The intention behind the survey of this literature is not to evaluate critically their substantive findings as such, but rather to identify the key concepts with which scholars, drawing on concepts that originated in the West, have sought to represent the Indian reality, to examine their internal variation and differentiation, and to explore the grounds of commensurability between their general approaches.

Four parameters underlie the classificatory scheme of the political process that characterises state–society relations suggested here. The first is the social vision, namely, the desired shape of the future which constitutes the objective of social transformation. The preferred values are to be realised through a set of instrumental values. These are: perception of the role of the state, perception of society and the institutional process through which social change is achieved. These, which constitute the other three parameters, specify the nature of the state structure and society, as they occur at the start of play, and the institutional process that is intended to suitably transform them for the realisation of the social vision. Using these criteria, the body of writings can be grouped into three broad streams, namely, developmental, functional and revolutionary. The positions they adopt on the key parameters are indicated in Table 10.2. The respective paradigms and their interconnectedness are discussed thereafter.

The Developmental Paradigm

Basic to this approach is a dichotomous view of the universe. On one side is to be found the world of tradition, woven together in the intricate web of reciprocal obligation into an organic

TABLE 10.2
**Competing Paradigms of State–Society Interaction:
A Classificatory Scheme**

	Perception of key parameters		
Paradigms	State	Society	Institutional process
Developmental	Hegemonic leader	Object of transformation	Bureaucracy, rational planning
Functional	Non-exclusive initiator	Object and initiator of transformation	Interpenetration, mutual accommodation of state/social system
Revolutionary	Epiphenomenon/ source of opposition	Epiphenomenon/ source of resistance	Class struggle/ revolutionary movement

Source Mitra 1999a: 45.

community, where life is ascription-oriented, particularistic and functionally diffuse. On the other side is the brave new world of functionally specific, universalistic, achievement-oriented society. The movement from one pole to the other is seen by the proponents of this paradigm as both a historical process and a moral imperative for those societies which are not yet modern.

The developmental paradigm, which aims to achieve modernisation for traditional societies, not only involves a change in psychological attitudes and the structure of social organisation, but also implies a radical change in the political process and economic organisation of society. Rapid economic growth, to be followed by political participation, are related concepts that provide the necessary linkage between the largely sociological writings on modernisation and the authors who address themselves essentially to development.

During the post-war period, it is the writings of Rostow that have been identified with the idea of economic growth as representing the quintessence of development. In the somewhat sparsely populated world of development 'theories', which have achieved broad acceptance by the non-economists, Rostow (1960) must certainly constitute an ideal exemplar. For evidence of acceptance of this framework, one needs only to consider such concepts as 'economic take-off', 'sustained growth', and 'preconditions for economic development', among others, which have now found their way into the everyday language of planners, captains of industry, as well as the taxpayer. In this much publicised work, Rostow defines the sweep of modern history as a set for stages of growth, essential for the process of transformation that a traditional society undergoes in order to reach modernity.

Though it is presented only as 'an economic historian's way of generalising', as one proceeds through the great five-fold scheme of the stages of growth through traditional society, the preconditions for take-off, take-off to sustained growth, drive to maturity and eventually, the age of high mass consumption, it gradually becomes clear that the formulations add up to more than mere description of a historical sequence. For what is being suggested here is not only the historical sequence of past events, but a developmental scheme with universal spatio-temporal dimensions. To generate the necessary momentum for this analytical descriptive scheme that alone can impart to it the character of the 'sweep to modern history', and thus reinforce its claim to be cross-culturally valid, Rostow identifies, in the cultural, social and political structures of societies that are fairly advanced in the scheme of the stages of growth, as well as those that are still groping their way towards it, certain forces that possess qualities akin to the forces that drive human beings towards a predetermined goal.

This goal, as indicated in the scheme, is the attainment of mastery over one's environment which, besides the immediate natural surroundings, eventually comes to include other people and also their natural surroundings. Political power in the hands of modernisers, with the state serving as the catalytic agent, is among the chief means towards the attainment of this goal. The modernising goal is achieved through the process of nation-building and economic growth, both of which involve the transformation of the production system towards greater productivity. These processes are complemented by the diffusion of entrepreneurial spirit and socio-cultural attributes collectively referred to as modernisation.[6]

Thus, viewed from the perspective of the developmental paradigm, political power in the hands of a modernising elite becomes a critical conceptual 'bridge' that links together the international state system and the developing world, whose members would secure full membership once their elites have succeeded in the political, economic and cultural transformation of their respective societies. It is this spirit that provides a unifying bond to such core writings on the developmental/modernisation paradigm as Huntington (1968), Myrdal (1968), as well as the influential series of volumes on Political Development brought out by the Social Science Research Council (New York).[7] In each of these works, India played the role of a critical empirical case for the concerned scientific paradigm, both as a source of supportive evidence, as well as a target of necessary advice in the form of policy implications for countries more or less in the position of India.

The vast majority of American scholars in the behavioural tradition, doing empirical work on India, placed themselves within the world-view of modernisation, either explicitly or implicitly. The application of this paradigm to Indian politics has been made, in a significant way, by Shils (1961) and Weiner (1962a, 1967, 1983), who extended the developmental paradigm to the field of electoral analysis.[8] Those, writing in this vein, have examined the relationship between modernisation and consolidation of democracy in India (Field 1980), diffusion of the norms of participatory democracy and institutionalisation of political competition and bargaining (Hardgrave and Kochanek 1993) and electoral competition and party politics (Eldersveld and Ahmed 1978; Palmer 1975; Weiner 1978, 1983), modernisation of religion (Smith 1963), interest groups and pressure groups (Weiner 1962b).

The 'pattern variables' of Parsons (1957), such as ascription/achievement, particularism/universalism, diffuseness/specificity, collective-orientation vs self/orientation and affectivity/neutrality, constitute the key parameters of the developmentalist paradigm. Though Parsons himself was cautious enough to admit the 'identification' of the universalistic-achievement pattern with the 'dominant American ethic',(Verney 1986), the same cannot be said of those who sought to apply this paradigm to India. In the brave new modern world envisioned by the developmentalists, they predicted 'a future in which caste as well as other "primordial" collectives would be superseded by individualistic modern associations' (Frankel and Rao 1989/90: 14). Growing economic differentiation and urbanisation, it was thought during the first decades following Independence, would lead to a decline of caste solidarity, resulting in greater secularisation of the political culture. According to Hardgrave, 'The differentiated political culture represents, perhaps most accurately, simply a foundation for the emergence of a political culture reflecting identities based on economic interests and growing political awareness' (Hardgrave 1969: 105).

Research on the consequences of modernisation has, however, shown a different picture. Exposure to modern methods of communication, growing affluence and the spread of literacy and migration to urban areas, have, in many cases, led to the spread of Sanskritic ideas and values (Beteille 1969). Singer (1980) has argued similarly that the spread of urbanisation, literacy, education and expansion of the mass media, represented a technical modernisation that was exploited in order to democratise the 'Great Tradition' and make it more accessible. These anomalous aspects of modernisation, marked by the spread of participation and political consciousness, have been pointed out by several authors including Madan (1987) and Nelson (1987).

The developments within Indian politics have witnessed both the spread of the norms of liberal democracy and its opposite, particularly methods of coercion and collective protest, to a degree where participation theory could not be explained within the paradigm of development. There were other anomalies as well. Whereas modernisation theory had confidently predicted the decline of political salience of religion and the transformation of primordial identities into civil loyalties, the politics of the 1980s and since, have been, if anything, dominated by religion, communal and caste conflict, and attempts by ethnic groups to carve out political territories for exclusive dominance.

Faced with these anomalies, the current version of the modernisation paradigm has found an explanation for India's problems in the 'theory' of deinstitutionalisation and criminalisation of politics, which suggests the moral case for the resurrection of the institutions of state to their original stature which they are presumed to have enjoyed during the Nehru era.[9] Once again, devoid of its empirical and theoretical arguments, the latest version of the modernisation paradigm can rely only on its moral core.[10] Being descriptive and essentially prescriptive in nature, the deinstitutionalisation thesis can only describe, but it fails to explain.[11]

The Functional Paradigm

The relative autonomy of politics from the social process and its ability to reformulate the rules of social transaction is the determining factor that we can use in our efforts to identify the authors who can be placed within this paradigm. Though identified widely with the work of Dumont (1966), who specifies a hierarchical social structure with the abstract values of *dharma* at the apex as the fundamental basis of Indian society, other major conceptual contributions to this approach include Bailey's notion of the peasant society as a multiplex of relations that selectively and rationally incorporates elements of modern life (Bailey 1970), Morris–Jones's concept of the three idioms of politics in India (Morris–Jones 1963, 1987), and the notion of the modernity of tradition put forward by Rudolph and Rudolph (1967). Bailey's theoretical formulations on a model of Indian politics, based on painstaking fieldwork, deserve careful attention. He describes the Indian political system as the aggregation of a set of interlocking and 'nested' arenas at the locality, district and regional levels. Each arena operates according to the rules specific to it, which is why there is no homogeneity across the larger political system. Therefore, issues of cross-systemic significance have to be 'translated into something else at constituency level and have to be translated yet again at village level' (Bailey 1970: 232). However, on the whole, while the functionalist arguments are effective in explaining the mutual accommodation of traditional social institutions and modern political processes, they are on weaker ground with regard to the political discontinuities and cases of system failure such as India has witnessed in the past decades.

The Paradigm of Revolution

A Marxist revolution, whose ultimate objective is to place Prometheus in the service of the toiling masses, has provided a rallying point for those dissatisfied with the inadequacies of the developmental and functional paradigms. Such influential works as pre-war Dutt (1940) and post-war Moore (1966), as well as more recent writers like Frankel (1978)[12] and Kohli (1987) broadly share some of the humanist and politically radical sympathies embodied in the Marxist paradigm. Kohli questions the incrementalism of the developmental models by referring to the unbroken exercise of power 'by an alliance of a nationalist political elite with entrepreneurial classes, capable of simulating economic growth' (Kohli 1987: 8), placed within a 'state supported capitalist economy' (Kohli 1987: 80).

> Those without property or other means of contributing to the process of production—which presumably provides the bonding principle for the rather different groups collectively referred to as India's ruling classes—can expect very little out of the political system. Mass poverty in India is therefore neither an accidental nor an incidental feature of the Indian political system, but its logical concomitant. The failure to mitigate even the worst of India's poverty is a consequence of the institutionalised patterns of dominance within India. (Kohli 1987: 8)

These themes find further reinforcement in Byres (1988), Harriss (1982) and a wide variety of writers both within and outside India. The wide-ranging nature of Marxist scholarship on the state and political discourse can be seen in the impact it has exercised on other aspects of Indian life. An impressive range of contributions, originally inspired by Guha, but which has increasingly been recognised as a distinct mode of analysis under the collective appellation of the 'Subaltern' school, has sought to overcome, in a more promising way, some of the limitations of what we have earlier referred to as Marxist political formulations on the state in India. These writers have attempted to incorporate endogenous political idioms within the Marxist paradigm in their efforts to locate collective protest in India within a revolutionary agenda.[13]

Rooted in a Marxist understanding of political change and evolution, but reinforced, nevertheless, 'with a wealth of empirical material and hard evidence'(Guha 1983), and drawing freely on a range of social sciences, Guha has succeeded in placing the specific historical conjuncture of colonial rule within a broader framework, in a manner where the categories of the actor and his political experience converge. As a result, subaltern research has extended the scope of social research into previously unexplored areas. However, having unleashed a rich stock of evidence at the level of individual consciousness, subaltern historiography demonstrates a tendency to slip back into orthodox Marxist political formulations when it seeks to place it within the context of macro-theory. The difficulty arises when attempts are made to impart a dynamic aspect to the analysis of the specific situation, almost to the extent that the description of the political negotiations and transactions that mark the post-insurrectionary situation is not possible without re-introducing the dreaded concept of false consciousness all over again.[14]

This brief and synoptic survey of the leading paradigms of discourse on Indian politics demonstrates two sets of difficulties. The first refers to those that characterise the normal functioning of a paradigm which serves to suggest an agenda, identify a community of scientists, specifies the puzzles, and lays down the criteria of acceptable rules of evidence. In the case of each of the paradigms examined here, we have identified its key concepts and parameters, its major puzzles and the degree of success it may have achieved in suggesting solutions to them. The inability of each of these 'flawed' paradigms to give a satisfactory account of reality, it is suggested here, is explained by the fact that the root concepts around which they are organised are not germane to the experience that comes under their domain.

One possible explanation for this intellectual shortcoming of the paradigms of politics might lie in their essential character as extensions of a 'western' *problematique* and a paradigm with which men and women sought to order their universe in the post-Enlightenment Europe. The consequence is a fatal dissociation between belief and practice, categories and experience and, most alarmingly, society and its intellectuals. Institutions, which provide the political context within which the dialectical interaction of ideas and experience takes place, are under considerable and increasing strain. The ironical consequence of this confusion is the rich abundance of terms of political discourse, where terms of discourse, jostling for public recognition, are engaged in competition. The exercise, undertaken in this chapter is intended to facilitate the search for a more effective paradigm, set within the terms of discourse derived from the Indian political experience and articulated in the endogenous political vocabulary.[15]

We have argued so far that the interaction of electoral democracy and social change is a complex process. Its significance and inherent contradictions are not always obvious even to those who are in daily and intimate touch with politics and social change. This renders the communication of the meaning, the potential resources, and the failings of India's democracy an uphill task, not only abroad, in the context of a western audience, but also at home. Something gets lost in the communication of the specialists' knowledge of the statistical and technical aspects of elections and democracy in India to the public. Commentators, in India and stable western democracies, who are happy to celebrate the success of the democratic form of government in India, are often not able to understand the best way to view its aberrations.

Western students of Indian politics have a special problem of cognition. At the level of their general public, two powerful obstacles interpose themselves between the Indian universe and its perception. The Indian world is seen alternatively either as organic or as morally anomic. They are two complementary myths. Whether it is seen in a well-meaning way—the Little Buddha syndrome—or as organically cohesive, bounded, collective identities, the Indian mind is seen as incapable of individual rationality, a necessary pre-requisite for sustaining the complex political institutions of democracy. Alternatively, when mass politics in India is conceptualised in terms of the individual calculations of interest, its limits are seen as restricted to the family, caste and tribe. The sum of these individual calculations could obviously not sustain democratic politics. From this follows the scepticism about the character of electoral democracy in India and the unreality—and unreliability—of elections. Western audiences, like sections of India's urban elites without close links to the electoral process, sometimes find it difficult to think of Indians as skillful political actors, with goals and strategies and enough information about others, against whom they are pitted in order to manoeuvre their way through choices they have to make.

Form and Content

In democracy, the process is the product. Our findings help us question the dichotomy between the procedural and the substantive views of democracy. The crucial task for the democrat is to bring full agency to the hands of men and women, so that, they can work out their ideal world in their everyday lives. To expect more out of democracy, points in the direction of totalitarian rule.

The main assumptions of this model are drawn from rational choice. They suggest, that the peasant (like the businessman) is also an optimiser, and both respond to changes in the institutional context which underpins their daily lives. Electoral information, just like participation, are political resources. Politicians, as well as electors, are engaged in purposive action, and their choices are based on a cost-benefit calculus. The implications, arising from these assumptions, will be looked at with the help of data emerging out of the survey. It is our hope to be able to share with the students of Indian politics our field experience of the electoral process and the keen interest that Indians take in politics. In the hands of ordinary men and women, politics has become the cutting edge of social change in India. It has become the fire which Prometheus stole from the gods to give to men so that through politics, they can give themselves what their gods have not given them![16]

India has not followed any pre-ordained path. The robust, vibrant Indian democracy has produced conditions where the modern and the pre-modern terms of the political discourse have intermeshed, to produce an authentic Indian modernity. The elite agency (Mitra 2008)—countervailing forces that have transformed India's marginal social groups into veto players—and the electoral process have played key roles in making this possible. This is a more reliable explanatory path than the repetition of the modernity of tradition, or India's unique diversity, because these are explanations that can shade off into the mysterious swamp of the 'genius of Indian culture' or crass populism.

In the final analysis, the success of Indian democracy owes much to the value added character of her leaders with regard to the creation of democratic structures and processes. More generally, we learn from the South Asian comparison that the normative content of democratic political systems is specific to culture and context, but the development and decay of democracy can be measured independently of the culture and context in which these systems are ensconced. History, memory, geography and the economy offer a set of cards; it is for the expert hand to play them properly. Democracy functions best where modern political institutions provide the space for the negotiation between adversaries. It is a game that one can learn, provided, one remembers that man makes [democratic] history within conditions imposed by history.

Notes

1. In the epilogue to the new edition of *The Government and Politics of India*, Morris–Jones talks about a major change in the tone and content of Indian politics during the last two decades. The 'peaceful interpenetration of tradition and modernity', which characterised the first two decades after Independence, has given way to a political context that is much more violent. The political landscape is increasingly taken over by the local protest movements, even internal war. The loss of coherence, and internal vitality that has affected the party system which had functioned remarkably well as an intermediary between the state and society, have grave implications for the political system as a whole. 'This is the basic loss suffered by the political system in the last two decades; it is this loss which has largely removed the nationwide stabilising element, without whose management capacity to contain particularist thrusts the system continually falls apart, with a centre which does not effectively hold' (Morris–Jones 1987:266).
2. *Gherao*: (in Hindi) surrounding a decision maker and pressuring him to negotiate.
   Dharna: literally, to sprawl one's self publicly on the ground, to bring pressure to bear on a decision-maker.
   Rasta roko: stopping traffic on main roads.
   Chakka jam: to seize crossroads and thus, stop traffic.
   Jail bharo: filling up jails by protesters to bring pressure to bear on the government.

244 When Rebels Become Stakeholders

3. Thus, Sathyamurthy (1989: 3) suggests:

> At the same time, a large number of economic and sociological terms are used to describe aspects of the political process which pertain to the subterranean reaches of politics rather than strictly to the sphere of formal institutional mechanisms (e.g., *dalal, mamul* Permit–Quota–Licence-Raj in discussions of corruption; *loan melas* in discussions of partisan favours in the economic sphere; and *chacha, dada, mastaan, Aayaa Ram Gayaa Ram* and *Garibi Hatao* in discussions about the manipulations of political and economic processes). These represent only a thin cross-section of the enormous range of the concepts of differing vitality and the imports that have arisen in discussions of Indian politics.

4. For comments on the 'derivative' discourse on politics in India, see Sathyamurthy (1989: 5). Commenting on the philosophical origins of the Western scholarship on South Asia, he suggests:

> Weber's work was used as the intellectual inspiration for functionalism and positivist sociology in post-war America, mainly by such scholars as Parsons and Shils and Merton and their students. Behaviourist, positivist and functionalist approaches to the study of society went hand in hand in the generation of 'comparative' studies purporting to provide typologies of different social and political systems based on common criteria... Over the years, the two broad perspectives—Marxist and Weberian, interpenetrated to varying degrees in the approaches adopted by social science researchers, although this may have led to a certain degree of eclecticism rather than to attempts at generating a third general alternative approach (Sathyamurthy 1986: 463).

5. Though the language is extreme and rather deliberately provocative, Naipaul's (1977: 18) comments on the perils of 'endogenous' models are not without justification.

> ...[I]ndependent India, with its five-year plans, its industrialisation, its practice of democracy, has invested in change. There always was a contradiction between the archaism of national pride and the promise of the new; and the contradiction has at last cracked the civilisation open. The turbulence in India this time hasn't come from foreign invasion or conquest; it has been generated from within. India cannot respond in her old way, by a further retreat into archaism. Her borrowed institutions have worked like borrowed institutions; but archaic India can provide no substitutes for press, parliament, and courts. The crisis of India is not only political or economic. The larger crisis is of a wounded old civilisation that has at last become aware of its inadequacies and is without the intellectual means to move ahead.

6. Rostow (1960) contains the most definitive, though not exclusive, statement of this position.
7. The reference here is to the Princeton series on political development which became a paradigmatic statement of the field in the 1960s. See, in particular, Pye and Verba (1965).
8. In a purely technical sense, the Indian applications of electoral forecasts have gone beyond the predictive accuracy achieved by their original Western inventors. The reference here is to the phenomenal success of electoral forecasts on the eve of the 1989 Indian parliamentary election.
9. The deinstitutionalisation thesis enjoys wide support among some leading students of Indian politics. See, for example, Manor (1983), Kothari (1982, 1983b) offers a similar explanation in elaborating his concept of the 'criminalization of politics'.
10. The moral argument comes out rather strongly in the 'explanation' of state degeneration given by Rudolph and Rudolph (1987).
11. It does not have the requisite theoretical depth to pose the all important question of the cause of the structural discontinuity, the symptoms of which are being referred to as deinstitutionalisation. To the extent that any attempts are made in this direction, its proponents are able to offer explanations only in terms of political styles and motives of key actors. Nor is the issue of the state's ability to regenerate itself raised with any degree of seriousness (Mitra 1988: 333).
12. In her recent work, Frankel has changed her methodological stance significantly. Instead of suggesting that the momentum for change could come only from a movement from below, she suggests the interaction between the state and society as a more feasible source of radical change in India. See Frankel and Rao (1989/1990).
13. The findings of the Subaltern school, in six volumes under Guha's general editorship, are published by Oxford University Press. For critical comments on their methodology, see Sathyamurthy (1990). A seventh volume (1992) has been added.
14. Thus, Hardiman (1987) concludes his analysis by attributing a consciously antibourgeois stance to the Adivasi uprising described in his work.
15. In a personal communication, Saberwal has indicated that this search would lead to a congruence between the observer's categories with the insider's 'lived-in' terms.
16. Prometheus symbolises the revolt of man against the gods. In his hands, ingenuity and treachery were powerful weapons. He managed to deceive Zeus himself and to bring humanity (it is claimed he was its very creator) all the good things refused it by the gods. All this was not achieved, however, without a price (Comte 1991: 168).

Appendix 1

Note on Methodology*

Drawing a random sample of the Indian population is made problematic by its sheer diversity. With 846 million people spread across 26 states and six union territories, India represents a very diverse society. Apart from numerous geographical divisions, it is a multi-cultural society. People are distributed in 16 major language groups. Smaller languages and local dialects are about 1000. Thousands of castes and sub-castes, distinguishing themselves in terms of pursuit of occupations, ritual practices, life style, food habits, and so on, make the country still more complex. Though Hindus constitute a vast majority (82 per cent), India is lived by almost all major religions of the world. With 100 million, 12.1 per cent Muslims, India ranks in the top, as far as total number of Muslims living in a country is concerned. In addition to Muslims, there is a sizeable population of Christians (2.3 per cent), Sikhs (1.9 per cent), Buddhists (0.8 per cent) and others (1.3 per cent), who do not only enjoy equality but minority safeguards are also granted to them.

These are, at the best, glimpses of the social diversities the Indian democracy is coping with. But more than these social diversities, economic inequality and its resultant effects are the greater cause of concern for the system. Regional imbalances, poor means of transport and communication, lack of literacy (as high as 47.8 per cent illiterates), over one-third of its population living below the poverty line, are all on the negative side of the democratic experiment. However, belying all popular myths about conditions hindering or helping the democratic experiment, India has not only ventured to defy these notions but has also succeeded, to a great extent, to integrate and unify them all through its democratic processes.

Since answers to questions posed here can be sought through ascertaining views from a wide variety of the country's population, only a survey method was found suitable for the purpose. The 1996 Lok Sabha

---

* For detailed methodological information on earlier and subsequent surveys, see 'National Election Study, 2004; An Introduction' in *Economic & Political Weekly*, December 18, 2004, pp. 5373–83.

elections provided the occasion and the entire Indian electorate, as they existed in this election, became the universe of this study. For reasons of abnormal law and order situation, it was decided to exclude the state of Jammu and Kashmir. That is, excluding the six Lok Sabha constituencies of Jammu and Kashmir, the remaining 537 constituencies falling in 25 states and six union territories of India constituted the universe. In other words, any person who figured on the electoral roll of these 537 constituencies was a potential subject for this study.

For a population of 846 million, a sample of 4000–5000 persons, chosen randomly, might be considered an appropriate size to derive generalizations at the national level. However, the concerns of the present study, aimed at analysing the data, not only at the state levels (at least for some of the states), but also at the level of the social groups and their comparison across as well as within the groups, necessitated a larger sample. It became all the more important because any stratification at the level of social groups was not possible at all.

Thus, we decided for a larger sample and aimed at a sample size of 9,000 plus completed interviews. In order to meet this target without any substitution, we had no option but to inflate the sample size to meet the short-fall caused by non-completion. The experience of previous surveys shows that, the rate of completion in similar surveys has varied between 55 to 70 per cent in different states. Considering the proportional contribution of each state, the national average works out to about 60 per cent. Given this rate of completion, if one has to meet the given target, the sample needs to be inflated by 66.67 per cent. Thus the original sample size of 9000 was inflated to 15,015 (9,000 × 0.6667 + 9,000 = 15,015) so that a completion rate of 60 per cent could give us 9,000 completed interviews, which was our target exactly.

Sample Units and Distribution of Respondents

Individual electors being the ultimate source of our information, a method had to be evolved to identify them in a manner that would make them the representatives of the universe. Since we had decided to examine our concerns through the prism of elections, each elector had to be located and traced through following different levels of electoral boundaries, namely, state, Lok Sabha constituency (PC), Vidhan Sabha constituency (AC), polling booth (PS), individual elector, that is, respondent. Following this track, and to give adequate coverage to each state or group of states and union territories, a quota of one-fifth of the constituencies from each state was fixed to be selected. Accordingly, excluding Jammu and Kashmir, a total of 108 out of 537 Lok Sabha constituencies had to be chosen first. Since Lok Sabha constituencies are constituted by different Vidhan Sabha segments in them, it was decided to select two ACs from each PC falling in the sample. That is, 216 Vidhan Sabha constituencies (108 × 2 = 216) were selected in the second step. Similarly, two polling booths from each of the chosen ACs, which makes 432 polling booths (216 × 2 = 432), were selected in the third step. Finally, in the fourth step, a fixed number of respondents from all the selected booths, sharing equally the quota proportionately allocated to each state, was selected from the most recent electoral roll of the sampled booth (see Table A1.1).

TABLE A1.1

State-wise Distribution of Sampled Units and Respondents

State and union territories	No. of PCs	No. of sampled PCs	No. of sampled ACs	No. of sampled booths	Proportion of national electorate	No. of respondents selected
Andhra Pradesh	42	8	16	32	.084	1264
Assam	14	3	6	12	.023	345
Bihar	54	11	22	44	.102	1529
Delhi	7	1	2	4	.014	210
Goa	2	1	2	4	.002	30
Gujarat	26	5	10	20	.051	765
Haryana	10	2	4	8	.019	286
Himachal Pradesh	4	1	2	4	.007	105
Karnataka	28	6	12	24	.054	810
Kerala	20	4	8	16	.035	524
Madhya Pradesh	40	8	16	32	.075	1128
Maharashtra	48	10	20	40	.092	1380
Orissa	21	4	8	16	.038	572
Punjab	13	3	6	12	.024	360
Rajasthan	25	5	10	20	.052	780
Tamil Nadu	39	8	16	32	.073	1096
Uttar Pradesh	85	17	34	68	.167	2499
West Bengal	42	8	16	32	.077	1152
North-East:	11				.010	
i. Meghalaya		1	2	4		75
ii. Tripura		1	2	4		75
Union Territories: Pondicherry	6	1	2	4	.002	30
All India	**537**	**108**	**216**	**432**	**1.001**	**15015**

Source Calculations based on the electorate figures for 1995 available with the Election Commission.

Sampling Procedure

In order to draw a representative sample of the Indian electorate, a multi-stage, stratified, random sampling procedure has been used, wherein we decided to select 20 per cent Lok Sabha constituencies from the list of all the constituencies in a state. The number of PCs thus selected from all the states and union territories of India (excluding Jammu and Kashmir) is 108. Selection of different sample units was done in different stages:

Stage One: Selection of Lok Sabha Constituencies

1. First of all, all PCs with their electorate in a state were serialised as per the Election Commission of India's Delimitation Order of 1976;
2. Cumulative total of the electorate was assigned against each constituency in an ascending order;
3. In order to avoid the selection of the contiguous constituencies, the total electorate in the state was divided by the number of constituencies to be selected from that state. It helped to create as many geographical zones as the number of sampled constituencies in the state. The figure thus obtained represents one zone and is called hereafter as 'constant';
4. Since the intentions were to give space to zonal representation too, we decided to select one PC from each such zone.

And, finally, to select individual PCs, a random number (using a Random Number Table) was chosen from within the constant and compared with the cumulative total of the electorate, listed against each PC. In whichever cumulative total it fell, the PC listed against that, was chosen as the first sampled Lok Sabha constituency of that state. Subsequent constituencies were selected by adding the constant to the random number. That is, one addition of the constant would give a second PC, an addition of two would give the third, and so on and so forth.

While this procedure provided adequate (geographical) coverage of the state, it also ensured a proportional chance to every constituency. That is, constituencies with a larger electorate enjoyed greater chance of selection in the sample and fulfilled the requirements of the PPS (Probability Proportionate to Size) sampling procedure.

These steps and the sampling procedure were repeated in each state to select a set of 108 Lok Sabha constituencies, and then repeated twice over to obtain two more such sets. Validation tests of the representativeness were then carried out by matching the mean score of these sample sets with the national average in terms of some key variables, such as voter turnout and the vote share of different political parties in the previous elections, proportion of reserved constituencies for the Scheduled Castes (SC) and the Scheduled Tribes (ST), share of the SC and ST population and the degree of urbanisation. The set which provided the best fit was thus selected. Table A1.2 presents comparable figures for the sample (the set which was finally selected) as well as of the universe, and validates the representative character of our sample to a great extent.

TABLE A1.2
Comparable Figures for the Sample and the Universe

Characteristics	Sampled constituencies	Universe
Percent Turn-Out	57.8	55.8
Votes Polled By		
INC	36.3	36.7
BJP	20.1	20.1
JD	12.1	11.8
CPI	2.2	2.5
CPM	6.0	6.1
Share of Reserved Constituencies for:		
Scheduled Castes	16	79
Scheduled Tribes	8	41
Share of Population (per cent):		
Scheduled Castes	14.1	14.4
Scheduled Tribes	6.4	6.5

Source CSDS data unit.

Stage Two: Selection of Vidhan Sabha Constituencies

1. All ACs with their electorate were serialised for every sampled PC in a state;
2. Cumulative total of the electorate was worked out and listed against each AC in ascending order;
3. The total electorate in a PC was divided by two (in the manner already stated earlier) to obtain a constant;
4. Drawing a random number from within the constant, the first AC was selected and the constant was added in the random number to select the second AC.

Like stage one, this procedure was repeated in each sampled PC to select the given number of ACs (No. of PC × 2) in a state. Similarly, like PCs, two more such sets were drawn to choose the best fit by following the same validation tests for Vidhan Sabha elections.

These steps were repeated for each state to select a final set of 216 Vidhan Sabha constituencies. Table A1.3 presents the list of sampled Lok Sabha and Vidhan Sabha constituencies.

Table A1.3
List of Sampled Constituencies Lok Sabha and Vidhan Sabha

Parliamentary constituency		Assembly constituencies	
ANDHRA PRADESH			
5	Bhadrachalam (ST)	38	Yellavaram(ST)
		274	Bhadrachalam(ST)
11	Eluru	67	Tadepalligudem
		70	Eluru
16	Bapatla	97	Ponnur
		113	Martur
21	Chittoor	140	Chittoor
		143	Punganur
26	Kurnool	177	Yemmiganur
		180	Pattikonda
31	Secunderabad	208	Sanathnagar
		213	Asafnagar
36	Peddapalli(SC)	248	Manthani
		251	Huzurabad
42	Miryalguda	283	Tungaturthi
		286	Miryalguda
ASSAM			
4	Dhubri	25	Golakganj
		39	Jaleswar
8	Mangaldoi	56	Kamalpur
		66	Sipajhar
13	Dibrugarh	117	Lahowal
		122	Tinsukia
BIHAR			
1	Bagaha(SC)	2	Bagha(SC)
		6	Lauria
6	Maharajganj	33	Maharajganj
		37	Masrakh
11	Sitamarhi	67	Sitamarhi
		72	Pupri
16	Rosera(SC)	87	Baheri
		101	Singhia(SC)
21	Madhepura	116	Singheshwar
		122	Kishanganj
26	Rajmahal(ST)	148	Borio(ST)

(Table A1.3 continued)

(Table A1.3 continued)

Parliamentary constituency		Assembly constituencies	
		151	Pakaur
31	Khagaria	169	Gopalpur
		182	Chautham
36	Arrah	213	Paliganj
		216	Arrah
40	Aurangabad	236	Nabinagar
		239	Rafiganj
45	Kodarma	270	Barkatha
		273	Jamua(SC)
49	Ranchi	305	Khijri(ST)
		308	Kanke(SC)
DELHI			
4	East Delhi	37	Trilok Puri(SC)
		47	Rohtas Nagar
GOA			
2	Mormugao	25	Vascoda Gama
		34	Cuncolam
GUJARAT			
6	Junagadh	38	Somnath
		42	Junagadh
11	Gandhinagar	67	Sabarmati
		79	Gandhinagar
16	Kapadvanj	107	Prantij
		128	Kathlal
22	Baroda	147	Baroda City
		150	Vaghodia
26	Bulsar(ST)	178	Bulsar
		182	Umberganon(ST)
HARYANA			
3	Karnal	11	Indri
		16	Assandh(SC)
8	Bhiwani	66	Bhiwani
		72	Hansi
HIMACHAL PRADESH			
3	Mandi	59	Karsog(SC)
		67	Darang
KARNATAKA			
2	Gulbarga	11	Shahabad
		15	Jewargi
7	Chitradurga	46	Molakalmuru

(Table A1.3 continued)

(*Table A1.3 continued*)

Parliamentary constituency		Assembly constituencies	
11	Kanakapura	51	Pavagada(SC)
		89	Uttarahalli
		100	Anekal(SC)
15	Chamarajnagar(SC)	112	Bannur
		120	Chamarajnagar
20	Chikmagalur	153	Mudigere(SC)
		157	Tarikere
25	Belgaum	194	Bailhongal
		200	Gokak(ST)
KERALA			
5	Manjeri	31	Wanchoor(SC)
		35	Kondotty
9	Trichur	58	Trichur
		65	Guruvayoor
15	Alleppey	98	Sherthalai
		102	Kuttanad
20	Trivandrum	136	Trivandrum East
		140	Parassala
MADHYA PRADESH			
3	Gwalior	16	Lashkar East
		21	Bhander(SC)
8	Satna	62	Chitrakoot
		204	Vijairaghogarh
13	Raigarh(ST)	98	Jashpur(ST)
		102	Lailunga(ST)
18	Mahasamund	139	Khallari
		144	Kurud
23	Balaghat	179	Kirnapur
		183	Balaghat
29	Hoshangabad	206	Bohani
		224	Itarsi
34	Khandwa	281	Harsud(ST)
		285	Nepa Nagar
39	Jhabua(ST)	306	Jhabua(ST)
		310	Ratlam Rural
MAHARASHTRA			
3	Kolaba	14	Mangaon
		17	Panvel
9	Bombay North	43	Malad
		45	Borivali

(*Table A1.3 continued*)

(Table A1.3 continued)

Parliamentary constituency		Assembly constituencies	
11	Dahanu(ST)	60	Bhiwandi
		65	Shahapur(ST)
16	Erandal	91	Parola
		96	Pachora
21	Amravati	120	Achalpur
		125	Badnera
26	Chandrapur	154	Rajpura
		159	Bhadrawati
31	Parbhani	177	Singnapur
		183	Pathri
36	Osmanabad(SC)	208	Paranda
		221	Barshi
41	Khed	242	Khed Alandi
		244	Mulshi
46	Sangli	271	Sangli
		275	Kavathe-Mahankal
MEGHALAYA			
1	Meghalaya	6	Nongbahi Wahiajer
		24	Sohryugkham
ORISSA			
5	Kendrapara	32	Rajnagar
		40	Mahanga
10	Aska	67	Suruda
		70	Kodala
15	Phulbani(SC)	102	Balliguda(ST)
		112	Sonepur(SC)
20	Sundargarh(ST)	137	Rajgangpur(ST)
		140	Raghunathpali(ST)
PONDICHERRY			
1	Pondicherry	14	Thirubuvanai(SC)
		27	Neduncadu(SC)
PUNJAB			
4	Jullundur	30	Jullundur North
		35	Nakodar
8	Patiala	72	Ghanaur
		76	Patiala Town
13	Ferozepur	92	Fazilka
		97	Zira
RAJASTHAN			
3	Churu	18	Ratangarh

(Table A1.3 continued)

(Table A1.3 continued)

Parliamentary constituency		Assembly constituencies	
		22	Sadulpur
7	Dausa	49	Lalsot(ST)
		54	Jamwa Ramgarh
13	Tonk(SC)	46	Dudu(SC)
		93	Malpura
18	Udaipur	139	Mavli
		143	Udaipur Rural(ST)
23	Barmer	177	Barmer
		181	Jaisalmer
TAMIL NADU			
3	Madras South	12	Triplicane
		19	Alandur
7	Vellore	36	Katpadi
		48	Vellore
12	Chidambaram(SC)	66	Bhuvanagiri
		70	Mangalore(SC)
17	Tiruchengode	98	Tiruchengode
		120	Erode
22	Palani	117	Kangayam
		147	Natham
27	Tiruchirapalli	159	Lalgudi
		168	Thiruverambur
32	Pudukkottai	190	Kolathr(SC)
		193	Arantangi
37	Tenkasi(SC)	214	Vasudevanallur(SC)
		217	Alangulam
TRIPURA			
2	Tripura East(ST)	38	Hrishyamukh
		52	Chandipur
UTTAR PRADESH			
2	Garhwal	5	Pauri
		424	Dehradun
7	Moradabad	31	Kunderki
		33	Moradabad
13	Pilibhit	57	Pilibhit
		60	Puranpur
18	Misrikh(SC)	77	Sidhauli(SC)
		83	Beniganj(SC)
23	Rai Bareli	109	Rae Bareli
		112	Dalmau

(Table A1.3 continued)

(*Table A1.3 continued*)

Parliamentary constituency		Assembly constituencies	
28	Faizabad	134	Ayodhya
33	Gonda	137	Sohawal(SC)
		159	Mankapur(SC)
38	Gorakhpur	162	Katra Bazar
		185	Gorakhpur
42	Salempur	193	Shyam Deurwa
		204	Bhatpar Rani
48	Jaunpur	222	Siar
		251	Mariahu
52	Varanasi	255	Rari
		241	Varanasi Cant
57	Chail(SC)	246	Gangapur
		278	Chail(SC)
62	Jalaun(SC)	281	Khaga
		332	Kanchi(SC)
67	Kannauj	335	Madhogarh
		307	Bidhuna
72	Firozabad(SC)	310	Chhibramau
		351	Firozabad
77	Khurja(SC)	360	Kheragarh
		379	Khurja
82	Muzaffarnagar	387	Dadri
		406	Jansath(SC)
		408	Muzaffarnagar
WEST BENGAL			
5	Raiganj	30	Karandighi
		42	Harish Chandrapur
10	Berhampore	64	Beldanga
		68	Bharatpur
15	Joynagar(SC)	100	Gosaba(SC)
		105	Canning West(SC)
20	Dum Dum	134	Khardah
		138	Dum Dum
25	Uluberia	171	Uluberia South
		174	Kalyanpur
31	Contai	209	Khajuri(SC)
		213	Egra
36	Vishnupur(SC)	245	Raipur(ST)
		254	Kotulpur
41	Bolpur	281	Mangalkot
		286	Dubrajpur

Source CDA data unit.

Stage Three: Selection of Polling Booths

Two polling booths were to be selected from each of the 216 ACs in our sample. These were selected by the simple random procedure. That is, the PPS method was not followed in the selection of polling booths. However, care was taken to avoid the selection of contiguous units. To do so:

1. Total number of polling booths in an AC was divided by two to make two groups and to obtain a number (constant) that would determine the distance between the two sampled booths;
2. First PS was selected by picking a random number from the first half; and
3. The second PS was selected by adding the constant to the serial number of the first booth.

Stage Four: Selection of Respondents

As stated earlier, the number of respondents to be interviewed in each state was determined by the state's share in India's total population (excluding Jammu and Kashmir). That is, the target of 15,000 respondents was proportionately (according to the 1991 Census) distributed in each state. The number thus obtained was divided by the total number of polling booths to be selected from that state to fix a quota for each sampled booth in the state (see Table A1.1).

To Select Individual Respondents from the Sampled Booth, the Following Steps were Followed:

1. The most recent electoral roll of the sampled booth was obtained from the local election office.
2. If required, the electoral roll was serialised for any deletion, addition, and of course, inclusion of list(s) from other electoral units, in case the booth covered more than one area.
3. The total number of electors in the booth was divided by the fixed quota of interviews to obtain a constant to divide the lowest sample unit (PS) into as many sub-units as the number of respondents allocated to a booth.

4. A random number was chosen from within the constant to select the first respondent from that locality. The constant was added to the random number to select the next respondent, and this exercise was repeated till the last respondent from that booth was selected.

This procedure was repeated for all the polling booths in each state and a list of 15,015 respondents was prepared to form a national representative sample for this study.

Research Instruments

A detailed interview schedule was prepared, involving scholars with considerable experience in survey research. Questions were tested and pre-tested in different socio-political milieus and were accordingly revised. The final version of the questionnaire was prepared in English (Appendix 2) and was translated into the local languages, which again was pre-tested for accuracy and standardisation across languages.

In addition to main questionnaire, two more data collection schedules were prepared.

1. *Village/town data schedule* was prepared to collect information about the locality from which our respondents were selected. Information like the social composition and infrastructural facilities of the area were thought to be of great use in enhancing our understanding of the data; and,
2. *Summary background data schedule.* This was prepared for those respondents whose interviews were not possible for one reason or the other. The information thus generated would help us to explain some methodological questions, for example, over-reporting in turnouts and distortion in the representative character of our sample, if any.

Training of Field Staff

The success of a large survey research lies in the quality of data collection. Since such surveys are conceived and designed by one person or a group of persons and carried out by different persons in the field, the investigators and other personnel associated with the fieldwork need to be adequately trained. They need to be trained to the extent that they are able to appreciate the basic concerns of the study, its relevance, and of course, why they have to follow the method, procedure and techniques they are told to. Accordingly, workshops were organised to train the trainers first, and they were equipped with the following:

1. Objective and focus of the study.
2. Objective of each question.
3. Sampling details.
4. Canvassing the questionnaire, editing and checking the recorded responses.
5. Coding.
6. Field logistics.

Training for field supervisors and field investigators were organised at different regional centres in which a group of trainers, associated with the study, participated. While the training covered all the aspects listed, special attention was given on rapport building and skills in canvassing the interview schedule, recording of answers, using probes and coding the responses in the columns provided for them.

A detailed manual for the interviewer was prepared in advance and was extensively used during the course of in-depth training.

Finally, to carry out the survey efficiently, the country was divided into 16 operational zones and as many 'state co-ordinators', drawn from the nationwide network of senior social scientists associated with the programme, were entrusted with the responsibility of co-ordinating the field-work and data collection in their respective areas.

Appendix 2

2.1 Survey Instrument, 1996

State   PC   PS   Res.

Centre for the Study of Developing Societies, 29 Rajpur Road, Delhi 110054

National Election Study, 1996
Post-Poll Survey

Interview's Introduction

I have come from Delhi—from the Centre for the Study of Developing Societies. We are studying the Lok Sabha elections and are interviewing thousands of ordinary voters from different parts of the country. The findings of these interviews will be used to write in books and newspapers without giving any respondent's name. It has no connection with any political party or the government. I need your co-operation to ensure the success of our study. Kindly spare some time to answer my questions.

Interview Begins

1. Let us first talk about this village/town you live in. How long have you lived here? (*If not all life, probe for number of years lived here*)
    1. Less than 10 yrs.   2. 10 yrs. or more   3. Entire life

IF NOT ENTIRE LIFE

   1a. From which village/town have you come?
       Name of village/town ....
       Name of district .... State ....

   1b. Where have you lived most of your life—in village or town?
       1. Village   2. Town   3. Both   9. Inapplicable

2. In talking to people about the recent elections to the Lok Sabha, we find that some people were able to vote and some were not able to vote. How about you? Were you able to vote or not?

    2. Yes   1. No   8. Not sure

2a. *(If yes)* Who did you vote for? Please mark your preference on this slip and put in this box. *(Supply the dummy ballot and explain the procedure)*

Ballot No.

FOR ASSAM, HARYANA, KERALA, TAMIL NADU, WEST BENGAL & PONDICHERRY ONLY

2b. And what about the assembly elections—who did you vote for? Please mark your preference on this slip and put in this box. *(Supply the dummy ballot and explain the procedure)*

Ballot No.

2c. *(If voted)* When did you finally make up your mind about who to vote for?

1. On the polling day
2. A few days before polling
3. As soon as the candidates were announced
4. Before the campaign
8. Can't say
9. Not Applicable

2d. *(If not voted)* What was the main reason you could not vote in this election?

1. Did not know I was a voter
2. Out of station
3. Not well
4. Have no interest/did not feel like voting
5. Prevented by some people from voting
6. Somebody had already voted before I went to vote
7. Fear of violence at polling station
8. Any other *(Specify)* ....
9. Not Applicable *(Yes in Q. 2)*

3. Keeping in view the election results, who do you think deserved to form the Government at the Centre?

1. Congress/Congress Led
2. BJP/BJP Led
3. NF-LF/Third Front
4. Others *(Specify)* ....
5. No one
8. D.K.

4. No single party has got a clear majority in Lok Sabha in this election. There are now two opinions about the formation of government. Some say that different parties should come together to form a coalition government. Others say that elections should be held again. What would you prefer—coalition government or fresh elections?

   1. Coalition Government   2. Fresh elections
   3. Others (*Specify*) ....   8. Can't say/D.K

5. In today's situation, who do you think can make the best Prime Minister of the country?

   1. P.V. Narasimha Rao   2. L.K. Advani
   3. Atal Bihari Vajpayee   4. V.P. Singh
   8. H.D. Deva Gowda   9. Can't say/D.K.
   13. Others (*Specify*) ....

6. Who won from this Parliamentary Constituency in this election?

   2. Correct   1. Incorrect/D.K.

7. Now let us talk about the campaign during this election: How interested were you in the election campaign this year—great deal, somewhat or not at all?

   3. Great deal   2. Somewhat   1. Not at all

8. How many of the election meetings that parties and candidates organised during the campaign did you attend?

   0. None   1. Some (one-two)   2. Many (more than two)

9. During the election people do various things like organizing election meetings, joining processions, participating in canvassing, contributing money, etc. to help a party or candidate. Did you do any such thing yourself during the recent election campaign?

   2. Yes   1. No

9a. (*If yes*) For which party or candidate? ....
9b. (*If yes in Q. 9*) And, what did you do (Multiple response possible)

   1. Helped organize election meetings   8. Distributed publicity material
   2. Joined processions   16. Contributed money
   4. Participated in canvassing   32. Other (*Specify*) ....

10. Did any candidate, party work or canvasser come to your house during the campaign to ask for your votes?

   2. Yes   1. No

10a. (*If yes*) From which parties or candidates did they come? (*Record first three in the order mentioned*)
   1. .... (Probe for 2nd, 3rd Party)
   2. ....
   3. ....

11. In deciding whom to vote, were you guided by any one?
      2. Yes   1. No

   11a. (*If yes*) Whose advice did you value most?
      1. Spouse   4. Friends/co-workers
      2. Other family members   7. Other (Specify)............
      3. Caste/community leaders 9. Inapplicable
                                     (No in Q. 11)

12. Now let us talk about relationship among the people in your village/town/city. Would you say that compared to five years ago, the relationship between various groups of people has become more harmonious, remained the same or tension among these groups has increased?
   1. More harmonious   2. Same as before
   3. Tension has increased   8. D.K.

   12a. (*If tension*) In your view, who among the following is best suited to resolve these tensions among various groups:
      1. Village Panchayat;   5. Caste/community
                                     leaders; or
      2. Government officials;   7. Any others (*Specify*)........
      3. Police;   8. D.K.
      4. Judiciary;   9. N.A.

13. Now I would like to read some statements about the relationship between different groups. Please tell me about each one whether you agree or disagree with it.

Statements	Agree	D.K./No opinion	Disagree
a. Relationship between different caste has become more harmonious *Do you agree to this or disagree?*	3	2	1
b. Tension between tribal and non-tribals has increased. *Do you......?*	3	2	1

c. Tension between different religious communities has decreased. *Do you........?*   3   2   1

d. Tension between dalit and non-dalits (Harijan and non-Harijans) has increased. *Do you ....?*   3   2   1

e. Tension between landowners and landless has decreased. *Do you ....?*   3   2   1

f. Relationship between people and the government officials has become more cordial. *Do you.......?*   3   2   1

g. Now there is more tension between the rich and the poor. *Do you ......?*   3   2   1

h. Police attitude towards common people has become more humane. *Do you ....?*   3   2   1

i. Compared to five years ago, life and property are less safe now than before. *Do you ....?*   3   2   1

j. The poor and deprived enjoy better social status now than before. *Do you ....?*   3   2   1

k. Condition of the poor has improved during last five years. *Do you ....?*   3   2   1

14. People hold different opinions about struggle. Some people say that struggle, even when it leads to violence, is a proper method for the people to fulfil their demands, while others say that struggle is not a proper method if it leads to violence. How do you feel—is struggle leading to violence proper or not a proper method for fulfilling people's demands?

    3. Proper   1. Not proper
    2. Other (*Specify*)................   8. D.K.

15. Generally speaking did most members of your caste group/community vote for one party or for different parties?

    2. Different parties   1. One party   8. D.K.

16. Do you think it is important or not important for you to vote the same way your caste group/community votes?

    2. Important   1. Not important   8. D.K.

17. Some political parties specially care for the interest of particular caste group or community, while others don't. How about your caste group/community? Is there any political party that looks after the interest of your caste group/community?

    2. Yes   1. No   8. D.K.

    17a. (*If yes*) Which party? ....

18. Now let us talk about the problems facing this country. What in your opinion are some of the major problems facing our country? (*Record exactly and in the order mentioned*)

    * 1...(Probe for 2nd & 3rd)
    * 2...
    * 3...

19. Which political party do you think can solve these problems better than others?
    ....

20. Leaving aside the period of elections, how much interest would you say you have in politics and public affairs, a great deal of interest, some interest, or no interest at all?

    3. Great deal   2. Some interest   1. No interest at all

21. How much in your opinion do political parties help to make government pay attention to the people—good deal, somewhat or not much?

    3. Good deal   2. Somewhat   1. Not much   8. D.K.

22. Is there any political party you feel close to?

    2. Yes   1. No

    22a. (*If yes*) Which is that party?...
    22b. (*If yes*) What are the things about (Name the party) which you like most? (*Record Exactly*)

    * ....

23. Is there any political party for which you will never vote?

    2. Yes   1. No

    23a. (*If yes*) Which is that party?..................................

    *23b. (*If yes*) What is it that you do not like about (Name the Party)?

    (*Record Exactly*)..

24. Now I would like to ask you about the things that were done by Narasimha Rao's government in Delhi during the last 5 years, that you may have liked or disliked. Was there any thing that Rao's Government did during the last 5 years that you particularly liked?

    2. Yes   1. No   8. Does not know about any work done by the government

    * 24a. (*If yes*) What was it? 1st..
    2nd..

    24b. Was there any thing in particular that you did not like?

    2. Yes   1. No   8. Does not know about any work done by the government

    * 24c. (*If yes*) What was it? 1st..
    2nd..

25. Do you think your vote has effect on how things are run in this country or you think your vote makes no difference?

    3. Has effect
    2. Others (Specify)..
    1. Makes no difference
    8. D.K.

26. Talking about the elections just completed what do you think was the main issue around which the election was fought this time (*Record exact answer*)

    * 1.. (Probe for 2nd & 3rd issue)
    * 2..
    * 3..

27. Suppose there were no parties or assemblies and elections were not held—do you think that the government in this country can be run better?

    2. Yes   1. No   8. Can't say/D.K.

28. I would like to read some statements we often hear. Would you tell me about each one whether you agree or disagree with it?

Statements	Agree	D.K./No opinion	Disagree
a. What this country needs more that all the laws and talk is a few determined and strong leaders *Do you agree to this or disagree?*	3	2	1
b. It is not desirable to have political parties struggling with each other for power. *Do you ....?*	3	2	1
c. Government policies are not responsible for the poverty of the people. *Do you....?*	3	2	1
d. Only educated people should have right to vote. *Do you......?*	3	2	1
e. Those who are not well educated should not be allowed to contest elections. *Do you.......?*	3	2	1
f. What people get in this life is the result of their KARMA in previous life. *Do you.....?*	3	2	1
g. Government generally takes care of the interests of the common people. *Do you...?*	3	2	1
h. Women should take active part in politics. *Do you.....?*	3	2	1
i. We should be loyal to our own region first and then to India. *Do you.....?*	3	2	1
j. Compared to national parties regional/local parties can provide better government in states. *Do you.....?*	3	2	1
k. It is the responsibility of the government to protect the interests of the minority communities. *Do you......?*	3	2	1

29. Have you heard of the disputed building (Babri Masjid) at Ayodhya?

    2. Yes   1. No

29a. (*If yes*) Some people say that the demolition was justified while others say it was not justified—what would you say—was it justified or not justified?

    3. Justified   2. Can't say/D.K.
    1. Unjustified   9. Inapplicable

29b. (*If heard about demolition*) What would you suggest should be built on that site now:

1. Neither mosque nor temple
2. Mosque should be built
3. Temple should be built
4. Both mosque and temple should be
5. Any other (*Specify*)..

30. Would you say that persons we elect by voting generally care about what people like you think, or that they don't care?

    2. Care   1. Don't care   8. D.K.

31. How much does having elections from time to time make the government pay attention to the people—good deal, somewhat or not much?

    3. Good deal   2. Somewhat
    1. Not much   8. D.K.

32. Peoples' opinions are divided on the issue of Kashmir problem—some people say that the government should suppress the agitation by any means while others say that this problem should be resolved by negotiation. What would you say—should the agitation be suppressed or resolved by negotiation?

    3. Should be suppressed   2. Cannot say
    1. Resolved through negotiation   7. Other (*Specify*)...............

33. During the last five years the central government has made many changes in our economy. Have you heard about them?

    2. Yes   1. No

33a. (*If yes*) What are these changes?
    * 1..
    2..

33b. (*If yes in Q.33*) On the whole do you approve or disapprove of these changes?

    2. Approve   1. Disapprove
    8. D.K.   9. Inapplicable

34. Let us now talk about some specific issues on which different people seem to have different opinions. I would read out some statements to which you may agree or disagree. Please tell me about each one whether you agree or disagree?

Statements	Agree	D.K./No opinion	Disagree
a. Backward caste should have reservation in government jobs. *Do you agree or disagree with this?*	3	2	1
b. There is no need for India to make atomic bomb. *Do you........?*	3	2	1
c. Foreign companies should not be allowed free trade in India. *Do you......?*	3	2	1
d. Like Gram Panchayats, there should be reservation for women in Assemblies and Parliament. *Do you.....?*	3	2	1
e. Government companies should be given into private hands. *Do you....?*	3	2	1
f. India should make more efforts to develop friendly relations with Pakistan. *Do you.....?*	3	2	1
g. The needs and problems of Muslims have been neglected in India. *Do you......?*	3	2	1
h. Every community should be allowed to have its own laws to govern marriage and property rights. *Do you......?*	3	2	1
i. Prohibition should be imposed all over the country. *Do you.....?*	3	2	1

35. Some people say that the government should pass legislation so that people are not allowed to own and possess a large amount of land and property. Others say that people should be allowed to own as much land and property as they can make/acquire. What would you say?

    3. Limit ownership   2. Other (*Specify*)....................
                                       1. Should not limit ownership

36. Some people say that whatever progress was the last few years through development, schemes and programmes of the government has benefited only the well-to-do. Others say no, the poor and needy have also benefited from them. What would you say? Have the benefits of development gone only to the well-to-do or have the poor and the needy also benefited.

  1. Benefits gone to well-to-do
  3. Poor and needy also benefited (If all, do not probe encircle 3)
  8. D.K.
  2. Other (*Specify*)..

37. People are generally concerned about what governments do—some are more concerned about what the government in Delhi does, others are more concerned with what the state government does. How about you? Are you more concerned about what the government in Delhi does or about what the (name the State government) does?

    1. Interested in neither   2. State Government   3. Both
    4. Government in Delhi   7. Other (*Specify*).........................

38. Government has initiated several schemes and programmes for the benefit of the people, such as housing schemes, employment schemes, old-age pension, loans/subsidies, etc. Have you or your family ever availed of such benefits?

        2. Yes   1. No   8. D.K.

  38a. (*If yes*) What type of benefits?

       1. Housing scheme
       2. Rojgar yojna
       4. Land allotment   (Multiple answers possible)
       8. Old-age pension
     16. Loan/subsidies
     32. Other (*Specify*)...

39. Thinking about the last ten years, would you say that the law and order situation in your area has improved, deteriorated or remained the same?

    3. Improved   2. Remained the same
    1. Deteriorated   8. D.K.

    39a. (*If deteriorated*) Why has it deteriorated?
         *...

40. I would like to seek your opinion about different institutions of India in which you may have good deal of trust, some trust or no trust at all.

Institutions	Great deal	Somewhat	Not at all
a. How much trust/confidence do you have in the central government–a great deal, somewhat or no trust at all?	3	2	1
b. How much trust/confidence do you have in the state government......?	3	2	1
c. How much trust do you have in local government/panchayat/municipality.....?	3	2	1
d. How much trust do you have in Judiciary......?	3	2	1
e. How much trust do you have in Election Commission......?	3	2	1
f. How much trust do you have in political parties......?	3	2	1
g. How much trust do you have in government officials......?	3	2	1
h. How much trust do you have in elected representative.......?	3	2	1
i. How much trust do you have in police.....?	3	2	1

41. Are you a member of any political party?

        2. Yes   1. No

    41a. (*If yes*) Which party?..

41b. *(If no)* Were you ever a member of any political party?

    2. Yes   1. No

41c. *(If yes)* Which party?...

42. Let us talk about associations and organisations other than political parties: are you a member of any religious or caste organisation?

    2. Yes   1. No

* 42a. *(If yes)* What are these 1..
*   2..

43. Aside from caste and religious organisation, do you belong to any other associations and organisations like the co-operatives, farmers' association, trade unions, welfare organisations, cultural and sports organisations, etc. *(Give two-three relevant examples of the locality)*

    2. Yes   1. No

* 43a. *(If yes)* What are these   1..
*   2..
        (Probe: Any other)...

44. There is quite a bit of talk these days about different social classes. Some people say they belong to the middle class, others say they belong to the working class, yet others say they do not belong to either of these classes but to some other class? Now thinking of people like you, to which class would you say you belong?

    1. Middle class   2. Working class   7. Other *(Specify)*.............

    44a. Do you think that the people of some other classes come in the way of progress and welfare of the people of your class, or do you think this is not the case?

        1. Come in way   2. Do not come in way

    44b. *(If come in way)* People of which class? *(Record exactly)*
        *...
        ....

45. During the last few years, has your financial situation improved, worsened, or has it stayed the same?

    3. Improved   2. Same   1. Worsened

46. In whatever financial condition you are placed today, on the whole, are you satisfied with your present financial situations somewhat satisfied?

    3. Satisfied   2. Somewhat satisfied   1. Not satisfied

47. Now looking ahead and thinking about the next few years, do you expect that your financial situation will stay about the way it is now, get better, or get worse?

    3. Better 2. Same 1. Worse

48. Looking to your needs and the needs of your household, how much income per month do you think you must have to meet your needs? (*Record exact answer*)

49. Do you think your children have better opportunities in life than you had?

    2. Yes 1. No 8. D.K.

50. Have you ever contacted any government official for any need or problem?

    2. Yes 1. No

51. Have you ever contacted any political leader for any need or problem?

    2. Yes 1. No

52. Do you personally know any party leaders or any of the candidates in this constituency?

    2. Yes 1. No

53. Who was your previous M.P. from this constituency?

    2. Correct 1. Incorrect/D.K.

54. Who is the Prime Minister of our country?

    2. Correct 1. Incorrect

55. And who is the Chief Minister of your State?

    2. Correct 1. Incorrect

56. Do you read newspaper?

    2. Yes 1. No

    56a. (*If yes*) How often—regularly, sometimes or rarely?

    3. Regularly 2. Sometimes
    1. Rarely 9. Inapplicable

57. Do you listen to Radio?

    2. Yes 1. No

    57a. (*If yes*) How often—regularly, sometimes or rarely?
    3. Regularly 2. Sometimes
    1. Rarely 9. Inapplicable

58. Do you watch T.V.?
 2. Yes 1. No
 58a. (If yes) How often—regularly, sometimes or rarely?
 3. Regularly 2. Sometimes
 1. Rarely 9. Inapplicable

59. Of those, on which source did you depend most for getting information about elections, parties and candidates?
 0 None 4. Newspaper and Radio
 1. Newspaper 5. Newspaper and T.V.
 2. Radio 6. Radio and T.V.
 3. T.V. 7. All three (Newspaper, Radio and T.V.)

60. This time the newspapers and magazines carried several surveys and forecasts about who will win the elections. Did you read it or hear about it?
 1. Read 2. Heard
 3. Neither read nor heard 8. D.K.

 60a. (If read or heard) Do you think your voting decision was influenced by it?
 2. Yes 1. No 8. D.K. 9. Inapplicable

 * 60b. (If yes) In what way?..

Background Data

1. Age (in completed years)..
2. Sex: 1. Male 2. Female
3. Marital Status: 1. Unmarried 2. Married 1. Divorced, etc.
4. Level of Education: Write appropriate category in relevant columns
 Level Respondent Spouse Father Mother
 1. Illiterate
 2. Literate—no formal education
 3. Primary
 4. Middle School
 5. High School
 6. College-no degree

7. College-degree
8. Post graduate/Professional
9. N.A.
5. What is/has been your main Occupation?..................................
6. What is/has been the main occupation of your husband/wife?......
   ....
7. What is/has been the main occupation of your father?...............
   ....
8. What is/has been the main occupation of your mother?...............
   ....
9. Total land owned by the respondent and his/her family:
   Total land...................Acres Irrigated land........................Acres
   (*Coding format xx.x*)
10. Do you or your family own any non-agricultural land for housing, etc.?
    2. Yes   1. No
11. Religion: 1. Hindu   2. Muslim   3 Christian   4. Sikh
               5. Buddhist 6. Jain   7. Parsi
               8. Other (*Specify*)..
12. Caste/Tribe:....................(*Write exact caste irrespective of religion*)
    12a. Also ascertain the caste group:
           1. SC   2. ST   3. OBC   4. Others
13. Do you or your family own the followings:
    a. House/Flat   2. Yes   1. No
    b. Car/Jeep/Tractor   2. Yes   1. No
    c. Pumping set/Tube well 2. Yes   1. No
    d. Scooter/Motor Cycle 2. Yes   1. No
    e. Bicycle   2. Yes   1. No
    f. Television   2. Yes   1. No
    g. Radio/Transistor   2. Yes   1. No
    h. Bullock-cart   2. Yes   1. No
    i. Buffalo/Cow   No. ....
    j. Bullocks   No. ....
    k. Goat/Sheep   No. ....
14. Source of drinking water: (Multiple source expected)
    1. Tap water   2. Handpump   4. Well   8. River/tank
    16. Other (*Specify*)..

15. Type of residential accommodation:
    1. Pucca
    2. Pucca–Kutcha mixed
    3. Kutcha
    4. Hut (Thatched house)
16. Ascertain sanitary condition of the living surrounding:
    1. Clean
    2. Average
    3. Unclean
    4. Very Unclean
17. Locality: 1. Rural   2. Urban

Not to be Asked

Date of interview....................Time of interview................Time taken

Place of Interview: 1. R's home   2. R's place of work
                      3. Public place   7. Other (*Specify*)..................

Was any one else present at the time of interview?

1. No one present (or only children under 14 present)
2. Others present but they took no part
3. Other took part

Was the respondent co-operative?

1. Very co-operative
2. Co-operative but did not seem actively interested
3. Unco-operative

Address

Name of Respondent ....S.No. on Electoral Roll.............
House No. & Street..
R's Village/Town..
District...State...........................
PC Name................................AC Name......................................
PS Name................................Official No....................................
Interviewer's Name...Signature.................
Checked by: Supervisor's Name...........................Signature...............

2.2 Survey Instrument, 2004

Centre for the Study of Developing Societies 29, Rajpur Road, Delhi 110054

National Election Study, 2004
Post-Poll Survey

Interviewer's Introduction

I have come from Delhi—from an educational institution called the Centre for the Study of Developing Societies (give your university's reference). We are studying the Lok Sabha elections and are interviewing thousands of voters from different parts of the country. The findings of these interviews will be used to write in books and newspapers without giving any respondent's name. It has no connection with any political party or the government. I need your co-operation to ensure the success of our study. Kindly spare some time to answer my questions.

Interview Begins

1. In the recently held Lok Sabha elections, throughout the country people voted by pressing a button on the Electronic Voting Machine (EVM). In your opinion, is the method of voting by pressing the button on the machine better or is the method of stamping the ballot paper better?
   1. Method of machine
   2. Method of ballot paper
   3. Voted for the first time, hence can't say
   4. No difference
   8. Don't Know (D.K.)

2. While talking to people about the recent elections to the Lok Sabha, we find that some people were not able to vote. How about you? Were you able to vote or not?
   1. Not able to vote (*Go to 2d*)
   2. Able to vote
   8. D.K.

2a. *(If yes)* Whom did you vote for? Please mark your vote on this slip and put it in this box. *(Supply white dummy ballot and explain the procedure)* ....

FOR ANDHRA PRADESH, KARNATAKA, ORISSA & SIKKIM ONLY

2b. And what about the assembly elections-who did you vote for? Please mark your vote on this slip and put it in this box. *(Supply pink dummy ballot and explain the procedure)* ....

2c. *(If voted)* When did you finally make up your mind about who to vote for—on the day of voting, a day or two before voting, during the campaign or even before the campaign started?

    1. On the day of voting   2. A day or two before voting
    3. During the campaign   4. Before the campaign started
    8. D.K.   9. Not Applicable (N.A.)

2d. *(If not voted)* What was the main reason due to which you could not vote in this election?

    1. Out of station
    2. Not well
    3. No interest/ did not feel like voting
    4. Prevented /Fear of violence
    5. No identity card/ identity proof
    7. Others *(Specify)* ....
    8. D.K.
    9. N.A.

3. *(If voted)* Did the election officers correctly put the mark on your finger? *(Please observe the marking and record)*

    1. Mark not found   2. Mark found   8. Could not check

4. After this election who would you prefer as the next Prime Minister of India? *(Do not offer any name & record exact answer)* .... *(Consult code book for coding)*

5. Now I would like to ask you about the 1999 Lok Sabha elections held five years ago. Were you able to vote? *(Distinguish from the recently held Vidhan Sabha elections)*

    1. No   2. Yes   8. Don't Remember

5a. *(If Yes)* Who did you vote for? *(Supply yellow dummy ballot and explain the procedure)* ....

6. Now let us talk about the election campaign during this election. How interested were you in the election campaign this year—a great deal, somewhat or not at all.

   1. Not at all   2. Somewhat   3. Great deal   8. D.K.

7. During the elections people participated in various activities. In the recent elections, out of the activities stated below, in which did you participate?

	No	Yes
a. Attended election meetings?	1	2
b. Participated in processions/rallies?	1	2
c. Participated in door to door canvassing?	1	2
d. Contributed or collected money?	1	2
e. Distributed election leaflets or put up posters?	1	2

8. Did any candidate, party worker or canvasser come to your house during the campaign to ask for your vote?

   1. No   2. Yes   8. D.K.

9. In deciding whom to vote for, whose opinion mattered to you most?

   1. Spouse
   2. Other family members
   3. Caste/community leaders
   4. Friends/neighbours
   5. Co-workers/colleagues
   6. No one, I voted on my own
   7. Others (*Specify*) ....
   8. D.K.

10. While voting, what is the most important consideration for you, the candidate, your caste community's interest or something else?

    1. Candidate   2. Party   3. Caste/Community
    4. Something else   8. D.K.

11. For you, in this election which were the biggest/most important issues? (*Record exactly in the order mentioned and probe for 2nd & 3rd response*)   (DO NOT CODE)

    1. ....
    2. ....
    3. ....

12. What is your opinion about the performance of the NDA Government during the last five years? Are you fully satisfied, somewhat satisfied, somewhat dissatisfied or fully dissatisfied?

    4. Fully satisfied   3. Somewhat satisfied
    2. Somewhat dissatisfied 1. Fully dissatisfied   8. D.K.

13. Now I will ask you to make a comparison between the Congress and the BJP. Tell me, on these issues which of these two is better?

	Congress	BJP	No Difference	No Opinion
a. For curbing corruption which party is better?	1	2	3	8
b. For good governance/administration ...	1	2	3	8
c. For good leaders which party is better?	1	2	3	8
d. For eradicating terrorism ...	1	2	3	8

14. Leaving aside the period of elections, how much interest would you say you have in politics and public affairs—a great deal of interest, some interest or no interest at all?

    1. No interest   2. Some interest   3. Great deal   8. D.K.

15. Is there any political party which you particularly like?

    1. No (*Go to Q16*)   2. Yes   8. D.K.

    15a. (*If Yes*) Which party? (*Record exact answer*) ....

16. Is there any political party which you particularly dislike?

    1. No (*Go to Q17*)   2. Yes   8. D.K.

    16a. (*If Yes*) Which party? (*Record exact answer*) ....

17. Are you a member of any political party?

    1. No (*Go to Q18*)   2. Yes   8. D.K.

    17a. (*If Yes*) Which party? (*Record exact answer*) ....

18. Other than political parties, are you a member of any religious/caste organisation or association?

    1. No   2. Yes   8. D.K.

19. Aside from caste and religious organisations, do you belong to any other associations and organisations like co-operatives, farmers' association, trade unions, welfare organisations, cultural and sports organisations, etc. (*Give two/three relevant examples in the locality*)

    1. No   2. Yes   8. D.K.

20. Now I will talk about the changes that have taken place in the country during the last five years. You tell me, in the last five years have the conditions regarding these issues improved or deteriorated?

	Improved	Same as before	Deteriorated	No Opinion
a. Curbing corruption	3	2	1	8
b. Security of the country/ National security	3	2	1	8
c. Employment opportunities.	3	2	1	8
d. India's image in the world.	3	2	1	8
e. Hindu-Muslim brotherhood	3	2	1	8
f. Development of the country	3	2	1	8

21. Do you think your vote has effect on how things are run in this country or you think your vote makes no difference?

    1. Has no effect   2. Has effect   8. D.K.

22. People's opinions are divided on the issue of the Kashmir problem, some people say that the government should suppress the agitation by any means while others say that this problem should be resolved through mutual dialogue. What would you say, should the agitiation be suppressed or resolved through negotiation?

    1. Should be suppressed
    2. Resolved through negotiation
    3. I have not heard of the Kashmir problem
    7. Other (*Specify*) ....
    8. D.K.

23. People have different opinions about democracy. Some people believe that democracy is better than any form of government. Others believe that dictatorship is better than democracy in certain conditions. And, others believe that it makes no real difference between a democratic or any other form of government. What is your opinion about it?

    1. Democracy is better   2. Dictatorship is better
    3. Makes no difference   8. D.K.

282 When Rebels Become Stakeholders

24. Now I will read out a few options. Tell me, to what extent do you agree with these options—fully agree, somewhat agree somewhat disagree or fully disagree?

	Agree Fully (4)	Agree Somewhat (3)	Disagree Somewhat (2)	Disagree Fully (1)	No Opinion (8)
a. We should be loyal to our own region first and then to the country.	4	3	2	1	8
b. One should vote in the same way ones caste/community votes.	4	3	2	1	8
c. Compared to national parties, regional/local parties can provide better government in states.	4	3	2	1	8
d. On the site of *Babri Masjid*, only Ram temple should be built.	4	3	2	1	8
e. Making of the atomic bomb has not benefitted the country.	4	3	2	1	8
f. The needs and problems of Muslims have been neglected in India.	4	3	2	1	8
g. Large states should be divided up and smaller states should be created.	4	3	2	1	8
h. Protecting the interests of the minorities is the responsibility of the government.	4	3	2	1	8
i. Country should increase spending on the army even if it increases the burden on ordinary people.	4	3	2	1	8
j. Those who are not well educated should not be allowed to contest elections.	4	3	2	1	8
k. War is the only solution to Indo-Pakistan problem.	4	3	2	1	8

25. While voting some people give more importance to the work done by the state government while others give more importance to the work done by the central government. While voting in this election, what mattered to you the most?
    1. Central Government in Delhi   2. State Government
    3. Both   4. Interested in neither
    7. Others (*Specify*) ....   8. D.K.

26. Now I would like to know your opinion about a coalition government. Some people believe that there is no harm in a coalition government. Others believe that in special circumstances there is no alternative to it. While, for others, a coalition government is not good in any case circumstances. What is your opinion in this regard?
    1. Nothing wrong in it   2. No alternative to coalition
    3. No coalition government in any circumstances   8. D.K.

27. Suppose there were no parties or assemblies and elections were not held—do you think that the government in this country can be run better?
    1. No   2. Yes   8. D.K.

28. There is quite a bit of talk these days about different social classes. Some people say they belong to the middle class, others say they belong to the working class, yet others say they do not belong to either of these classes but to some other class? Now thinking of people like you, to which class would you say you belong?
    1. Middle class   2. Working class
    7. Other(*Specify*) ....

29. People have different opinions about the NDA Government. Some people believe that the economic policies of this Government have brought prosperity to the whole country, whereas some believe that only the rich have benefited and others believe that no one has benefited. What is your opinion—the whole country has become prosperous, only the rich have benefited or no one has benefited?
    1. Prosperity has come   2. Only rich have benefited
    3. No one has benefited   8. D.K.

30. Now I will read out a few statements regarding the economic policy of the country. You tell me, do you fully agree, somewhat agree, somewhat disagree or fully disagree with these statements?

	Agree Fully (4)	Agree Somewhat (3)	Disagree Somewhat (2)	Disagree Fully (1)	No Opinion (8)
a. There should be a ban on possessing land and property above a limit.	4	3	2	1	8
b. The number of government employees should be reduced as paying their salaries is costly for the country.	4	3	2	1	8
c. The government factories and businesses should be sold/handed over to private companies.	4	3	2	1	8
d. Foreign companies should not be allowed free trade in India.	4	3	2	1	8
e. People themselves are responsible for their poverty not the government.	4	3	2	1	8
f. Government hospitals should offer better treatment even if it means charging high/costly fees.	4	3	2	1	8

31. During the past five years, has your financial situation improved, worsened, or has it remained the same?

1. Worsened   2. Same   3. Improved   8. D.K.

Appendix 2

32. In whatever financial condition you are placed today, on the whole, are you fully satisfied, somewhat satisfied, somewhat dissatisfied or fully dissatisfied?
    4. Fully satisfied
    3. Somewhat satisfied
    2. Somewhat dissatisfied
    1. Fully dissatisfied
    8. D.K.

33. Now looking ahead and thinking about the next few years, do you expect that your financial condition will improve, deteriorate or remain the same?
    1. Worsened
    2. Remain the same
    3. Improve
    8. D.K.

34. Now I will ask you about a few religious activities. You tell me how often do you practice them—daily, weekly, only on festivals or never?

	Daily	Weekly	On festivals	Never
a. Prayer (*puja, namaz,* etc)	4	3	2	1
b. Visiting temple, mosque, church, *gurudwara,* etc.	4	3	2	1

34a. And what about these, how often do you practice them—frequently, occasionally, rarely or never?

	Frequently	Occasionally	Rarely	Never
a. Participating in *kathas, sangats bhajan-kirtans, jalsas,* church services etc.	4	3	2	1
b. Giving donations for religious activities.	4	3	2	1
c. Keeping fasts, *rozas,* etc.	4	3	2	1

35. Considering all the things I mentioned, tell me, during the past ten years has your or your family's engagement in religious activities increased, decreased or is same as before?
    1. Decreased
    2. Same as before
    3. Increased
    8. D.K.

286 When Rebels Become Stakeholders

36. Now I will talk about some issues/opinions. Tell me, to what extent do you agree with these statements—fully agree, somewhat agree somewhat disagree or fully disagree with these statements?

	Agree Fully (4)	Agree Somewhat (3)	Disagree Somewhat (2)	Disagree Fully (1)	No Opinion (8)
a. Every community should be allowed to have it's own laws to govern marriage and property rights.	4	3	2	1	8
b. Marriage of boys and girls from different religions should be banned.	4	3	2	1	8
c. Seats should be reserved for women in Lok Sabha and Vidhan Sabha.	4	3	2	1	8
d. There should not be caste-based reservations in jobs.	4	3	2	1	8
e. Higher education is not good for women.	4	3	2	1	8
f. In a democracy, it is appropriate that the opinions of the majority community should prevail.	4	3	2	1	8
g. Like men, women also have the right to work.	4	3	2	1	8
h. There should be a legal ban on religious conversions.	4	3	2	1	8
i. Marriage of boys and girls from different castes should be banned.	4	3	2	1	8
j. Doing politics is not meant for women.	4	3	2	1	8

37. Have you heard the name of Sonia Gandhi?

    1. No   2. Yes   8. D.K.

37a. Lets assume that in this election, Sonia Gandhi was not the leader of the Congress. Whichever party you voted for, instead of that party, would you have voted for some other party or this would have made no diference on your decision?

    1. No effect   2. Would have effected
    8. D.K.   9. N.A.

37b. What would have been the change in your voting decision?

    1. BJP to Congress   2. Other party to Congress
    3. Congress to BJP   4. Congress to other party
    8. D.K.   9. N.A.

38. Have you heard the name of Atal Behari Vajpayee?

    1. No   2. Yes   8. D.K.

38a. Lets assume that in this election, Atal Behari Vajpayee was not the leader of the NDA. Whichever party you voted for, instead of that party, would you have voted for some other party or this would have made no diference on your decision?

    1. No effect   2. Would have effected
    8. D.K.   9. N.A.

38b. What would have been the change in your voting decision?

    1. Congress to BJP   2. Other party to BJP
    3. BJP to Congress   4. BJP to other party
    8. D.K.   9. N.A.

39. About two years ago, a train was burned near Godhra station in Gujarat and many people were burnt to death. Have you heard about it?

    1. No   2. Yes   8. D.K.

39a. (*If yes*) Mostly who were killed in the Godhra incident—Hindus or Muslims?

    1. Hindus   2. Muslims
    3. Both   8. D.K.

40. After the Godhra incident, riots took place in many areas of Gujarat in which many people were killed. Have you heard about it?

   1. No   2. Yes   8. D.K.

   40a. *(If yes)* Mostly who were killed in the riots—Hindus or Muslims?

   1. Hindus   2. Muslims
   3. Both   8. D.K.

41. Who do you think was primarily responsible for the riots in Gujarat—the Government, Muslim extremists, Hindu extremists or someone else?

   1. The Government   2. Muslim extremists
   3. Hindu extremists   7. Others *(Specify)* ....
   8. D.K.

42. Thinking of the way elections are conducted in India, what do you feel—are elections fair, somewhat fair or unfair?

   1. Not at all fair   2. Somewhat fair
   3. Fair   8. D.K.

43. Now compare the recently held election in your area with elections held in the past. Do you think in this election things like rigging, fraud and other malpractices have increased, decreased or remained the same?

   1. Increased   2. Same as before
   3. Decreased   4. Malpractices never take place
   8. D.K.

44. Do you read newspapers?

   1. No *(Go to Q46)*   2. Yes

   44a. *(If yes)* How often do you read the newspaper—daily, often, once in a while?

   1. Daily   2. Often
   3. Once in a while   9. N.A.

45. Which newspapers do you read? *(Record name of the newspaper)*

   1. ....   2. ....

46. Do you listen to Radio?

   1. No *(Go to Q47)*   2. Yes

46a. (*If yes*) How often do you listen to news on the radio—daily, often, once in a while?

    1. Daily   2. Often   3 Once in a while
    4. Never   9. N.A.

47. Do you watch television?

    1. No (*Go to Q48*)   2. Yes

47a. (*If yes*) How frequently do you watch news on T.V.—daily, often, once in a while?

    1. Daily   2. Often   3. Once in a while
    4. Never   9. N.A.

47b. Which channels do you watch for news?

    1. ....   2. ....
    3. ....

48. Which source did you trust most for election related news—Newspaper, T.V. or radio? (*Ask for only one response*)

    1. None   2. T.V.
    3. Newspaper   4. Radio

49. During the recent India-Pakistan cricket series how many matches did you watch on television or listened to the commentry on the radio—almost all, most of the matches, only a few matches or none?

    1. Almost all   2. Mostly   3. Few
    4. None   8. D.K.

50. Do you think that the Vajpayee led NDA government should get another chance?

    1. No   2. Yes   8. D.K.

51. Who do you think is most likely to win from your parliamentary constituency? (*Record exact party or candidate and consult the party code*) ....

Background Data

Personal Data

1. Now let us talk about this village/ town you live in. How long have you lived here? (*If not all life, probe for number of years lived here*)

1. Less than 10 years   2. Ten years or more   3. Entire life

1a. (*If not all life*) Where did your ancestors (grand parents) live? Name of State .... Name of district ....

2. What is your age (in completed years) ....

3. Gender: 1. Male   2. Female

4. Till what level have you studied .... (*Record exactly and consult code book*)

   4a. Till what level have your father and your mother studied? Father .... Mother ....

5. What is your main occupation? ....
   (*Record exactly and consult code book & if retired, try to ascertain his/her previous occupation*)

   5a. (*If the respondent is not the main earner*) What is husband/wife's occupation? (*Record exactly and consult the code book*) ....
   ....

   5b. What is/has been the main occupation of the respondent's father (*Record exactly and consult the code book*) ....
   ......

6. What is your Caste/Jati-biradari/ Tribe name (*Probe further, if R mentions ambiguous surname*) ....
   (*Consult state code book, or master list*) And your sub-caste ....
   .... (*Not to be coded*)

   6a. And what is your Caste group: (*Ascertain and consult SC/ST/OBC list for the state*)

   1 SC   2 ST   3. OBC   4. Others

7. Which religion do you follow?

   1. Hindu   2. Muslim   3. Christian   4. Sikh
   5. Buddhist   6. Jain   7. Parsi
   8. Other (*Specify*) ....

8. Generally, which language is spoken in your house? ....
   .... (*Record exactly & consult code book for coding*)

   8a. How is your command on English?

      1. Can speak fluently
      2. Can speak somewhat
      3. Can understand but not speak
      4. Can even not understand

9. Have you got a voter's photo identity card?
    1. No card, not photographed
    2. Photographed, but card not issued
    3. Card issued but defective
    4. Yes, R has proper card
    5. Card issued but lost
    6. Any other (*Specify*) ....

Household Data

10. Locality:
    1. Village
    2. Town (below 1 Lakh)
    3. City (above 1 Lakh)
    4. Big city (above 10 Lakhs)

    (*If in doubt consult the electoral roll or census. If not stated on either then it is classed as a village*)

    10a. (*If Town/City*) Type of house where R lives (own or rented)
        1. House/Flat/Bungalow with 4 or more bedrooms
        2. House/Flat with 3 or 4 Bedrooms
        3. House/Flat with 2 Bedrooms (With kitchen and bathroom)
        4. House/Flat with 2 *Pucca* rooms (With kitchen)
        5. House/Flat with 2 *Pucca* rooms (Without kitchen)
        6. House with 1 *Pucca* rooms (With kitchen)
        7. House with 1 *Pucca* rooms (Without kitchen)
        8. Mainly *Kutcha* house
        9. Slum/Jhuggi Jhopri/fully *Kutcha*

    10b. (*If Village*) Type of house where R lives (own or rented)
        1. Pucca (both wall and roof made of pucca material)
        2. Pucca-Kutcha (Either wall or roof is made of pucca material and of other kutcha material)
        3. Kutcha (Both wall and roof are made of kutcha material other than materials mentioned in category 4)
        4. Hut (both wall and roof are made of grass, leaves, mud, un-burnt brick or bamboo)

11. Total agricultural land .... (*in local units*)

    11a. Irrigated land .... (*in local units*)

12. Number of rooms used in the household? ....

13. Total number of family members living in the household (Adult .... Children ....)
14. Do you have a latrine in the household   2. Yes   1. No
15. Do you or your family own the following   Yes   No
    a. Car/Jeep/Van (*Record exact number of cars*) ....
    b. Tractor   1   0
    c. Colour or B/W Television 2 Colour   1 B/W   0 No
    d. Cable Television   1   0
    e. Scooter/Motorcycle/Moped   1   0
    f. Telephone   1   0
    g. Mobile telephone   1   0
    h. Electric fan/cooler   1   0
    i. Bicycle   1   0
    j. Radio/Transistor   1   0
    k. Pumping set   1   0
    l. Fridge   1   0
    m. Camera   1   0
    n. Goat/Sheep (*Record exact number of goat/sheep*) _____
    o. Cow/Buffalo (*Record exact number of cow/buffalo*) _____
16. Most important source of drinking water:
    1. Tap inside the house   2. Tap outside the house
    3. Tube well   4. Well
    5. Hand pump   6. Natural source
                                     (Pond/Lake/Stream/River/Spring)
    7. Any other (Tank/ canal) (*Specify*) ....
17. Most important source of lighting:
    1. Electricity   2. Kerosene
    3. No lighting   4. Other
18. Most important source of fuel used for cooking:
    1. LPG/Gas   2. Electricity
    3. Kerosene   4. Coal/lignite/charcoal
    5. Others bought (Firewood/Crop residue/Cow dung cake)
    6. Others not bought (Firewood/Crop residue/Cow dung cake)
    7. Other (*Please specify*) ....
19. Total Monthly household income (in Rs.)
    1. Up to Rs.1000   2. Rs.1001–Rs.2000
    3. Rs.2001–Rs.3000   4. Rs.3001–Rs.4000
    5. Rs.4001–Rs.5000   6. Rs.5001–Rs.10,000
    7. Rs.10,001–Rs.20,000   8. Rs.20,001 and above.

Not to be Asked

Was the respondent cooperative?
    1. Very cooperative   2. Somewhat cooperative
    3. Not at all cooperative
Date of Interview .... Interviewer's name ....
Name of respondent .... A.C.Name ....
P.S. Name .... Landmark ....

2.3 Accommodation

The objective of this scale called *Accommodation* is to measure along an inclusiveness–exclusiveness dimension of the willingness of the Indian electorate to accommodate minority and related interests. At one extreme of the scale are those who want a strong, nationalistic-culture, elitist and patriarchal state, and at the other extreme are those who prefer a multi-cultural, gender-sensitive and non-elitist society.

The following variables (attitudinal data) have been selected to form the index of accommodation. The 'no responses' and missing values have been regrouped in the middle (value = 1) and recoding has been done in order to adjust the direction of answers (inclusive = 0; exclusive = 2).

Table A2.3.1
Questions for Accommodation Scale

Number	Question
28d	Only educated people should have the right to vote. Do you agree or disagree?
28e	Those who are not well educated should not be allowed to contest elections.
28k	It is the responsibility of the government to protect the interests of the minority communities. Do you agree or disagree?
29a	Some people say that the destruction (of the disputed building [Babri Masjid]) was justified while others say it was not justified. What would you say? Was it justified or not justified?
34a	Backward castes should have reservation in government jobs. Do you agree or disagree?
34b	There is no need for India to make the atomic bomb. Do you agree or disagree?
34d	Like Gram Panchayats, there should be reservation for women in assemblies and parliament. Do you agree or disagree?
34f	India should make more efforts to develop friendly relations with Pakistan. Do you agree or disagree?
34g	The needs and problems of Muslims have been neglected in India. Do you agree or disagree?
34h	Every community should be allowed to have its own laws to govern marriage and property rights. Do you agree or disagree?

The scale has been generated on the basis of the following correlations:

> Accordingly, the values of these 10 variables have been added up, so that one gets a scale from min = 0 (inclusive to max = 20 (exclusive). Graphically, one can see the distribution of the whole sample and two sub-populations, namely, the age cohorts as developed in Chapter 2 and the voters of the Left Front and the BJP.

Appendix 3

Tables

TABLE A3.1
Election Data, Indian Parliamentary Elections, 1952–2004

Year	Seats	Candidates	Polling stations	Electorate (in millions)	Votes polled (in millions)	Turnout (%)
1952	489	1,874	132,560	173.2	79.1	45.7
1957	494	1,519	220,478	193.7	92.4	47.7
1962	494	1,985	238,355	217.7	120.6	55.4
1967	520	2,369	267,555	250.6	153.6	61.3
1971	518	2,784	342,944	274.1	151.6	55.3
1977	542	2,439	373,908	321.2	194.3	60.5
1980	529	4,629	434,742	363.9	202.7	56.9
1984	542	5,493	479,214	400.1	256.5	64.1
1989	529	6,160	579,810	498.9	309.1	62.0
1991	534	8,780	588,714	511.5	285.9	55.9
1996	543	13,952	767,462	592.6	343.3	57.9
1998	539	4,708	765,473	602.3	373.7	62.0
1999	543	4,648	774,651	619.5	371.7	60.0
2004	543	5,435	687,473	671.5	389.9	58.1

Source Data Unit, CSDS, Delhi.

TABLE A3.2
Participation Trends in Major Assembly Elections, 1952–2006

Year of election	States	Total seats	Turnout (%)	Total contestants	Contestants per seat total	Contestants per seat independents
1952	22	3,283	45	15,361	4.7	1.9
1957	13	2,906	48	10,176	3.5	1.4
1960–62	15	3,196	58	13,665	4.3	1.3
1967	20	3,487	61	16,507	4.7	1.9
1971–72	21	3,131	60	13,768	4.4	1.6
1977–78	24	3,723	59	22,396	6.0	2.2

(Table A3.2 continued)

(Table A3.2 continued)

Year of election	States	Total seats	Turnout (%)	Total contestants	Contestants per seat total	Contestants per seat independents
1979–80	16	2,589	54	17,826	6.9	3.2
1984–85	18	3,131	58	26,963	8.6	5.4
1989–90	18	3,028	60	35,187	11.6	7.0
1993–95	16	2,770	64	40,773	14.7	9.1
1996–1998	18	2602	64	25,184	9.7	5.1
1999–2001	15	2383	66	17,427	7.3	2.8
2003–05	19	2580	61	21,773	8.4	3.2

Source Yadav 1996a.
Note A 'major' round of Assembly Elections is defined here as one which involved, within a year or two, elections to at least 2,000 Assembly constituencies.

TABLE A3.3
Percentage Turnout in Assembly Elections, 1984–2006

States	1984–85	1989–90	1993–95	1996–98	1999–2001	2002–06
Andhra Pradesh	66.7	67.6	71.1		69.1	69.3
Arunachal Pradesh	76.3	68.9	81.4		69.4	63.6
Assam				78.3	75.1	75.7
Bihar	55.1	62.2	61.8		62.6	46.5
Chattishgarh						71.3
Delhi	55.6	54.3	61.8	49.0		53.4
Goa	71.9	68.7	71.7		63.6	68.8
Gujarat	47.4	51.1	64.7	59.3		61.5
Haryana				70.5	69.0	71.9
Himachal Pradesh	69.6	66.7	71.7	71.2		74.5
Jammu & Kashmir				53.9		73.1
Jharkhand						56.9
Karnataka	66.3	63.8	68.8		67.7	64.9
Kerala				71.2	72.5	72.3
Madhya Pradesh	48.6	52.8	59.0	60.2		67.4
Maharashtra	58.3	61.1	72.0		60.9	63.4
Manipur	87.3	80.6	88.8		89.9	90.2
Meghalaya				74.5		70.4
Mizoram	70.6	80.4	80.8	76.3		78.7
Nagaland				22.2		87.9
Orissa	51.4	55.5	73.8		59.1	65.9

(Table A3.3 continued)

(*Table A3.3 continued*)

States	1984–85	1989–90	1993–95	1996–98	1999–2001	2002–06
Pondicherry				75.3	72.5	85.7
Punjab				68.7		65.1
Rajasthan	54.0	56.5	60.6	63.4		67.2
Sikkim	62.6	69.5	81.0		81.8	
Tamil Nadu				66.9	59.1	70.8
Tripura				80.8		78.7
Uttar Pradesh	44.8	48.5	57.1	55.7		53.8
Uttaranchal						54.3
West Bengal				82.9	75.2	81.9
Bihar (October 2005)						45.9
Total	**55.3**	**60.3**	**64.2**	**64.4**	**66.1**	**62.8**

Source Data Unit, CSDS, Delhi.

TABLE A3.4
Summary of Lok Sabha Elections, 1952–1971
(Seats and per cent of Vote)

Party	1952	1957	1962	1967	1971
INC(1)	364	371	361	283	352
	(45.0)	(47.8)	(44.7)	(40.8)	(43.7)
BJS/BJP	3	4	14	35	22
	(3.1)	(5.9)	(6.4)	(9.4)	(7.4)
JP/JD	–	–	–	–	–
CPM	–	–	–	19	25
				(4.4)	(5.1)
CPI	26	29	29	23	23
	(3.3)	(8.9)	(9.9)	(5.0)	(4.7)
BKD/LD/SJP	–	–	–	–	1
					(1.8)
INC(2)	–	–	–	–	16
					(10.4)
Soc.	21	19	18	36	5
	(16.4)	(10.4)	(9.5)	(8.0)	(3.4)
Swatantra	–	–	18	44	8
			(7.9)	(8.7)	(3.1)
Regional parties	14	20	20	32	41
	(14.1)	(6.2)	(8.9)	(9.1)	(8.4)
Independents	38	42	20	35	14
	(15.9)	(19.4)	(11.1)	(13.7)	(8.4)

(*Table A3.4 continued*)

(*Table A3.4 continued*)

Party	1952	1957	1962	1967	1971
Others	23	9	14	13	11
	(2.2)	(1.4)	(1.6)	(1.1)	(3.6)
Total	**489**	**494**	**494**	**520**	**518**

Source Data Unit, CSDS, Delhi.

TABLE A3.5
Summary of Lok Sabha Elections, 1977–2004
(Seats and per cent of Vote)

Party	1977	1980	1984	1989	1991	1996	1998	1999	2004
INC (I)	154	353	415	197	244	140	141	114	145
	(34.5)	(42.7)	(48.0)	(39.5)	(36.6)	(28.8)	(25.8)	(28.3)	(26.5)
BJS/BJP	–	–	2	86	120	161	182	182	138
			(7.4)	(11.5)	(20.0)	(20.3)	(25.6)	(23.8)	(22.2)
JP/JD/JD(U)	295	31	10	142	59	46	6	21	8
	(41.3)	(19.0)	(6.7)	(17.7)	(10.8)	(8.1)	(3.2)	(3.1)	(2.4)
CPM	22	36	22	33	35	32	32	33	43
	(4.3)	(6.1)	(5.7)	(6.5)	(6.1)	(6.1)	(5.2)	(5.4)	(5.7)
CPI	7	11	6	12	14	12	9	4	10
	(2.8)	(2.6)	(2.7)	(2.6)	(2.5)	(2.0)	(1.8)	(1.5)	(1.4)
BKD/LD/SJP/ JNP	–	41	3	–	5	17	1	–	–
	(0.1)	(9.4)	(5.7)	(0.1)	(3.3)	(2.9)	(0.1)	(0.1)	(0.1)
INC (2)	3	13	5	1	1	4	–	–	–
	(1.7)	(5.3)	(1.6)	(0.3)	(0.4)	(1.5)			
Regional parties	49	34	73	27	51	118	117	174	179
	(8.8)	(7.7)	(13.3)	(10.5)	(13.3)	(20.6)	(24.2)	(32.0)	(33.4)
Independents	9	9	5	12	1	9	6	5	5
	(5.5)	(6.4)	(8.1)	(5.3)	(3.9)	(6.3)	(3.2)	(2.6)	(4.3)
Others	3	1	1	19	4	4	49	10	15
	(1.0)	(0.8)	(0.8)	(6.1)	(2.1)	(3.3)	(10.9)	(3.2)	(4.0)
Total	**542**	**529**	**542**	**529**	**534**	**543**	**543**	**543**	**543**

Source Data Unit, CSDS, Delhi

Notes 1. Abbreviations.: BJS-Bharatiya Jana Sangh; BJP-Bharatiya Janata Party; BKD-Bharatiya Kranti Dal; CPI-Communist Party of India; CPM-Communist Party of India (Marxist); INC(1)-Indian National Congress (-1967), Congress (Requisionist) (1971), Congress (Indira) (1980); INC (2)-Congress (Organisation), Congress (Urs) (1980), Congress (Socialist) (1984-); JD-Janata Dal; JP-Janata Party; LD-Lok Dal; SJP-Samajwadi Janata Party.

2. The 'Socialist' category includes the Socialist Party, the Kisan Mazdoor Party, the Praja Socialist Party, and the Samyukta Socialist Party.

TABLE A3.6
Multiple Correlation of the Components of Democracy and Social Change (1996)

	Political legitimacy	Political exposure	Political efficacy	Financial efficacy	Institutional trust	Political information	Economic liberalisation	Law and order	Social harmony
Political legitimacy	1.00								
Political exposure	.12	1.00							
Political efficacy	.15	.16	1.00						
Financial efficacy	.06	.12	.08	1.00					
Institutional trust	.06	.21	.15	.19	1.00				
Political information	.05	.38	.09	.21	.24	1.00			
Liberalisation	.03	.00	-.05	-.02	.00	-.01	1.00		
Law and order	.00	-.01	.06	.06	.05	-.07	.02	1.00	
Social harmony	.02	-.03	.06	.10	.09	-.03	.01	.18	1.00

Source Data Unit, CSDS, Delhi.

Note All correlations are significant at the .000 level. N > = 9000.

Bibliography

Ahmed, Bashiruddin. 1971. 'Political Stratification and the Indian Electorate', *Economic & Political Weekly*, VI(3–5): 251–58.
Ahmed, Bashiruddin and Samuel. J. Eldersveld.1978. *Citizens and Politics: Mass Political Behavior in India*. Chicago: University of Chicago Press.
Ahmed, Bashiruddin and V. B. Singh. 1975. 'Dimensions of Party System Change: the Case of Madhya Pradesh', in Sheth (ed.), *Citizens and Parties: Aspects of Competitive Politics in India*, pp. 165–205, New Delhi: Allied.
Akbar, M.J. 1988. *Riot after Riot: Reports on Caste and Communal Violence in India*. Delhi: Penguin.
Ali, Tariq. 2007. 'The General in His Labyrinth', *London Review of Books*, 29(1): 21–24.
Almond, Gabriel and G. Bingham Powell. 2008. *Comparative Politics Today*. New York: Harper Collins.
Almond, Gabriel and Sidney Verba (eds). 1989. *The Civic Culture Revisited*. London: Sage.
Ambedkar, B.R. *Debates of the Constituent Assembly*, Vol VII(1): 39.
Apter, D.E. (ed.). 1964. *Ideology and Discontent*. New York: The Free Press of Glencoe.
———. 1965. *The Politics of Modernisation*. Chicago: University of Chicago Press.
———. 1971. *Choice and the Politics of Allocation: A Development Theory*. New Haven: Yale University Press.
———. 1987. *Rethinking Development: Modernization, Dependency and Post-Modern Politics*. Beverley Hills: Sage.
Austin, Granville. 1966. *The Indian Constitution*. Oxford: Oxford University Press.
Bachrach, P. 1962. 'Elite Consensus and Democracy', *Journal of Politics*, XXIV (August): 155–163.
Bailey, Frederic. G. 1957. *Caste and the Economic Frontier: A Village in Highland Orissa*. Manchester: Manchester University Press.
———. 1970. *Politics and Social Change: Orissa in 1959*. Berkeley: University of California Press.
Banfield, Edward. 1958. *The Moral Basis of a Backward Society*. New York: The Free Press.
Bardhan, Pranab. 1984. *The Political Economy of Development in India*. New York: Basil Blackwell.
Barth, Hans. 1960. *The Idea of Order: Contributions to a Philosophy of Politics*. Dordrecht, Holland: D. Reidel.

Basu, Sajal. 1982. *Politics of Violence: A Case Study of West Bengal*. Calcutta: Minerva Associates.
Bayley, David H. 1969. *The Police and Political Development in India*. Princeton, N.J.: Princeton University Press.
———. 1983. 'The Police and Political Order in India', *Asian Survey*, 23(4), April: 486–96.
Beethan, David. (ed.). 1994. *Defining and Measuring Democracy*. London: Sage.
Bendix, Reinhard. 1964. *Nation-Building and Citizenship: Studies of Our Changing Social Order*. New York: John Wiley and Sons.
Bernstorff, Dagmar. 1981. 'India's 7th General Elections: The Forgiving Electorate', *Asien. Deutsche Zeitschrift für Politik, Wirtschaft und Kultur*, 1(October): 7–31.
Beteille, A. 1969. *Castes Old and New: Essays in Social Structure and Social Stratification*. Bombay: Asia Publishing House.
Bettelheim, C. 1968. *India Independent*. London: McGibbon & Kee.
Bhagwati, Jagdish. 1986. 'Rethinking Trade Strategy', in Joh Lewis and V. Kallab (eds), *Development Strategies Reconsidered*. Washington, DC: Overseas Development Council.
Bhatt, Anil. 1973. 'Caste and Political Mobilization in Gujarat District', in Rajni Kothari (ed.), *Caste in Indian Politics*. New Delhi: Orient Longman.
Bhattacharyya, Harihar. 1997. *Post-colonial Context of Social Capital and Democratic Governance: The Case of West Bengal in India*. Unpublished Research Report. Burdwan: University of Burdwan.
Bhattacharyya, Dwaipayan. 1993. 'Agrarian Reforms and the Politics of the Left'. Unpublished Ph.D. Dissertation, submitted to Cambridge University.
———. 1996. 'Social Capital, Redistributive Reforms, Panchayati Democracy and Norms of Justice in West Bengal', in Hans Blomquist 'Agora Project: Democracy and Social Capital in Segmented Societies'. Working paper for the Conference on Social Capital and Democracy at Toshali Sands, Orissa, Uppsal, India. Unpublished paper.
Bhattacharyya, Harihar. 1998. *Micro Foundations of Bengal Communism*. Delhi: Ajanta.
Bjorkman, James (ed.). 1988. *Fundamentalism, Revivalists and Violence in South Asia*. Riverside, Md: Riverdale Publishing Co.
Blomquist, Hans. 1996. 'Agora Project: Democracy and Social Capital in Segmented Societies', Working Papers from the Conference on Social Capital and Democracy at Toshali Sands, Orissa, Uppsala, India.
Bondurant, Joan V. 1958. *Conquest of Violence: The Gandhian Philosophy of Conflict*. New Jersey: Princeton University Press.
———. 1958. *Regionalism versus Provincialism: A Study in Problems of Indian National Unity*. Berkeley: University of California Press.
Brass, Paul R. 1984. 'National Power and Local Politics in India: A Twenty-year Perspective', *Modern Asian Studies*, 18(1): 89–118.
Brass, Paul. 1997. 'National Power and Local Politics in India: A Twenty-year Perspective', in Partha Chatterjee (ed.), *State and Politics in India*, pp. 303–35. Delhi: Oxford University Press.

Brass, Paul R. and Francis Robinson. 1987. *The Indian National Congress and Indian Society, 1885–1985: Ideology, Social Structure and Political Dominance*. Delhi: Chanakya Publications.

Brechon, Pierre and Subrata Mitra. 1992. 'The National Front in France: The Emergence of an Extreme Right Protest Movement', *Comparative Politics*, 25(1): 63–82.

Burns, James MacGregor and Jack Walter Peltason. 1963. *Government by the People: The Dynamics of American National, State, and Local Government*. New Jersey: Prentice Hall, Inc.

Byres, T.J. 1988. 'A Chicago View of the Indian State: An Oriental Grin without an Oriental Cat and Political Economy without Classes', *The Journal of Commonwealth and Comparative Politics*, 26(3): 246–69.

Centre for the Study of Developing Societies (CSDS). 2008. *The State of Democracy in South Asia*. Delhi.

Chatterjee, Partha. 1986. *Nationalist Thought and the Colonial World: A Derivative Discourse*. London: Zed Books.

———— (ed.). 1997. *State and Politics in India*. Delhi: Oxford University Press.

Chenery, Hallis, Montek S. Ahluwalia, C.L.G Bell, John H. Duloy and Richard Jolly. 1974. *Redistribution with Growth*. Oxford: Oxford University Press.

Chum, B.K. 1996. 'Akali Dal Goes for Mainstream Politics', *Deccan Herald*. Bengaluru, 27 February.

Cohen, Jean and Andrew Arato. 1992. *Civil Society and Political Theory*. Cambridge: Massachusetts Institute of Technology Press.

Cohen, Stephen. 1988. 'India's Military', in Atul Kohli (ed.), *India's Democracy: An Analysis of State–Society Relations*, Princeton, pp. 99–144. New Jersey: Princeton University Press.

Comte, Fernand. 1991. *The Wordsworth Dictionary of Mythology*. Hertfordshire: Wordsworth Editions.

Dahl, Robert. 1989. *Democracy and its Critics*. New Haven: Yale University Press.

Das Gupta, J. 1970. *Language Conflict and National Development: Group Politics and National Language Policy in India*. Bombay: Oxford University Press.

Datta-Ray, S. 1990. 'Politics and Morality: Can V.P. Singh afford Devi Lal?', *The Statesman Weekly*, Kolkata, March 17.

De Souza, Peter. 2007. 'The Indian Commonsense of Democracy', *Seminar 576*, August: 34–35. Delhi: Seminar Publications.

Deutsch, Karl W. 1961. 'Social Mobilization and Political Development', *American Political Science Review*, LII (September): 218–20.

Devadas, David. 1996. 'Left, Right or Centre?', *Business Standard*. Delhi, April 16.

Dixit, J.N. 1996. 'Wisner's Assessment: Elections and Image', *The Indian Express*. New Delhi, 23 April.

Downs, Anthony. 1957. *An Economic Theory of Democracy*. New York: Harper and Row.

Drèze, Jean and Amartya K. Sen. 1995. *Economic Development and Social Opportunities*. Oxford: Oxford University Press.

Dumont, Louis. 1966. *Homo Hierarchicus: The Caste System and its Implications*. Chicago: University of Chicago Press.
Dutt, R.P. 1940. *India Today*. London: Gollancz.
Easton, David. 1957. 'An Approach to the Analysis of Political Systems', *World Politics*, IX(April): 383–400.
Economic & Political Weekly. 2004. 'National Election Study, 2004: An Introduction', *Economic & Political Weekly*, Dec. 18, 2004, 5373–83.
Eisenstadt, S.N. 1965. 'Transformation of Social Political and Cultural Orders in Modernization', *American Sociological Review*, XXX(October): 659–70.
Eldersveld, Samuel J. and Bashiruddin Ahmed. 1978. *Citizens and Politics: Mass Political Behaviour in India*. Chicago: University of Chicago Press.
Encyclopaedia Britannica 1974. Vol 16.
Field, J.O. 1980. *Consolidating Democracy: Politicization and Partisanship in India*. New Delhi: Manohar Publications.
Finer, S.E. 1970. *Comparative Government*. London: Allan Lane the Penguin Books
Fox, R.G. 1969. 'Varna Schemes and Ideological Integration in Indian Society', *Comparative Studies in Society and History*, 11: 27–44.
Fox, R. 1970. 'Avatars of Indian Research', *Comparative Studies in Society and History*, 12(1): 59–72.
Frankel, Francine. 1989/1990. 'Caste, Land and Dominance in Bihar', in Francine Frankel and M.S.A. Rao (eds), *Dominance and State Power in Modern India: Decline of a Social Order*, Vol 1: 46–132. Delhi: Oxford University Press.
———. 1978. *India's Political Economy, 1947–77: The Gradual Revolution*. Princeton, New Jersey: Princeton University Press.
Frankel, Francine. and M.S.A. Rao (eds). 1989/90. *Dominance and State Power in Modern India: Decline of a Social Order* (two volumes). Delhi: Oxford University Press.
Geertz, Clifford. 1964. 'Ideology as a Cultural System', in D.E. Apter (ed.), *Ideology and Discontent*. New York: The Free Press of Glencoe.
Gilmour. 1992. *Riots, Rising and Revolution: Governance and Violence in Eighteenth-Century England*. London: Hutchinson.
Gould, Harold. 1990. *The Hindu Caste System*. Delhi: Chanakya.
Government of India. 1956. *Balwant Rai Mehta Committee Report*. New Delhi: Planning Commission.
———. 1965. *Report of the Commitee on Panchayati Elections 1965*. New Delhi: Ministry of Community Development and Cooperation.
———. 1978. *Report of the Committee on Panchayati Raj Institutions*. New Delhi: Ministry of Agriculture and Irrigation, Department of Rural Development.
Graff, Violette. 1987. 'The Muslim Vote in Indian Lok Sabha Elections of December 1984', in Paul R. Brass and Francis Robinson (eds), *The Indian National Congress and Indian Society, 1885–1985: Ideology, Social Structure and Political Dominance*, pp. 427–69. Delhi: Chanakya Publications.
Guha, Ranajit. 1983. *Elementary Aspects of Peasant Insurgency in Colonial India*. Delhi: Oxford University Press.

Bibliography

Hardgrave, Robert. 1968. 'The Breast Cloth Controversy', *Indian Economic History Review*, 5 (June): 171–87.
———. 1969. *The Nadars of Tamilnadu: The Political Culture of a Community in Change*. Berkeley: University of Callifornia Press.
Hardgrave, Robert and Stanley Kochanek. 2008. *India: Government and Politics in a Developing Nation*. Fort Worth: Harcourt.
Hardiman, D. 1987. *The Coming of the Devi: Adivasi Assertion in Western India*. Delhi: Oxford University Press.
———. 1992. 'Harijans and their Influence on the Elections in Uttar Pradesh', in Subrata Kumar Mitra and James Chiriyankandath (eds), *Electoral Politics in India: A Changing Landscape*, pp. 241–58. New Delhi: Segment Books.
Harrison, Selig. 1960. *India: The Most Dangerous Decades*. Princeton, New Jersey: Princeton University Press.
Harriss, J. 1982. *Capitalism and Peasant Farming, Agrarian Structure and Ideology in Northern Tamil Nadu*. Delhi: Oxford University Press.
Hasan, Zoya. 1996. 'The Regionalisation of Politics', *The Hindu*, Chennai, 23 April.
Hause, E.M. 1961. 'India Under the Impact of Western Political Ideas and Institutions', *Western Political Quarterly*, XIV(December): 879–95.
Haynes, Douglas and Gyan Prakash (eds). 1991. *Contesting Power: Resistance and Everyday Social Relations in South Asia*. Berkeley: University of California Press.
Heimsath, Charles H. 1964. *Indian Nationalism and Hindu Social Reform*. New Jersey: Princeton University Press.
Hobsbawm, Eric. 1995. *Age of Extremes: The Short Twentieth Century, 1914–1981*. Delhi: Viking, Penguin.
Hobsbawm, Eric J. and George Rudé. 1968. *Captain Swing: A Social History of the Great Agrarian Uprising of 1930*. New York: Pantheon.
Huntington, Samuel P. 1968. *Political Order in Changing Societies*. New Haven: Yale University Press.
———. 1996. *The Clash of Civilisations and the Remaking of World Order*. New York: Simon and Schuster.
Inden, Ronald. 1990. *Imagining India*. Oxford: Blackwell.
India Today. 1996. 'Different Strokes', *India Today*, 15 July, pp. 32–36.
Inkeles, Alex. 1969. 'Making Men Modern', *American Journal of Sociology*, LXXV (September): 208–25.
Irschick, Eugene. 1969. *Politics and Social Conflict in South India*. Berkeley: University of California Press.
———. 1994. *Dialogue and History: Constructing South India, 1795–1895*. Delhi: Oxford University Press.
Jain, Meenakshi. 1991. *The Congress Party, 1967–1977: The Role of Caste in Indian Politics*. Delhi: Vikash.
Jayal, Niraja Gopal and Sudha Pai (eds). 2001. *Democratic Governance in India: Challenges of Poverty, Development and Identity*. New Delhi: Sage.
Johnson, Chalmers A. 1983. *MITI and the Japanese Miracle: the Growth of Industrial Policy, 1925–1983*. Stanford, California: Stanford University Press.

Joshi, Ram and R.K. Hebsur (eds). 1987. *Congress in Indian Politics: A Centenary Perspective*. Bombay: Popular.
Kaase, Max. 1972. *Political Ideology, Dissatisfaction and Protest*. Mannheim: Institut für Sozialwissenschaften.
Keane, John (ed.). 1988. *Civil Society and the State*. London: Verso.
Khanna, B.S. 1994. *Panchayati Raj: National Perspective and State Studies*. Delhi: Deep and Deep.
Khare, Harish. 1997. 'The Union Endures, the Federation Flourishes', *The Hindu*, New Delhi: Special issue of 15 August, 39.
Khilnani, Sunil. 1997. *An Idea of India*. London: Hamish Hamilton.
Kirchheimer, Otto. 1966. 'The Transformation of the Western European Party Systems', in La Palombara and Weiner (eds), *Political Parties and Political Development*, pp. 177–200. Princeton, New Jersey: Princeton University Press.
Kogekar, S.V. and Richard L. Park (eds). 1956. *Reports on the Indian General Elections 1951–52*. Bombay: Popular Book Depot.
Kohli, Atul. 1983. 'Parliamentary Communism and Agrarian Reforms: the Evidence from India's Bengal', *Asian Survey*, 23(7): 783–809, July.
———. 1987. *The State and Poverty in India: The Politics of Reform*. Cambridge: Cambridge University Press.
———. (ed.). 1988. *India's Democracy: An Analysis of Changing State–Society Relations*. Princeton, New Jersey: Princeton University Press.
———. 1990. *Democracy and Discontent: India's Growing Crisis of Governability*. Cambridge: Cambridge University Press.
———. 2001. *The Success of India's Democracy*. Cambridge: Cambridge University Press.
Kothari, Rajni. 1964. 'The Congress "System" in India', *Asian Survey*, 4(12): 1161–63.
———. 1970. *Politics in India*. Boston: Little, Brown.
———. 1973. *Caste in Indian Politics*. Delhi: Orient Longman.
———. 1974. 'The Congress System Revisited. A Decennial Review', *Asian Survey*, 14(12): 1035–54.
———. 1982. 'Towards Intervention', *Seminar* 269(January): 22–27.
———. 1983a. 'A Fragmented Nation', *Seminar* 281(January): 24–29.
———. 1983b. 'The Crisis of the Moderate State and the Decline of Democracy', in P. Lyon, and J. Manor (eds), *Transfer and Transformation: Political Institutions in the New Commonwealth*, pp. 24–29. Leicester: Leicester University Press.
———. 1988. *State Against Democracy: In Search of Humane Governance*. Delhi: Ajanta Publications.
Krishna, Daya. 1979. *Political Development: A Critical Perspective*. Delhi: Oxford University Press.
Krueger, Anne. 1974. 'The Political Economy of Rent-seeking Society,' *American Economic Review*, 64(3): 291–304.
Kuhn, Thomas. 1962. *The Structure of Scientific Revolutions*. Chicago: University of Chicago Press.

La Palombara, Joseph and Myron Weiner. 1966. 'The Origin and Development of Political Parties', in La Palombara and Weiner (eds), *Political Parties and Political Development,* Princeton, New Jersey: Princeton University Press.

La Palombara, Joseph and Myron Weiner. 1972. *Political Parties and Political Development.* Princeton, New Jersey: Princeton University Press.

Lacy, Creighton. 1965. *The Conscience of India: Moral Traditions in the Modern World.* New York: Holt, Rinehart and Winston.

Lakatos, I. and A. Musgrave (eds). 1970. *Criticism and the Growth of Knowledge.* Cambridge: Cambridge University Press.

Lawson, Kay (ed.). 1994. *How Political Parties Work: Perspectives from Within.* Westport: Praeger.

Lewis, John P. 1962. *India: A Quiet Crisis.* Delhi: Oxford University Press.

———. 1995. *India's Political Economy: Governance and Reform.* Oxford: Oxford University Press.

Lewis, John and V. Kallab (eds). 1986. *Development Strategies Reconsidered.* Washington, D.C.: Overseas Development Council.

Lijphart, Arendt. 1996. 'The Puzzle of Indian Democracy: A Consociational Interpretation', *American Political Science Review,* 90(2): 258–68.

———. 1984. *Democracies: Patterns of Majoritarian and Consensus Government in Twenty-one Countries.* New Haven: Yale University Press.

Lipset, Seymour M. 1959. 'Some Social Requisites of Democracy: Economic Development and Political Legitimacy', *American Political Science Review,* LIII(March): 69–105.

Long, N. 1977. *An Introduction to the Sociology of Rural Development.* London: Tavistock.

——— (ed.). 1989. *Encounters at the Interface: A Perspective on Social Discontinuities in Rural Development.* Wageningen: Agricultural University.

Luthera, Ved Prakesh. 1964. *The Concept of the Secular State and India.* Calcutta: Oxford University Press.

Lyon, P. and J. Manor (eds). 1983. *Transfer and Transformation: Political Institutions in the New Commonwealth.* Leicester: Leicester University Press.

Madan, T.N. 1987. 'Secularism in its Place', *The Journal of Asian Studies,* 46(4): 747–59.

Maheshwari, Shriram. 1963. *The General Election in India.* Allahabad: Chaitanya Publishing House.

Malenbaum, Wilfred. 1962. *Prospects for Indian Development.* London: G. Allen and Unwin.

Manor, James. 1983. 'Anomie in Indian Politics: Origins and Potential Impact', *Economic & Political Weekly,* 18(1–2): 725–34.

———. 1987. 'Appearance and Reality in Politics: The 1984 General Election in the South', in Paul R. Brass and Francis Robinson (eds), *The Indian National Congress and Indian Society, 1885–1985: Ideology, Social Structure and Political Dominance.* pp. 400–26. Delhi: Chanakya Publications.

———. 1998. 'A Coming Asian Tiger in India', *The International Herald Tribunal.* 7 January.

Marsh, Alan. 1977. *Protest and Political Consciousness*. Beverley Hills: Sage.
Masterman, M. 1970. 'The Nature of a Paradigm' in I. Lakatos and A. Musgrave (eds), *Criticism and the Growth of Knowledge*. pp. 59–89. Cambridge: Cambridge University Press.
Mehrotra, N.C. 1980. *Political Crises and Polls in India*. New Delhi: Deep & Deep.
Mehta, V.R. 1987. 'Political Science in India: In Search of an Identity', *Government and Opposition*, 22(3): 270–81.
Merkl, Peter H. 1967. *Political Continuity and Change*. New York: Harper and Row.
Migdal, Joel S. 1988. *Strong Societies and Weak States: State–Society Relations and State Capability in the Third World*. Princeton: Princeton University Press.
———. 1988. 'The Paradox of Power: Political Science as Morality Play', *The Journal of Commonwealth and Comparative Politics*, 26(3): 318–37.
———. 1990. *Post-colonial state in Asia: Dialectics of Politics and Culture*. Hemel Hempstead: Harvester.
———. 1991. 'Room to Maneuver in the Middle: Local Elites, Political Action and the State in India', *World Politics*, 43(3), pp. 390–414.
———. 1992. *Power, Protest, Participation: Local Elites and the Politics of Development in India*. London: Routledge.
———. 1994a. 'Caste, Democracy and the Politics of Community Formation in India', in Mary Searle-Chatterjee and Ursula Sharma (eds), *Contextualising Caste: Post-Dumontian Approaches*, pp. 49–71. Oxford: Blackwell/The Sociological Review.
———. 1994b. 'Party Organization and Policy Making in a Changing Environment: The Indian National Congress', in Kay Lawson (ed.), *How Political Parties Work: Perspectives from Within*, pp. 153–77. Westport: Praeger.
———. 1997a. 'Legitimacy, Governance and Political Institutions in India after Independence', in Subrata Kumar Mitra and Dietmar Rothermund (eds), *Legitimacy and Conflict in South Asia*, pp. 17–49. Delhi: Manohar.
———. 1997b. Nation and Region in Indian Politics. *Asien, Afrika, Lateinamerika*. 25: 499–519.
———. 1999a. *Democracy and Social Change in India*. New Delhi: Sage.
———. 1999b. *Culture and Rationality, the Politics of Social Change in Post-Colonial India*. New Delhi: Sage.
———. 2005. *The Puzzle of India's Governance: Culture, Context and Comparative Theory*. London: Routledge.
Mitra, Subrata Kumar. 2008. 'India', in Gabriel Almond and G. Bingham Powell (eds). *Comparative Politics Today*, pp. 608–59. New York: Harper Collins.
Mitra, Subrata Kumar and Dietmar Rothermund (eds). 1997. *Legitimacy and Conflict in South Asia*. Delhi: Manohar.
Mitra, Subrata Kumar and James Chiriyankandath (eds). 1992. *Electoral Politics in India: A Changing Landscape*. New Delhi: Segment Books.
Mitra, Subrata Kumar and R. Alison Lewis (eds). 1996. *Subnational Movements in South Asia*. Boulder: Westview Press.

Mitra, Subrata Kumar, Mike Enskat and Clemens Spiess. 2004. *Political Parties in South Asia*. Westport: Praeger.

Moddie, A.D. 1968. *The Brahmanical Culture and Modernity*. Bombay: Asia Publishing House.

Moore, Barrington. 1966. *Social Origins of Dictatorship and Democracy: Lord and Peasant in the Making of the Modern World*. Boston: Beacon Press.

———. 1967. *The Social Origins of Dictatorship and Democracy: Lord and the Peasant in the Making of the Modern World*. London: Allen Lane.

Moore, Wilbert E. 1960. 'A Reconsideration of Theories of Social Change', *American Sociological Review*, XXV(December): 810–18.

Morris–Jones, W.H. 1963. 'India's Political Idioms', in C.H. Philips, (ed.), *Politics and Society in India*, pp. 133–54. (London: George Allen Unwin).

———. 1987. *The Government and Politics of India*. Wistow: Eothen Press.

Mukherjee, N. 1994. *Decentralisation of Panchayats in the 1990s*. New Delhi: Vikas.

Mukherjee, N. and D. Bandopadhyay. 1994. 'New Horizons for West Bengal Panchayats', in N. Mukherjee, *Decentralisation of Panchayats in the 1990s*, pp. 215–82. New Delhi: Vikas.

Myrdal, Gunnar. 1968. *Asian Drama: An Inquiry into the Poverty of Nations* (3 vols). New York: Pantheon.

Naipaul, Vididhar Surajprasad. 1964. *An Area of Darkness*. London: Penguin.

———. 1977. *India: A Wounded Civilization*. London: Andre Deutsch.

———. 1990. *India: A Million Mutinies Now*. London: Heinemann.

Nanda, B.R. 1995. *Jawaharlal Nehru: Rebel and Statesman*. Delhi: Oxford University Press.

Nehru, Jawaharlal. 1947. 'Tryst with Destiny', *The Hindu*, 15 August. Reprinted in *The Hindu*, 15 August, 2007.

———. 1960. *A Bunch of Old Letters*. New York: Asia Publishing House.

Neiburg, H.L. 1962. 'The Threat of Violence and Social Change', *American Political Science Review*, LVI (December): 865–73.

Nelson, J. 1987. *Access to Power: Politics and Urban Poor in Developing Nations*. Princeton: Princeton University Press.

Nettl, J.P. 1967. *Political Modernization: A Sociological Analysis of Methods and Concepts*. London: Faber and Faber.

Nicholson, N.K. 1968. 'India's Modernizing Faction and the Mobilization of Power', *International Journal of Comparative Sociology*, IX (September–December): 302–17.

North, Douglass C. 1990. *Institutions, Institutional Change and Economic Performance*. Cambridge: Cambridge University Press.

Norton, P. 1991. *The British Polity*. London: Longman.

O'hanlon, R. 1988. 'Recovering the Subject: Subaltern Studies and Histories of Resistance in Colonial South Asia', *Modern Asian Studies*, 22(1): 189–224.

Organski, A.F.K. 1965. *The States of Political Development*. New York: Alfred A. Knopf.

Pai, Sudha. 1996. 'Panchayats and Grassroots Democracy: The Politics of Development in Two Districts of Uttar Pradesh', in Hans Blomquist 'Agora Project: Democracy and Social Capital in Segmented Societies'. Working paper for the Conference on Social Capital and Democracy at Toshali Sands, Orissa, Uppasal, India. Unpublished paper.

Palmer, N.D. 1975. *Elections and Political Development: the South Asian Experience.* Durham, North Carolina: Duke University Press.

Parekh, B. 1989. *Colonialism, Tradition and Reform: An Analysis of Gandhi's Political Discourse.* New Delhi: Sage.

———. 1994. 'Cultural Diversity and Liberal Democracy', in David Beetham (ed.), *Defining and Measuring Democracy*, pp. 199–221. London: Sage.

Parmanand, P. 1985. *New Dimensions in Indian Politics: A Critical Study of the Eight Lok Sabha Election.* Delhi: UDH Publishers.

Parsons, Talcott. 1957. *The Social System.* Glencoe, Illinois: the Free Press.

Philips, C.H (ed.). 1963. *Politics and Society in India.* London: George Allen Unwin.

Plamenatz, J.P. 1960. *On Alien Rule and Self-Government.* New York: Longman.

Poplai, S.L. and V.K.N. Menon (eds). 1957. *National Politics and 1957 Elections in India.* Delhi: Metropolitan Book.

Poston, R.W. 1962. *Democracy Speaks Many Tongues.* New York: Harper and Row.

Powell, G. Bingham. 1982. *Contemporary Democracies: Participation, Stability and Violence.* Cambridge, Massachusetts Harvard University Press: 1982.

Putnam, Robert D. 1993. *Making Democracy Work: Civic Traditions in Modern Italy.* Princeton: Princeton University Press.

Pye, Lucian and Simon Verba (eds). 1965. *Political Culture and Political Development.* Princeton: Princeton University Press.

Quigley, Declan. 1993 *The Interpretation of Caste.* Oxford: Clarendon Press.

———. 1994. 'Is a Theory of Caste Still Possible?', in Searle-Chatterjee, Mary and Ursula Sharma (eds), *Contextualising Caste: Post-Dumontian Approaches*, pp.25–48. Oxford: Blackwell/The Sociological Review.

Ranade, Sudhansu. 1991. 'Competitive Democracies: The Case of Integrated Transfers in India,' Doctoral dissertation submitted to Woodrow Wilson School of International and Public Affairs, Princeton University.

Rao, B.S. 1960. 'The Future of Indian Democracy', *Foreign Affairs*, XXXIX (October): 117–35.

Ray, Ramashroy. 1972. *The Uncertain Verdict: Study of the 1969 Elections in Four Indian States.* Berkeley: University of California Press.

Reddy, Rama and K Hargopal. 1985. 'The Pyraveekar: The Fixer in Rural India', *Asian Survey,* 25(11): 1148–62.

Riggs, Fred W. 1961. *The Ecology of Public Administration.* Bombay: Asia Publishing House.

———. 1964. *Administration in Developing Countries: The Theory of Prismatic Society.* Boston: Houghton Mifflin.

Riker, William and Peter Ordeshook. 1973. *An Introduction to Positive Political Theory.* Englewood Cliffs: Prentice Hall.

Robinson, Marguerite. 1988. *Local Politics: The Law of the Fishes. Development through Political Change in Medak District, Andhra Pradesh (South India)*. Delhi: Oxford University Press.
Rosen, George. 1966. *Democracy and Economic Change in India*. Berkeley: University of California Press.
Rostow, Walt W. 1960. *The Strategy of Economic Growth: A Non-Communist Manifesto*. Cambridge, Massachusetts: Cambridge University Press.
Rothermund, D. 1962. 'Constitutional Reforms versus National Agitation in India', *Journal of Asian Studies*, XXI (August): 505–22.
Rudolph, Lloyd and Susanne H. Rudolph. 1960. 'The Political Role of India's Caste Associations', *Pacific Affairs*, XXXIII(March): 5–22.
———. 1967. *The Modernity of Tradition: Political Development in India*. Chicago: The University of Chicago Press.
———. 1971. 'The Change to Change: Modernization, Development and Politics', *Comparative Politics*, 3: 286–322, April.
———. 1987. *In Pursuit of Lakshmi: The Political Economy of the Indian State*. Chicago: University of Chicago Press.
Rushdie, Salman. 1981. *Midnight's Children*. London: Vintage Books.
Rushdie, Salman and Elizabeth West (eds). 1997. *The Vintage Book of Indian Writing, 1947–1997*. London: Vintage.
Saberwal, S. 1986. *The Roots of Crisis*. New Delhi: Oxford University Press.
Sadasivan, S.N. 1977. *Party and Democracy in India*. New Delhi: Tata McGraw-Hill Publishing Company.
Said, Edward. 1978. *Orientalism*. New York: Pantheon.
Sathyamurthy, T.V. 1971. 'American Science of Indian Politics: An Essay in the Sociology of Knowledge', *Economic & Political Weekly*, 6(23): 1131–33.
———. 1986. 'Contemporary European Scholarship on Political and Social Change in South Asia: An Essay in the Sociology of Knowledge', *Economic & Political Weekly*, 22(11): 459–65.
———. 1989. *Terms of Political Discourse in India*. York: University of York.
———. 1990. 'Indian Peasant Historiography: A Critical Perspective on Ranajit Guha's Work', *The Journal of Peasant Studies*, 18(1): 90–144.
Scott, James. 1985. *Weapons of the Weak: Everyday Forms of Peasant Resistance*. New Haven: Yale University Press.
Searle-Chatterjee, Mary and Ursula Sharma (eds). 1994. *Contextualising Caste: Post-Dumontian Approaches*. Oxford: Blackwell/The Sociological Review.
Selig, Harrison. 1960. *India: The Most Dangerous Decades*. Princeton: Princeton University Press.
Seligman, L.G. 1964. 'Elite Recruitment and Political Development', *Journal of Politics*, XXVI(August): 612–26.
Sen Gupta, Bhabani. 1996. *India: Problems of Governance*. Delhi: Konark Publishers.

Sen, Amartya. 1981. *Poverty and Famines: An Essay on Entitlement and Deprivation.* Delhi: Oxford University Press.
Shah, A.B. and C.R.M. Rao (eds). 1965. *Tradition and Modernity in India.* Bombay: Manaktalas.
Shastri, K.N. Ramannah (ed.). *An Analytical Study of 1967 General Elections in India.* Agra: Educational Publishers.
Shekhar, G.C. 1996. 'Jayalalitha–Karunanidhi: Fight to the Finish', *India Today.* May 15, 36–37.
Shepperdson, Mike and Colin Simmons (eds). 1988. *The Indian National Congress and the Political Economy of India, 1885–1995.* London: Avebury.
Sheth, D.L. 1975. *Citizens and Politics: Aspects of Competitive Politics in India.* Delhi: Allied.
———. 1996. 'The Prospects and Pitfalls', *India Today,* 31 August, p. 37.
———. 1997. 'Caste: The Challenge of Stratification', *The Hindu,* Chennai, 15 August.
———. 2005. 'Consideration for a Policy Framework', *Seminar* 546 (May).
Shils, Edward. 1961. *The Intellectuals Between Tradition and Modernity: The Indian Situation.* The Hague: Mouton and Company.
———. 1962. *Political Development in the New States.* The Hague: Mouton and Company.
Singer, M. 1980. *When a Great Tradition Modernizes: An Anthropological Introduction to Indian Civilization.* Chicago: University of Chicago Press.
Singh, Manmohan. 2005. Speech delivered at the Asian-African Conference on 23 April 2005. Available online at http://meaindia.nic.in/speech/2005/04/23ss01.htm (accessed on February 2005)
Singh, N.K. 1996. 'BJP: Confident by Default', *India Today,* 30 April, pp. 26–27.
Singh, V.B. 1974a. 'Changing Pattern of Inter-Party Competition in Uttar Pradesh: An Analysis of 1974 Elections', *Economic & Political Weekly,* Special Number, 9(August): 32–34.
———. 1974b. 'Party Fortune in the Uttar Pradesh Election: A Case of Azamgarh', *Economic & Political Weekly,* 9(February): 6–8.
———. 1996. 'Grass Roots Political Process: Atrantia Constituency', *Economic & Political Weekly,* January, 13–20.
Singh, V.B. and Shankar Bose (eds). 1984. *Elections in India: Data Handbook on Lok Sabha Elections, 1952–80.* Delhi: Sage Publications.
Sirsikar, V.M. 1995. *Politics of Modern Maharashtra.* London: Sangam Books.
Sisson, Richard and Stanley Wolpert (eds). 1988. *Congress and Indian Nationalism: The Pre-independence Phase.* Berkeley: University of California Press.
Smith, D.E. 1963. *India as a Secular State.* Princeton, New Jersey: Princeton University Press.
Smruti Koppikar. 1995. 'Shiv Sena: Blowing Hot and Cold', *India Today,* August 15, pp. 40–41.
Srinivas, M.N. 1967. *Social Change in Modern India.* Berkeley: University of California Press.
———. 1987. *The Dominant Caste and Other Essays.* Delhi: Oxford University Press.

Suri, Surindar. 1962. *Elections: A Political Analysis*. New Delhi: Sudha Publications.
Tharoor, Shashi. 1997. *India: From Midnight to the Millennium. Indien: Zwischen Mythos und Moderne.* New York: Harper Perennial.
Thorson, Thomas Landon. 1962. *The Logic of Democracy.* Holt: Rinchart and Winston.
Tilly, Charles. 1975. *The Rebellious Century, 1830–1930.* Cambridge: University of Chicago Press.
——— (ed). 1985. *The Formation of National States in Western Europe.* Princeton: Princeton University Press.
Toennies, F. 1971. *On Sociology: Pure, Applied and Empirical.* Chicago: University of Chicago Press.
Vanderbok, William and Richard Sisson. 1987. 'The Spatial Distribution of Congress Electoral Support: Trends from Four Decades of Parliamentary Elections', in Paul R. Brass and Francis Robinson (eds), *The Indian National Congress and Indian Society, 1885–1985: Ideology, Social Structure and Political Dominance,* pp. 373–99. Delhi: Chanakya Publications.
Varshney, Ashutosh (ed.). 1989. *The Indian Paradox: Essays in Indian Politics.* New Delhi: Sage.
———.2007. 'India's Democratic Challenge', *Foreign Affairs,* 86(2): 93–106.
Verney, D. 1986. *Three Civilisations, One State: Canada's Political Traditions.* Durham, North Carolina: Duke University Press.
Waldron, Arthur. 1997. '"Eat People"—A Chinese Reckoning', *Commentary,* 104(1), July.
Washbrook, D.A. 1989/90. 'Caste, Class and Dominance in Modern Tamil Nadu: Non-Brahmism, Dravidianism and Tamil Nationalism', in Francine Frankel and M.S.A. Rao (eds), *Dominance and State Power in Modern India: Decline of a Social Order,* pp. 46–132. Delhi: Oxford University Press.
Weiner, Myron. 1962a. 'Political Parties and Panchayati Raj', *Indian Journal of Public Administration,* VII(4), reprinted in T.N. Chaturvedi and R.B. Jain (eds), 1981, *Panchayati Raj* (Delhi: IIPA): 93–98.
———. 1962b. *The Politics of Scarcity: Public Pressure and Political Response in India.* Chicago: University of Chicago Press.
———. 1966. *Modernization: The Dynamics of Growth.* New York: Basic Books.
———. 1967. *Party Building in a New Nation: The Indian National Congress.* Chicago: University of Chicago Press.
——— (ed.). 1977. *Electoral Politics in the Indian States: The Impact of Modernization.* New Delhi: Manohar.
———. 1978. *India at the Polls: The Parliamentary Elections of 1977.* Washington, DC: American Enterprise Institute.
———. 1983. *India at the Polls, 1980: A Study of the Parliamentary Elections.* Washington, DC: American Enterprise Institute.
———. 1989. 'India in the mid-seventies: A Political System in Transition', in Ashutosh Varshney (ed.), *The Indian Paradox: Essays in Indian Politics,* pp. 263–91. Princeton: Princeton University Press.

Weiner, Myron and Rajni Kothari. 1965. *Indian Voting Behaviour. Studies of the 1962 General Elections*. Calcutta: Firma K.L. Mukhopadhayay.

White, Gordon. 1994. 'Civil Society and Democratization, I: Clearing the Analytical Ground', *Democratization*, 1(3): 48–65.

White, Gordon. 1995. 'Civil Society and Democratization, II: Two Case-Studies', *Democratization*, 2(2), Summer: 56–84.

White, Gordon, Howell, Jude and Xiaoyuan Shang. 1996. *In Search of Civil Society: Market Reform and Social Change in Contemporary China*. Oxford: Clarendon Press.

Wittfogel, Karl August. 1957. *Oriental Despotism: A Comparative Study of Total Power*. New Haven and London: Yale University Press.

Wood, J.R. 1985. *State Politics in Contemporary India: Crisis or Continuity?* Boulder: Colorado: Westview Press.

Woodley, H. 1990. 'The Press during the Emergency', unpublished undergraduate Honours dissertation, submitted to University of Hull, Great Britain.

Yadav, Yogendra. 1996a. 'Elections 1996: Towards a post-Congress Polity', *The Times of India*, Gurgaon, March 30.

———. 1996b. 'Reconfiguration in Indian Politics: State Assembly Elections 1993–95', *Economic & Political Weekly*, 2–3, 13–20 January.

Index

achievement–deprivation index, 157
anti-Emergency movement, 207
Asian Drama: An Inquiry into the Poverty of Nations, 90
Asoka Mehta Committee, 181

Bage Subcommittee of 1973, 189
BSP (Bahujan Samaj Party), as party of Scheduled Castes, 101
Balawant Rai Mehta Committee, recommendations of, 180, 181, 209
BJP (Bharatiya Janata Party), 101
    participation in demolition of Babri Mosque, 110
British colonial rule, liberalisation of Indian economy and, 24
British system, of parliamentary democracy, 88
bullock capitalists, 135

Campaign Exposure, index of, 70–72
caste
    cross-tabulation of, 152
        with education, 153
    hierarchy, 215
    and political competition, 216
    war, 212
ceteris paribus, 156
Citizens and Parties, 10
Civil Code, for every community, 117
coalition of minorities, 100
communal accommodation, 138
communal cohesion, 178
communal riots, 177
communities, formation of, 216
    politics of, 217
competitive elections
    and *indigenisation* of party system in India, 87–95
    and interest articulation, 95–102
competitive party system, 92
competitive politics, primordial identities and, 214–16
Congress system, 92, 178

data collection schedules
    training of field staff for, 258–59
    types of, 258
democracy, and politics of liberalisation, 165–69
democracy and social change
    impact of economic conditions on, 78–79
        current financial situation, 80–81
        financial prospects, 81–82
        financial situation, improvements in, 79–80
    neo-institutional model of, 9–12
    politics of, 1
    public opinion, survey research and social dynamics influencing, 12–17
    roles of state in development of, 6
democratic decentralisation, in India, 180
democratic politics, 176
    and trust in institutions, 37–38
deprivation
    combined measures of, 157–61
    levels of, 157
    'objective' and 'subjective' measurement of, 151–57
    social profiles of, 158–59

developing country, and policies of state, 9
dharma, values of, 238
differential mobilisations, 30, 215
  and electoral campaigns, 33
DRDA (District Rural Development Agency), 182
'divide and rule' policy, 178
Dumont's theory of caste, 214

election campaign, 67–68
  and advice on vote, 74–77
  importance of house to house contact in, 72–74
  involvement or motivation in politics, 69
  micro-political considerations for, 127–32
  peoples' orientation and exposure to, 70–72
  reformulation of regionalisation conjecture for, 132–33
  social profile of regionalists for, 133–135
Election Commission of India's Delimitation Order of 1976, 249
elections, competitive. *See* Competitive elections
electoral democracy, 15
electoral mobilisation, 215
electoral process
  and election meetings, 68–70
  and voting decisions, 64–67
electoral sociology, 29
electors, opinions and attitudes of, 127–32

financial satisfaction, index of, 82–84
'first–past–the post' system, political systems with, 95
'Food for Work' programme, 181
'Freedom at Midnight,' 10, 24, 148, 211

Gandhi–Nehru legacy of social justice, 20

generation-based conflict, 42
government companies, privatisation by social background, 169
Gram Panchayats, 45, 187, 189
Great Leap Forward, 20
Green Revolution, 181

Hindu fundamentalism, 110
homo hierarchicus, 214
horizontal mobilisation, 30, 215

India
  British constitutionalism as applied to, 232
  centrality of stakeholders in, 224–25
  character of electoral democracy in, 241
  colonial rule, legacy of, 21
  community and conflict in, 177–79
  concept of social change during post-independence, 7
  and conceptualisation of 'Congress System,' 9
  democratic politics and, 210–14
  democratisation compared to South Asia, 229–30
  economic change and political discontent in, 147–51
  economic development and community formation in, 184
  elections and indigenisation of party system in, 87–95
  electoral participation at central and regional levels in, 46
  during emergency of 1975–1977, 26
  'grey area' of multi-party democracy in, 207
  Indian National Congress and its political influence on, 8
  influence of exceptionalism on structural changes in, 5–9
  interfacing institutions and politics in, 37–38
  issue of inter-generational continuity in, 41

liberalisation of economy and globalisation in, 4
liberalisation policy of, 170
mass democracy, introduction of, 10
as multi-cultural society, 246
multi-party democracy of, 144
and outbreak of inter-community violence, 28
political community and political culture in, 5
political system, stakeholders of, 14
and post-colonial society, 44
radical–liberal ideology and its development in, 27–28
sample units and distribution of respondents in, 247–48
social base of citizenship, 16
social changes and democracy in, 1
social justice, normative basis of, 161–65
society and hierarchy of caste status in, 7
socio-demographic features in, 160
state–society relations and inter-communal relations in, 137
strategies combining political action with rational protest, 10
surveys of social and political attitudes in, 13
in twentieth century vs. eighteenth century Europe, 2–5
universal adult franchise, influence of, 25
India: A Quiet Crisis, 173
Indian electorate, random sampling procedure for, 249–57
Indian National Congress
and anti-colonial movement against British colonial rule, 44
during emergency of 1975–1977, 26
under leadership of Indira Gandhi, 26
rule during 1947–1957, 26
one-party-dominance

Indian politics
affects of political attitude on, 23
after Independence, 34
age cohorts and salient elements of, 43–49
and attitudes towards
Ayodhya incident, 53
social conflict and discrimination, 53–57
central politics of, 220–24
conservative dynamism of, 42–43
influence of value conflict and partisan competition on, 110–16
influence on age cohorts and economy, 57–58
economic satisfaction by generation, 58
liberalisation of economy, 58–59
inter-generational attitudes towards institutionalisation and participation, 50–52
level of education, 49–50
on issue of
reservation for women, 56
separate civil code, 56
methods of state integration and, 138–40
and need of
atomic bombs, 55
neglected Muslims, 57
participation and partisanship in, 60
and policy towards Pakistan by generation, 54
political structure and social change in, 28–35
and resolution of Kashmir issue, 55
and second phase of political change, 91
and social conflicts, 63
'India Shining' campaign, 102
India's Political Economy: Governance and Reform, 173
India: The Most Dangerous Decades, 90
Indo–Pak relations, influence of Kashmir problem on, 114

In Pursuit of Lakshmi, 6
IRDP (Integrated Rural Development Programme), 173
inter-community riots, 63

Jajmani system, 91
   and political influence of 'pyramid of dominance,' 31
   representation of, 31
   social and economic interests influence on, 33
   social system based on, 30
   and vote bank based vertical mobilisation, 35
   vote bank system, 30
jotdars, 190

karma, 162
kar sevaks, demolition of Babri Mosque, 110
Kashmir problem
   Indo–Pak relations on resolution of, 114
   partisan opinion on resolution of, 113
   regionalists' attitudes towards, 139

labour market regulation, reforms in, 229
liberalisation, policy of, 165–69
licence–permit–raj, 150
Little Buddha syndrome, 241
Lok Sabha, 128
   constituencies, selection of, 249–50
   list of sampled constituencies of, 251–56

Marxist revolution, 239
'Midnight's Children,' concept of, 43, 49
'Million mutinies'
multi-party democracy, 95
multi-party system, political legitimacy and effectiveness of, 104–10

neo-institutional model
   based on structural parameters of action, 13
   for democracy and social change, 9–12

Panchayati democracy, 190
Panchayati Raj, 34, 176
   and building of civil society, 179–182
   elements of, 182
   implementation of, 186
   introduction in
      Bihar, 188–189
      Maharashtra, 187
      West Bengal, 187–188
PPN (*Panchayat Parichalona Nirdeshika*), 191
panchayats, 177, 186
   Bengal 'model' of community building through, 190
Panchayat Samiti, 189
parliamentary communism, 190
parliamentary democracy, British system of, 88
Political Order in Changing Societies, 90
political parties
   legitimacy of, 107
   social bases of, 97–99
   usefulness of, 106
political systems
   democratic, 35
   evaluation of, 108
   with 'first–past–the post' system, 95
   legitimacy in India, 14
politics, and developmental sociology, 6
polling booths, selection of, 257
Poona Pact of 1935, 178
post-colonial state
   social agenda of, 24–26
   and utilitarian philosophy, 25
poverty alleviation, programmes for, 181

poverty index, 151
PPS (Probability Proportionate to Size) sampling procedure, 249
pseudo-secularism, 57
purusakara, 162

Redistribution with Growth, 173
regionalists
    attitudes towards Kashmir issue, 139
    financial efficacy in, 136–37
    and partisan preference, 140
    re-invention of nation from regions, 141–143
    sense of efficacy in, 136
    social background of, 132
        by caste, 133
        by level of education, 135
        by religion, 134
    social profile of, 133–35
    and their attitudes towards communal accommodation, 138
regional movements, 140
respondents, selection of, 257
ryotwari land relations, 161

Sepoy Mutiny of 1857, and affects on social reforms, 25
social and economic development, levels of, 120
social conflict, and Indian politics, 63
social diversity, political aggregation in context of, 64
social justice, normative basis of, 161–65
Social Origins of Dictatorship and Democracy: Lord and Peasant in the Making of the Modern World, 90–91

social policy, deprivation and attitudes towards, 171
social revolution
    and changes in social hierarchy, 1
    in India, 1
    influence of political phenomenon on, 1
SEZ (Special Economic Zones), 189
state–society interaction, competing paradigms of, 234
swadeshi concept, and policy towards liberalisation, 168

transitional societies, politics in, 3
Tryst with Destiny, 24
Tyagi Subcommittee of 1973, 189

universal adult franchise, 36, 179
    democratic constitution and, 184
    and development of political process in India, 26
    introduction in India, 45, 90
universal adult suffrage, 215
Untouchability Offences Act 1955, 214

vertical mobilisation, 215
    and influence on vote banks, 29
Vidhan Sabha
    constituencies, selection of, 250–56
    list of sampled constituencies of, 251–56
village councils, 45
vote banks, 29
    and *Jajmani* system, 30
V. P. Naik Committee report, 181

zamindari systems, of land tenure, 161
Zila Parishad, 189

About the Authors

Subrata K. Mitra is Professor and Head, Department of Political Science at the South Asia Institute, Heidelberg University, and a Visiting Fellow at the Centre for the Study of Developing Societies, Delhi. His published work includes *The Puzzle of India's Governance: Culture, Context and Comparative Theory* (2005). He is the editor of *Heidelberg Papers in South Asian and Comparative Politics* and the academic editor of the series *Advances in South Asian Studies*. He was the President of the Research Committee on Political Sociology of the International Political Science Association and the International Sociological Association (2002–06).

V.B. Singh is Honorary Fellow at the Centre for the Study of Developing Societies, Delhi. His published works include *Profiles of Political Elites in India and Elections in India: Data Handbook on Lok Sabha Elections 1986–91* (1984); *Hindu Nationalists in India: The Rise of BJP* (1994 and 1995); and *Elections in India: Data Handbook on Vidhan Sabha Elections, 1952–85* (Five volumes) (1994). He has been the Director of the Centre for the Study of Developing Societies from 1997 to 2002.